WEERANE

MOHAMED BARUD ALI

The Mourning Tree

An Autobiography and a Prison Memoir

"Rag & Dumar" – Men and women is a series of biographies or autobiography of men and women whose their life influenced the history of the Somaliland nation. The series is directed by Jama Musse Jama and published and distributed by Ponte Invisibile (redsea-online.com).

REDSEA-ONLINE.COM Publishing
Daarta Oriental Hotel
Hargeysa, Somaliland
telephone: 00 252 2 525109
email: bookshop@redsea-online.com

Ponte Invisibile
Inqueries to the editor
Jama Musse Jama
Via Pietro Giordani 4, 56123 Pisa, Italy
email: editor@redsea-online.com

First Edition 2010

ISBN 88-88934-12-X
EAN 9788888934129

Cover design Sola Arts
www.solaarts.org

Photo of Mohamed Barud Ali by
Ismahan Rashid

Printed in Italy

www.redsea-online.com/books

This book is the first of Rag iyo Dumar (men and women) series of selected biographies.

To the heroes in my family: all of them women: my mother who gave birth to me under the acacia tree in the most harrowing circumstances; my sister Fadumo, who became our surrogate mother at the tender age of nine; my indomitable aunt Aisha, who moulded me into a man and made me laugh even when she could not feed me; my wife, who persevered under impossible conditions during Siyaad Barre's time.

M.B.A

Acknowledgements

I sincerely thank Catherine Michael Mariano who initially suggested that I write about our experience in prison. I wrote a few pages and she took them out of Mogadishu and gave them back to me in Djibouti. Jama Musse Jama made me believe that as a Somali, from an oral society, I may be able to write and Ayan Ashur pushed me to finish the manuscript. I am grateful to both of them. Also thanks are due to Dr Mpalive Msiska, Birkbeck, University of London for looking at the manuscript.

Other people who encouraged me to write this memoir include, but are not confined to, Ahmed Abdi Jama, Mohamoud Arreyeh, Adan Dhoolla-yare, Abdirahman tube, Osman Adam Robleh, Yussuf Gaidh, Ahmed Abdirahman, Gahnoug Osman Dubad, Muse Ahmed and Ahmed Ilmas. I thank them all for their support and encouragement. Thanks also due to Prof. Mohamed Dirie for editing the manuscript in a professional manner.

We would like to thank the numerous groups and individuals who have selflessly fought to publicize our suffering and contributed immensely to the international pressure which finally resulted in our release from prison. We are grateful, not only because their noble endeavour had succeeded in our case, but also because General Siyaad Barre and other repressive leaders had been compelled to yield to the will of humanity. The final victory will come when the dictators learn that any harm done to a single one of their countrymen affects the rest of humanity and their misdeeds and follies can no longer be tolerated.

The people who campaigned on our behalf are too numerous to be mentioned in this short exposition. Many people, including our loved ones, have suffered a great deal simply because they were related to us. Organizations such as Amnesty International and National Academy of Science, Human Rights Group and Africa Watch have consistently opposed tyranny and violations of human rights all over the world. We thank all the individuals, organizations and governments for their humane actions, in the name of all those who have been, and still are, under the yoke of oppression.

I was reminded of my Quranic School teacher Aw Adan who, when he was upset with one of his pupils, used to say: "When I punish you, you will be reminded of the milk you had suckled from your mother's breasts." At Labaatan-Jiraw prison, I was not exactly reminded of my mother's milk, but of many things that would not be remembered except in difficult situations.

When you have all the time in the world you reminisce about the minute details of your past, knocking on the wall all day and all night and telling each other stories and events that you would not talk about under normal circumstances. We exhausted our store of stories and experiences within a few months. But we never got tired of the repeats because no new portraits were being painted in our minimalist living conditions. We squeezed and extracted the most enjoyment from these repeats. When you have so little, you find joy in insignificant things. Preoccupations of everyday life are forgotten. That is why we were able to push the limits of our stories. And we could remember more and much further than we would under ordinary circumstances.

We learnt to tell each other our innermost secrets and feelings. Maybe it was easy to tell or divulge your secrets and most personal feelings to someone, across an impregnable concrete wall, whose expression of horror or disgust you were not able to see and who, in your darkest moments, you thought you may never see again. We were able to expose our souls. All kinds of pretences and reservations were thrown to the wind. The stories we told each other and the discussions we had were all enriched by our improved perceptions.

Perceptions that seemed to have been heightened so dramatically that our thoughts were articulated with exceptional clarity. These hitherto undiscovered qualities of clarity of thought, exceptional memory and ability to focus were definitely aided by the isolation. Our faculties of sight and hearing were underused and our brains, naturally, diverted the powers in those to imagination and thought. It was probably why most thinkers worked in isolation, albeit voluntary isolation.

The will to survive was vital and it helped me come through that ordeal.

But also religious faith, which all prisoners possess, at least when they are inside, kept me going through the seeming hopelessness of the long years in prison.

1

Beginnings

I was born in 1950 near Aware town, in what is now the Somali Region of Ethiopia, about 150kms south of Hargeisa, the capital of Somaliland. According to my father, we were on the move during autumn to bring the livestock herds to a better grazing area, and my mother, who was nearing her time, went missing with labour pains. My father and a relative, Jibril Botan, went looking for her in the seemingly identical fields of tall grass punctuated by pockets of acacia trees. They occasionally climbed one of the acacia trees to gain a bird's-eye view of the surrounding landscape calling her name but getting no response.

The shadows were getting longer in the late afternoon and they were getting worried and were about to go to two different directions when Jibril, my relative, started shouting with alarm. He was pointing high at the distant horizon. My father looked at the direction Jibril was pointing. He was frightened. High up where they were looking was one of the most ominous signs of this *terra incognito*—a group of falcons flying in circles on the same spot. Without asking questions, they started in the direction of the falcons. Moving fast in the effortless nomadic fashion, they were soon approaching the target area. There was a relatively large acacia tree right in front of their path, and, through the tall grass, my father, who was leaving Jibril behind, saw some movement at the trunk of the big tree. Suddenly breaking into a run, he was there next to the trunk of the big tree and, lo and behold, there was my mother. Leaning against the trunk of the tree serenely holding in her lap and wrapped up in the lower parts of her single white cotton wrap-around, was all of me, a tiny bubble of humanity that attracted the attention of all. My mother sighed "it is a boy," answering the question in their eyes. My father, despite his happiness at finding us safe and being the father of a third son, did not hug her nor did he offer to hold me. This was a tough environment and men were not expected to display their emotions.

The placenta which had attracted the birds of prey and served as our rescue at the same time was lying about ten meters away where my mother had dragged it. The men started digging the ground, with sharpened acacia sticks, for a hole to serve as a burial ground deep enough for the placenta not to be eaten by scavengers. We all left after burying the placenta, my mother carrying me and slowly following the two men, until we reached the new encampment. The address where I was born at was not any old acacia tree. The tree under whose shade my mother had chosen to rest and against whose supportive trunk she had given birth to me was steeped in clan folklore. It was called "*Weerane*" -the Mourning Tree. Two men of my father's clan had been killed by a group of men from my mother's clan in an act of revenge and their white cotton clothing had been thrown on top of the tree for all to see. The rags stayed there for many years, white being the mourning colour for Somalis.

My beloved mother died of a bout of untreated malaria about 2½ years later, six months after giving birth to my youngest brother, Adan. I was the last but one of five children, one girl and four boys. At the time of my mother's premature death, Adan, the youngest, was only six months old; I was two and half years old; Jama, the middle one, was five years old; Hassan-the second oldest was eight and Fatima, who was the oldest, was 10 years old.

Despite dreaming of my mother, in Labaatan-jiraw prison, entreating me to take care of her daughter when I left prison, I do not claim to remember my mother. Recently, reading a serial article by one of the local newspapers, I was able to look back at that dream with interest. The feature writer, quoting a leading Muslim scholar and an authority on the interpretation of dreams, explained that dreaming about your mother when you are in a difficult and life threatening situation meant you were going to survive that ordeal.

The first incident I can clearly recall occurred when I was three and a half years old. We were on the move, again. That evening three middle-aged men had come back from their reconnaissance trip, briefed the elders and made recommendations to move camp. Summer winds were starting to blow and humans and their livestock needed protection from the prevailing winds. The elders made their decision for a move.

Moving camp normally occurs during the second half of the night, around four o'clock. Kids under five, who are too heavy to be carried on the back of their mothers, and too weak to walk, are transported on the back of camels. Not exactly on their backs but an enclosure is made on one side of the pack camel carrying parts of the hut. And on the other side the three cooking stones are put for balance. The camel used to transport the kids is the tamest, most docile, steadiest and least excitable pack camel that would not be disturbed even by the roar of a lion.

We moved before dawn when the eastern star (Venus) appeared on the eastern horizon before the Mullah called for morning prayers. We moved out of the old encampment with old men heralding for the pack camels to move first, the newly born sheep and goats to follow with the main flock coming last. Our caravan moved, led by the youngest, unbroken male camel, its rope held tightly by my aunt, my uncle's wife, who was acting as a surrogate mother for us. We moved out to the sounds of camels gurgling, sheep and goats bleating and goat-herders singing nervously to keep the flocks together, and for the foxy one and other predators to keep away (*naa hooy dayooy heedhe, dayo caliyee*.......).

Very soon I was lulled into sleep by the rolling gait of the camel. The first thing I distinctly remember when I woke up is the pain on my side. I was fully awake but I was confused. One minute I had been in a warm, womb-like and safe nest, the next minute I found myself on the ground naked, barefooted, cold and alone with pain on my side as if a camel had kicked me. I stood up. I did not cry, looked around and followed the caravan slowly. Just after dawn, my sister Fadumo, looking after the newly born sheep and goats, was frightened by the sound of breaking branches behind her. She turned around and was shocked to see me naked, barefooted and alone. She came running and she hugged me closely feeling me all over as if to reassure herself that I was whole.

She was crying and for the first time I started crying with her. Carrying me on her back, she shouted for the camel caravan to stop and I was put back on the camel. From that moment onwards Fadumo, my sister, would not leave the side of the camel, continuously speaking to me.

When we arrived at our new camp, I was taken off the back of the camel and my sister made me sit under the shade of a big acacia tree. She stayed with me for the whole day massaging my tender feet and removing the thorns from my feet. Soon after we settled in our new encampment, the news of what had happened to me reached my father who was in Hargeisa.

In the camel-denominated nomadic communities, your status and your word, under the acacia tree, where affairs of the clan are discussed and decided, weighed as much as the number of camels you owned. My father had no livestock of his own and with no influence and prestige in the nomadic communities he had decided earlier to seek his fortune in the town. When news of this incident reached him, he decided to take three of us with him to Hargeisa. Fadumo, our sister, could not come to the town without a chaperone, such as a mother; Aden was too young to be uprooted and taken away from his surrogate mother. We travelled to Hargeisa, about 150kms away; I on my father's shoulders and my two elder brothers, Hassan and Jama, walking for the two weeks it took us to reach Hargeisa.

Upon our arrival we stayed at my uncle Abdilllahi's camp near Hargesia Airport. The camp served as a half-way camp for livestock where nomads left their livestock overnight with uncle Abdillahi who would bring them to the market the next day. Livestock merchants also collected their livestock at uncle Abdillahi's for transportation to Berbera Port for eventual shipment and export to Saudi Arabia. My two brothers stayed with my uncle but I was taken to Aunt Asha in the middle of the town in a quarter called Jameeco Weyn.

As I already said, my father had come to Hargeisa to seek his fortune. He knew no trade other than being a pastoralist. On top of that there were many like him, unemployed and impoverished, competing for the few opportunities that came by way of unskilled labour. But my father did not become a labourer. My father, being a proud nomad, looked down on manual labour as disgraceful and beneath his clan honour. So my father worked as an intermediary between nomads bringing their livestock to the market and livestock traders. The livestock was entrusted to the intermediaries on strictly clan and sub-clan basis. The chances of my father landing 2 heads of sheep a week were slim and few. Even when he was lucky to find 2 heads of sheep to sell for a week, they earned him less than 2 dollars at today's rate.

My father's office, where he met nomads who brought their sheep and goats to the market was a small teashop, Ina Gamur's, frequented by his clansmen. His tools of trade consisted of a metre long rope, to secure the one sheep or goat that irregularly came his way through a relative bringing one to the market, and a shepherd's crook, to fend off the fierce competition. Because he did not earn enough to pay for his daily expenses, my father always owed the owner a few shillings for tea and bread.

My father left my two older brothers with my uncle and he entrusted me with Aunt Asha since he could not pay for our upkeep and had no reliable income of his own. This lack of income on the part of my father was the reason that I nearly missed out on going to school. When I enrolled in elementary school in Dec. 1959, the school fee for a term was twenty shillings (about seven dollars then). My father was unable to pay that kind of money and it was touch and go that I would drop out of school, even before I finished the first class, if it was not for the intervention of four of my better-off clansmen (Ali Botan, Arrale Dolal, Abdi Elmi-Abdi Tumal, Hassan Hussein (Hassan Tule), each of whom contributed five shillings to pay for the first term. Luckily the new Somali government declared free lower primary education before the generosity of my clansmen was severely tested. After the lower primary, I was able to finish my schooling due to two factors: my father possessed no camels of his own to send me off to look after them; I was able to maintain my position as one of the top five students in the class who, as a result, were exempted from paying school fees.

Aunt Asha was about 70 and had three grown-up sons. She was very religious in that fanatical uncompromising way that Somalis can be about Islam without actually comprehending its teachings. She frequented the "*Sitaad*", a quasi-religious gathering of elderly women, where drums were played, frankincense filled the air and raw coffee (Khashar) was consumed in large quantities. The women sang in frenzy, in praise of Ali's wife, Fatima, the prophet's daughter, asking for her intervention on their behalf on the Day of Judgment:

Sitooy Faadumo nabaay sowjadii Calaay,
maalinta bacadka kulul biyo qabow na sii,
oo maalinta lays xisaabaayo noo xil qari.

Staying with aunt Asha was memorable, enjoyable and instructive. She had no income of her own. Two of her three sons were relatively well-off, owning businesses in Hargeisa. But they did not take care of all her needs. Occasionally, she sold some tomatoes and sometimes few eggs laid by her three hens. But somehow she made sure she fed me. Despite this poverty aunt Asha used to buy the Somali National League Newspaper (SNL) paper, called *Qarnu Ifriqia* (the Horn of Africa) without fail, every Thursday. This was her contribution to the cause of freedom and her party because neither of us could read the newspaper. We would often fill the newspaper in the many holes of our hut.

I hardly ever saw her eat. She mostly drank Khashar (raw-coffee). On the rare night when my aunt was not able to scrounge to feed me, she would make me lay my head on her lap and massaging my head, feeling for lice, she would regale me with stories, sometimes sad but often funny. She often succeeded in making me forget about my hunger and fall asleep. My aunt was often nostalgic about her past. She told me about her three sons now grown-up, the youngest of whom was a seaman. This youngest absent son stole her heart. He wrote her irregularly but he was never more than a heartbeat away from her mind. She expected him to knock on our door any day and lavish us with gifts and wealth.

My aunt was the oldest of twelve siblings of my grandfather's and my father was the youngest. She would often remind me about this when we discussed issues concerning religion. I was six and was going to Quranic School. Because of my new learning, I argued with her constantly, confident I knew all. On such occasions, she would laugh serenely and pushing back her head scarf from her temples, she would say: "Look here young man. Look at my grey hair. I am the oldest of my father's children and your father is the youngest and you are a mere nothing. I come from a religious family. My brother Hassan, bless his soul, was a great imam. I live in a religious community-Jameeco Weyn- and you dare talk to me about religion." Yet my aunt Asha had the most endearing and eccentric mixture of superstitious and religious beliefs. She insisted that her old cronies call her Hajia Asha, an appellation for those who had gone to Mecca on pilgrimage. We all knew she had not been to Mecca but my aunt insisted that she be called Hajia by her peers otherwise she would not acknowledge them or their greetings. The reason she must be called Hajia, she said, was because she had been to Sheikh Yusuf Al-kownain's (aka Aw-Barkhadle-the blessed one) place of burial- three times. Somalis believed that Sheikh Yusuf had brought Islam to them. As a result a tomb had been built for him at a village which carries his name about 35 km on the tarmac road between Hargeisa and Berbera.

My aunt was not alone in her belief that Sheikh Yusuf Al-kownain was a saint as attested by the thousands of people who came from all corners of the Horn of Africa including Djibouti and Diredawa, Ethiopia, to pay their homage to his burial place annually, performing at his tomb many of the rituals and trappings observed during pilgrimage to Mecca. My aunt on greeting her cronies would say she was fine and that she did her four obligations. I knew she never missed one of the five obligatory prayer times a day, but she somehow forgot to add up her prayer times. When I asked her about this misrepresentation about her prayer times, she would never answer me directly but would smilingly allude to my tender years compared to her advanced aged.

When aunt Asha came home from the *Sitaad* gatherings in the evening she would have a far-away look in her eyes and be very quite and still. If I tried to speak to her, she would put her index finger against her lips, silently warning me not to disrupt her spell and contact with the other-worldly forces, otherwise I might be harmed by those forces. According to my aunt, the presence of those forces in our midst, benevolent ones on this occasion, was proven by an incident that occurred on the last day but one of Ramadan, the holiest month in the Muslim calendar, when the holy Quran was revealed to the Prophet Mohamed through Archangel Jibrael. As a result, Muslims are more devout during the month of Ramadan and in particular on the odd-numbered days in the last fifteen days of Ramadan so as not to miss the night of revelation (*Laylatal Qadr*) when the heavens are open and prayers are certain to be accepted.

On this day aunt Asha had asked me to go to Jawahir's, a Harari lady who had a mini-market in her bedroom, selling everything, complete with hand-held weighing scales, to buy her a slice of hard soap to wash my only khaki shorts and white shirt, the school uniform, so that I could celebrate Eid-al-Fidr- the end of Ramadan- with the other kids. I was despondent because many of my friends in the neighbourhood had already been bought new and colourful clothes by their parents. I was dragging my feet as I went past the Jameeco Weyn mosque, reputedly the oldest building in Hargeisa, when I saw, to my amazement, three new notes of East Africa money (sixty shillings), held by the wind against the thorny fence of the mosque. My legs became leaden and refused to move. I had never handled so much money before in my life. The notes were crackling new. I finally picked them up. I ran back to aunt Asha in record time. She shot up standing when I entered the hut and showed her the money. She stared behind me to see what demons were chasing me. When I breathlessly told her what had happened, she seemed to sag and sat heavily with a sigh. She did not speak but signalled for me to sit next to her and, holding me against her bosom, she started to cry. She was sure this was a sign of divine intervention and that her prayers had been answered.

According to the popular radio serial producer, the great Somali comedian, poet and playwright, Mohamed Omer "Huryo",

I had met *Laital-khadar*, the flesh and blood personification of the heavens and I was lucky to have met the man with the boneless right thumb and fleshy handshake on the last day but one of Ramadan. Needless to say that aunt Asha made sure I was the happiest and best dressed boy in our neighbourhood on that particular Eid, complete with my first pair of shoes. Aunt Asha and I lived in a small dome-like hut (Aqal) two meters in diameter and a meter high. It was made up of bits and pieces of the roots, branches and the soft inner bark of acacia trees and tall grass quilted together. The material was so full of holes that in the morning we would be woken up by rays of sunlight made by the rising dust and the light coming through the numerous holes. Our tiny hut had a thorny acacia bush fencing to stop thieves and other intruders because, although this was the least attractive area for thieves, it was also the least policed.

Aunt Asha was bulky and often asked me to message her back by walking slowly over her back while she lay on her stomach fully dressed. She oohed and aahed with pleasure while I maneuvered perilously on her mountainous frame.

During my stay with aunt Asha, I went back to the nomadic community when I was twelve and on school leave. In the nomadic community, the herds of camels that are no longer giving milk are kept far away from the main dwelling areas in camel camps. There are no women and huts in these camel camps. One of the she-camels lost its newborn calf. The nomads removed the skin of the dead calf and dried it. This dried skin was held in front of the camel, in lieu of its calf, during milking. Without this skin the she-camel would not settle to be milked.

During the nomads' frequent movements, I was obliged to carry the skin as the youngest person and as a result the camel would follow me around, sometimes physically and sometimes with its eyes. I lost the skin during one of these movements but the chief camel herder was not upset as I expected him to be. When the turn of the particular she-camel came to be milked, he would ask me to stand in front of the camel. The camel would lower its long neck towards me, gurgle with satisfaction and settle to be milked. After that the camel not only accepted me in place of its dead calf not only during milking but it would also sit very close to the campfire during the night where it could reach me with its long neck and make sure I was there. Sometimes one of the older boys would playfully chase me around and the she-camel would come running, frothing at the mouth, ready to defend me and chase away the offender.

At the end of the school holidays, when it was time for me to go back, the nomads would not understand why I wanted to go back. The camel's milk will dry up when you leave, they argued. Going to school, to them, was a waste of time and effort. In the minds of the nomads, three categories of youths were sent to town to learn the Quran: Those whose fathers did not own camels, the mentally slow, who would not be trusted with camels, and the disabled. The unfortunate whom God had not bestowed with camels, the only animal praised in the Quran, the weak and those with disabilities went to towns to beg. The fact is that there were not many people with disabilities to be seen in the nomadic communities. There were few permanent settlements or water sources between Hargeisa and Aware about 150 km distance, and people with disabilities were a burden on the meagre resources of nomads. They could not look after the livestock let alone grow up to go on raiding parties for camels.

When a baby with a disability was born to a nomadic family it was considered a curse on them. They will tolerate this while the baby was still young and manageable and there was hope that the baby will grow to be normal. They will read the Quraan to bless the baby and chase away the devil (*shaitan*). But very soon, the baby became heavier and a burden to move around. During the next long trek, the young person with disability would be abandoned, thrown to the dogs as it were, in this case the hyenas, put under a shade of a tree with some food and water, if he or she was lucky. The next season, when nomads came back to the area, the bare bones will be found scattered around the old encampment. Even those people with infectious diseases, like smallpox, measles and cholera were left to fend for themselves. The lucky ones among the disabled were taken to the towns to be looked after by a relative or to beg. That is why, before the deluge of beggars from Ethiopia and Southern Somalia, most of the beggars you saw in Hargeisa and other towns were disabled.

My first Quranic school was run by two disabled teachers. Ma'allin Curyan was completely disabled; yet he was intelligent, proud and ruled his domain with an iron fist. Ma'allin ismail was blind and recited the Quran from memory. I was fortunate that my father had no camels of his own to keep me in the countryside. I went back to Hargeisa with the experience of a lifetime to tell my school friends who had never ventured outside the town. The one reason I was sorry to leave the countryside was the delicate attachment of such a seemingly awkward animal. I was certain that it would search for me, in vain, for many days to come.

I stayed with aunt Asha until I finished primary education in Hargeisa and went to boarding school at Sheikh in September, 1966. Sheikh is a small, sleepy and beautiful town high up in the Golis mountains, about fifty miles south of the Red Sea port of Berbera. The student population, numbering two hundred boys, came from all the regions of Somaliland and even from the neighbouring Somali regions of Ethiopia and Djibouti where there were no secondary schools. The teachers in the school were a microcosm of the British Colonial Office, Britons (Mr. R.R. Darlington, the English Geography and sports master; Mr. McKinley, the History and Geography master; Mr. D.N.W. Feiller, the English master), the Indians, (Mr. Ilyas, the Physics and Chemistry master; Mr. Paul Singh, the Chemistry master; Mr. Daniel, the Biology master), the Africans, in this case the Somalis, (Mr. Galib Musa, the Head master and History teacher; Mr. Ahmed Sheikh Adan, the Classical Arabic master; and Mr. Ali Abdulkadir, the English master).

The school was practically run by an old India hand, a British military officer, who had fought with Somalis in the Burma theatre, in the Second World War. Mr. R.R. Darlington, universally known as *Gacmadhere* (the long armed one) had lead the Somali regiment in the War and often spoke about their great courage in battle, their disdain for authority and their puzzling and open admiration for the enemy, the Japanese, whose soldiers never retreated or flinched in hand-to-hand combat. Mr. Darlington was about seventy, tall, gaunt and idiosyncratic. He possessed, what I later found out to be, a very unique British sense of humour and he treated all the boys as his sons. He was the coach to both the football and hockey teams. He contributed all the magazines and newspapers to the reading rooms. He belonged to all kinds of book clubs which regularly sent him new novels which he donated to the school library.

The school curriculum was not intellectually inspiring for such a hallowed institution. It was stable and solid and served the purpose of preparing its graduates for higher education while the country desperately needed technical and professional cadres. In my third year at Sheikh on October 21, 1969, the civilian president of the Somali republic, Abdirashid Ali Sharmaarke, was fatally shot in Las Anod, in the north of the country, by one of the presidential security detail. Five days later, an armed forces cabal, headed by Siyaad Barre, staged a coup and ruled or misruled Somalia for the next twenty one years.

I first met Siyaad Barre, in 1967, in Sheikh, when he was the army commander and on a visit to the Army Training School based in Sheikh. His visit coincided with the announcement of disputed results of a referendum in Djibouti, *Cote Françoise des Somalis, CFS,* (French Somali Coast) which had asked whether the territory retained its links with the French republic. Earlier in 1966, Charles de Gaulle, the French president, on an official visit to the Djibouti, was met by demonstrators demanding independence. On September 1966 the French announced that the voters would be consulted about whether CFS would remain as part of the French Republic. The referendum was held on March 19, 1967 and showed that 22,000 voted yes and 14,000 voted no, with the Afars favoring links with France and the French having rigged the elections in their favour by expelling thousands of Somalis from the territory before the referendum was brought to the polls (*Encyclopedia of African History*). In July 1967, the territory was renamed as the Territoire Françoise Afar des Somalis, TFAS (French Territory of the Afar and Issas) and was given internal rule. As a result there were demonstrations across Somalia supporting independence. The students went to demonstrate in support of those seeking independence and in reply to a speech by one of the older boys, Siyaad Barre made a stirring speech about the Somali armed forces being equal to the task of defending all Somali territories, including Djibouti, and we as students should concentrate on our studies because that was the major war.

I thrived in the new camaraderie atmosphere of the school with so many boys of my age, who professed to enjoy the same interests, after years sparring with my old aunt. By all accounts I was one of the best footballers that passed through the gates of the school. I became a member of the school committee in the last year and I graduated as one of the top two students in the final year not only in my school but in the country. My first day in school was quite memorable and inspiring. Mr. Feiler, the English master, asked our class to write an essay on four people stranded on a cliff and their attempts to attain safer ground. When he distributed the marked essays, there was a comment on each paper. I will never forget the comment on my paper which was: "Do not use a ten-letter word where a four-letter word will do." I like to think that I have used that motto since then and that it was the reason that I passed English with the highest marks that year. The top ten students who passed English were sent to the UK for further education.

Before our departure for the United Kingdom, a reception was held for us at the British Embassy in Mogadishu. A film was shown to us depicting the culture of Britain and its people and I remember the commentator's words on one particular issue that made us all laugh:" Do not ask an English man about his sex life or about his income."

2

England and the Pepper Wars

When we arrived in the UK, we were taken to Brighton, Sussex, a town on the southern coast of England, about 55 minutes by train from Victoria station in London. We were enrolled in Davies School of English in Brighton and Hove to refine our spoken English and to mingle with the many foreign tourists who descended on Brighton every summer to visit the numerous tourist attractions in the area and to improve their English. Brighton was, and still is a popular tourist destination for people from all parts of the world but particularly from more affluent parts including North America, Western Europe, the Middle East and Japan. We stayed in a Catholic hostel for young people on Marine Parade on the sea front in Brighton. We were there for only about two weeks when a fellow Somali, Mohamed Ali Atteye, an old boy from Sheikh, who was in England a year before us, arrived early one evening at our hostel, while we were all watching this unusual contraption called TV, accompanied by a Somali girl. They told us excitedly about a close encounter they had had with skin-heads. Skin-heads were a new phenomenon in Britain; menacing looking, tattooed working class kids with shaven heads and wearing combat boots. They indulged in random violence and attacked foreigners in what they called Paki-bashing orgies of violence. They did not attack only Pakistanis but all dark skinned foreigners. If they did not find dark skinned foreigners, they would attack those with a different accent than theirs or those from a different country or from a different part of England or even Brighton. They were bent on venting their anger on someone different.

On this occasion, Mohamed Ali and his companion were quite visibly different than the skin-heads and were inviting an attack by the skin-heads when they went to a night club frequented by these thugs. The skin-heads attacked them as soon as they entered the night club. Mohamed and his companion were saved by the grace of God through the intervention of the bouncers working for the establishment. When they came to our hostel and recounted to us what had happened to them, we were very offended and, like the nomads we were, we made preparations for a counter attack to strike a blow and save a face (*dheg* in Somali) for Somalis. Our preparations were meticulous. We were told that we could not enter the night club without a formal dress code. We all went out and bought ties since most of us did not have ties. But the most memorable item of our preparations was what was given to each of us just before we departed for the battle ground, the night club. Someone, I do not remember exactly who, maybe Rashid Awleed, had bought a pound of pepper powder and wrapped it up in tiny conical pieces of paper, folding and securing it at the top like the shopkeepers did with tea leaves in Hargeisa. Each of us was given one of these conical missiles without any instructions on how to use it.

As soon as we entered the club, before we even discovered our bearings in this sea of people, light and sound, people started pushing and heckling us. We were typical Somalis whose pride had been injured and who were spoiling for a fight. But we did not know who to fight. We were in a sea of white faces all of them potential enemies and we were easily distinguishable from the rest and were targets for a get-the-boot-in massacre. The bouncers came to our rescue again. They took us to a corner, watched on threateningly not only by the skin-heads but by all the clientele of the club. They reasoned with us to leave the club for our safety. We obstinately resisted first but we left when the bouncers told us wisely that they will repay our entrance fees making our exit more dignified and palatable.

When we came out of the club at ten o'clock in the evening, it was still daylight in mid-August which in itself was quite disorienting and confusing to us. We held a council of war, and after a short meeting, we decided that we were not going to leave until we had our revenge. We waited in the narrow Brighton lanes until midnight when the club clientele poured out into the empty streets in waves. The skin-heads saw our two scouts and shouting: "there they are", they came running at us. The two obvious leaders took off their coats, gave them to their girl friends and entered the lanes to flush us out. But as soon as they entered the lanes they came out shouting as if being chased demons and there was a stampede and people were trampled upon. Soon, the two leaders were lying at the entrance of the lanes, holding their heads with their hands, crying for help and not knowing what had hit them, black magic, Voodoo. Many of us also did not know what had happened. One minute we were being chased by a horde, not knowing where to hide, the next minute we were chasing the hordes, victorious but magnanimous in victory, not hitting those lying on the ground now protected by their girl friends who kept saying: "please leave them alone. They are helpless."

The rest of the skin-heads never looked back, and despite their ostentatious toughness, never had the courage to take their war wounded. The wounded were taken by ambulance to a hospital. They were released from the hospital soon after because there was no damage to their eyes. The chief constable of Brighton and Hove later invited us to police headquarters together with representatives from the skin heads. He talked to us for an hour about the importance of tourism to the area and the hitherto unblemished record of race relations in Brighton and Hove. When we were leaving the police headquarters, one of the officers said to one of my friends:" I don't know what you boys have done to them (the skin heads), but they have not been the same since. Every police man wants to congratulate you and hug you. You have managed to accomplish what the police department had failed to do."

We were transferred from Brighton to different parts of the country in September 1971. Four of us went to Bath, Somerset to do our G.C.E. A levels for the next two years at Bath Technical College; they were:

1. Ahmed Haji Abdillahi (Sufi)
2. Mohamed Mohamoud (Kitable)
3. Ibrahim Mohamoud Sh. Musa
4. Myself.

Ahmed Sufi and I stayed with a Mrs. Gruppo, an Irish widow with two children of Italian-Irish descent, Tina, six, and Patrick, four. She lived across the River Avon Bridge on 77 Shakespeare Avenue. She was very friendly and her two kids treated us naturally after an initial period in which Tina occasionally rubbed her arms against ours to see if our colour was real.

We were not the only boarders with Mrs. Gruppo. Two Mormon students Mathew and Alex stayed with us for a year. Both were nineteen and over six feet tall and very heavy. They were not only huge physically, but they also talked big. The US was the mightiest country in the world; we have the largest army in the world; we are the richest country in the world; and finally the state of Utah from which they hailed, with its honey and milk, was the best place to live in the US. We had no responses to such an onslaught, being so starved and puny and coming from a camel country.

The first winter that we stayed in the UK was severe. We all suffered mild cases of culture shock. The weather, the food, the multiplicity of accents and the completely different cultural and social environment in which we found ourselves were sources of confusion and disorientation that caused us difficulties even in our studies. When we finally adjusted to the situation, we were able to appreciate and enjoy the beauty of the city of Bath and the surrounding areas. People came from all over the UK and from around the world to visit the Roman Baths and the fine Roman architecture of Bath that regularly won it the accolade of the most beautiful city in Europe.

We were even able to laugh at the slave trade era street names of Bristol, the nearest big city, including "Black Boy Hill", "White Ladies Road" when we visited it during week-ends. We had a generous host, Yassin, a former seaman, who always welcomed us wholeheartedly and took us to Indian and Chinese restaurants and West-Indies night clubs. The Somali community then in the area consisted of Yassin and a guy called Ismail and his family in Bristol. But there was a larger community in the general area of Cardiff, Wales. We paid a visit to Cardiff in the summer of 1972 where the Somalis and Yemenis were concentrated in the Tiger Bay area, near the docks. The seamen we met there were a throwback to the nomads back home yesteryear. They would not speak to us until they had found out about our clan affiliations; they cooked the same meat and rice fare, which we nostalgically enjoyed, in their restaurant; they talked about the old country as if they had left it only yesterday, and their bags were packed to go back home any day.

After finishing A levels, I went to Sunderland in county Durham in 1973. Sunderland was one of the most depressed areas in England. The traditional industries of ship-building, coal mining and glass-making were going out of business, overtaken by more competitive industries in other countries. Sunderland was much colder than Bath in the south, but Sunderland was much warmer as far as human contact was concerned. I have life-long friends in that region. I loved the Geordie accent when they supported Sunderland football team "haway the lads". "Or how is the bern?" "Poorly like" or "Canny like". When I went back to Sunderland in 1993, after coming out of prison, Sunderland was booming with the largest Nissan factory in the area and it was one of the most connected areas in England. Not only that but my best friends who were of working class origin, all went back to school and were working for major institutions in the country. Irene Liddy was the head of the YMCA in Birmingham; Moira Hague, who had two boys, Hassan and Adam, with a Somali classmate, Rashid Samatar, was head of Nike Sports-wear Company in north-west England and was based in Manchester; Jean Hague was a professor of English language at Sunderland University. Jean's son, who was attending Liverpool University at the time, interviewed me on his amateur radio, heard throughout Sunderland. They all took time off from their busy schedule to welcome me as their long lost son.

I left Sunderland after earning a degree in Geology and Chemistry in 1977. Before leaving the UK I stayed in London for few weeks. One day while sitting on a bench outside the Times building with some friends, we saw the headline "Somalia at war with Ethiopia". We were shocked and we talked about this heatedly for sometime. In the middle of our discussion, I recalled a BBC 1 program called "this year, next year". I watched on 31st

December, 1976. The Program, speaking about" war clouds gathering in the Horn", showed the Somali army marching in the streets of Mogadishu with Mig fighters flying over the city. The commentator said this was one of the poorest countries in Africa and yet they had one of the best trained armies in black Africa. Finally, asking himself rhetorically where this army was going, he answered himself prophetically that there was no were else other than Ethiopia. And sure enough there was un-winnable deadly war between the neighbours.

After the defeat of the Somali army by Ethiopia, albeit with the help of Russia, Cuba and the Yemen, there was chaos in the ranks of the Somali army. There was a coup attempt by army officers in 1978, the Western Liberation army, who were fighting alongside the Somali army, behaved as occupying armies in the north with the blessing of Siyaad Barre and opposition movements were born. This was definitely the beginning of the death knell for Siyaad Barre and his regime.

I went back to Somalia at the end of 1978. I went to Mogadishu because it was the only place where there was an opportunity for employment in the country. I was employed by the new Juba Sugar Project (JSP) of Mareery, near Kismayo. The head of the JSP, who was the minister for industry at the same time, Mr. Ali Khalif made me a team leader for a group of Suju (Somalis from east Africa) secondary school leavers to be trained as factory operators in the Jowhar Sugar factory near Mogadishu while the JSP was under construction. We all got jobs because we spoke English which was critical since the company that was contracted to implement the project was a British Company called Booker McConnell. We stayed in Jowhar for eleven months, learning the rudiments of sugar technology. At the end of the year, the whole team was offered up to six month's further training in sugar technology in a small factory town, near Aswan, in southern Egypt called Komombo.

Before we went to Egypt, I met my future wife and we got engaged, with my best friend, Osman Adan Roble, as the best man. Osman can remember the type and colour of shirt everyone in his class wore thirty years ago. We got engaged on January 4,

1980. When we went to Egypt, we arrived in Cairo in transit to Aswan in southern Egypt. It was really cold. But the image I still carry from that trip is of the majestic River Nile. A long, winding strip of green in the midst of a shimmering and desolate whiteness of the desert. I was able to appreciate the Egyptian saying that the Nile was synonymous with life in Egypt. God ordained that there be life in the desert and there was the Nile. I do not know if the life of any other nation depended as much on the existence of a single entity as that of the Egyptians did on the Nile. Talk about diversification. When we arrived in Aswan, we were taken by train along the Nile north to komombo, a small factory village whose whole workforce was employed by the sugar factory. There is nothing romantic about a sugar factory. But between our training and work in the factory, and making friends with Egyptians, we were able to visit some of the fabulous sights of ancient Egypt. We were taken every other weekend to the historic monuments and sights of ancient Egypt.

On one of the most memorable visits to the Valley of the Kings and Queens, we were at the palace of Queen Hatshepsut. Queen Hatshepsut was one of the few women kings in ancient Egypt. She was an absolute ruler, both politically and religiously. In fact she was considered a deity. She ruled for twenty-two year, between 1472 and 4152 BC. We were owed by the incredible mountain palaces with the narrow passages and such deep chambers on either side. We were told that the bones of would-be robbers were piled-up that they had to be removed once so often. Frightening pictures, looking like they were drawn yesterday, were expected to frighten robbers who managed to find those well-camouflaged palaces. On this occasion, when we visited Queen Hatshepsut's palace, we were with a group of tourists from North America and Western Europe. We were guided by two young Egyptians who graduated from Egyptian universities on Egyptian culture and tourism.

Taking us through the palace, they deciphered for us the Hieroglyphics depicting the history and biography of the queen. The high point of this visit came when the young man guiding us suddenly mentioned "present day Somalia". I woke up from my reverie, imagining what life was like for those Pharaohs and their subjects who lived 3000-4000 years ago. He pointed at a boat in the Gulf of Aden on its way to the Somali coast. On the boat was a delegation sent by Queen Hatshepsut to the land of Punt (the so called land of the Gods). On land, on the Somali side, there was a picture of a very fat black woman with a huge leg, obviously suffering from Elephantiasis, sitting on a chair under the shade of an acacia tree, attended by three guards, wearing only white clothing on their loins and carrying spears. On top of the tree there was what looked like a hut (Aqal, in Somali). The guide explained that the hut on top of the tree signified, in hieroglyphics, that there were wild, man-eating animals in the area. The delegation was sent by Queen Hatshepsut to the potentate of the land of Punt who also happened to be a woman. The delegation brought with them gifts of spices and varieties of fish and messages of future trade and friendship. The Egyptian delegation was sent back bearing with them gifts of frankincense, and myrrh and some animals, including leopards, monkeys and exotic birds and similar messages of friendship and future trade.

We stayed in Cairo for two days and went back to Mogadishu on July 14th. Before going back to Mareery I took a three week holiday and went to Hargeisa with my wife to seek the blessing of our parents for our engagement. While in Hargeisa, I met an old friend, Mohamed Abu-Site, who was the head of the Pepsi-Cola bottling plant in Hargeisa. He invited me to lunch and later showed me around the plant. Compared to the sugar factories I worked in, this looked like a small corner shop as opposed to a huge super market. At the end of our conversation, Mohamed told me that they needed someone to manage the plant for them. He offered me a very enticing package of treble the salary I was getting at Mereery and other benefits including housing. After discussing it with my wife, I accepted his offer on condition that I go back to Mogadishu and seek a release from my employer. My resignation was accepted and I started working at the Pepsi-Cola plant on September 1st, 1980.

In early 1981, two events had occurred at about the same time that changed the political, economic and social landscape of the whole north. First, on April12 1981 the formation of the Somali National Movement was announced in London by a group of northern politicians and military officers as an opposition movement dedicated to overthrow the repressive regime in Somalia. The second was the naming of General Mohamed Hashi Gani as the commander of the Somali Armed Forces and virtual governor of the north. As a close relative of the Siyaad Barre, he had an unequalled access to his court and his word and advice about the north was unquestioned. He was notorious for his inflammatory language and behaviour and his unabashed pride in his role as the virtual ruler of the north. As soon as he arrived in Hargeisa, he transferred most of the senior officers who were from the north, many of them senior to him but under his command because of his meteoric rise to generalship.

One of his most provocative actions to the people of the north was accusing Colonel Abdillahi Siyaad, one of the most popular officers in the Somali Army, of treason and summarily executing him in the bush. Most of his fellow officers were outraged but were unable to help him. That is why people started calling him *Derie* (the one who unwittingly raised people's awareness). While this was going on in the political and military spheres, in the economic and social sectors things were deteriorating. There were food shortages throughout the country because all food exporting activities were nationalized and handed over to an autonomous government agency, ENCE (National economic and commercial agency). There are a lot of stories and anecdotes about the proverbial inefficiency of this agency. My favourite is the story about the group of flying fish that would fly in the air in unison and sing the revolutionary song every morning, (haay haay weligaa haay) meaning for the regime to stay in power because ENCE would be responsible for food, including fishing, and fish would thrive in those conditions.

To address those difficult conditions, a local voluntary social services committee was established by a group of business people and other community leaders. They had the consent of local authorities before the arrival of Gani and it did not seem at the time that they would need the military commander's agreement to help their communities. This voluntary committee and Dr. Adan Yussuf Abokor, who was the director of Hargeisa Group Hospital, invited a group of teachers, doctors and others in early July, 1981 to a meeting to explain to them the deteriorating conditions of social services in Hargeisa, particularly Hargeisa Group Hospital. This was done in the presence of and with the support of local and regional authorities. They explained the lack of electricity, of mattresses of medicine and the total absence of proper sanitation and water. The most poignant illustration of this was the fact that husbands who brought their pregnant wives to the hospital to be delivered would be asked by the mid-wives to switch-on their headlights and direct them at their wives, as they were being attended to by medical personnel, because there was no electricity.

There were international organizations and UN agencies in the area but they were specifically for the hundreds of thousands of refugees around Hargeisa and other parts of the north. The refugees were initially welcomed by the local populace, but there was soon resentment in the air when the locals perceived that the government and international agencies were giving refugees preferential treatment over them. The German Emergency Doctors (GED), a German agency headed locally by Abdikarim Aw Rally, was one of the few agencies that appreciated the unique nature of the situation where the government was bolstering the general economic and social situation of the refugees to punish its own people. The GED understood that by helping improve conditions in Hargeisa Hospital, they were simultaneously improving referral conditions for refugees.

Enter Gani and his high-handedness. According to many who knew him well, Gani was a very ambitious man and as one of the youngest generals, he expected no hurdles in his way to the highest office. And of course the old wily general would tap him on the shoulder that he was his sole heir. In his preparations to come to Hargeisa in early 1981, Gani met a number of old friends who he wanted to help smooth his way in his new job in the north. One of the people he trusted most was unfortunately in prison in the basement of the Somali Socialist Revolutionary Party (SSRP) headquarters for corruption charges. A number of people had already been sentenced to death on similar charges for embezzling 100,000 Somali Shillings or more. The most well-known case was that against Jibril Amin, a first cousin (*Ina-abti*) of President Hassan Guaid of Djibouti. President Gulaid was said to have pleaded with Siyaad Barre until the last moment, even flying to Mogadishu, to grant his cousin amnesty or at least commute his sentence to a long sentence. Sources close to President Gulaid affirm that he slept well the last night because Siyaad Barre promised him he will respect his wishes. But the next morning Jibril was shot promptly.

Knowing all this, there had been a shuttle of elders and community leaders for many months from Hargeisa to save Faisal Ali Warabe who was in the basement of the SSRP headquarters. Gani went to see Siyaad Barre and told him what President Gulaid had apparently failed to tell him. He came away with Faisal, a free man. Obviously, with God's help, Gani was his saviour. The next time Faisal visited Hargeisa it was on the invitation of his Friend Gani. Many of the people in UFFO (Hargeisa Group) and others who were not imprisoned met Faisal on a couple of occasions during Ramadan that year. This may not be verbatim because it is such a long time ago but this is the gist of his message: "Gani is an old friend. He saved my life. If you got to know him, you will agree with what I am saying. He wants to know young community leaders of the Issaq. The government is at war with the Majerteen, but not the Issaq. He has the ear of his uncle and he can do a lot for the north. Let us accept him as an ally, not an enemy."

Our response was that we were all new to the country and that the elders are all in the major towns and that the political leaders are in Mogadishu. So none of us ever met Gani except in court when he would drop in on court proceedings in full regalia, softly beating his baton against the palm of his left hand accompanied by his body guards, say a few words to the court officials and leave. According to court proceedings, when Faisal went back to Mogadishu, he gave Gani the names of two trusted friends who would cooperate with him. He in turn passed them on to Colonel Mohamed Samater, head of military intelligence or HANGASH. Samater passed the names to Major Ibrahim Cid, head of HANGASH in Hargeisa. Major Cid testified in court that the names of those accused were given to him by these two men and that he gave them forty thousand Somali Shillings (Four Thousand Dollars then) as a reward. Neither of them was in court to be questioned, but despite strenuous objections by the lawyers, the court accepted as evidence our names with some vague accusations that we used to have QAT sessions in the same houses and that we discussed government failings. The names are in the court transcript: Adan Ali Guhad and Abdi Aw Adde (Langadhe). Adan died with Mohamed Moge when a group of SNM officials were ambushed near Aware by sympathizers of Siyaad Barre. Abdi also went to fight with the SNM and is now a respected elder in Hargeisa.

3

The Arrest

The knock came just after 2:00 a.m. Although I had expected them to come any day because a friend had been arrested on 2nd November and had heard there was a list of people to be detained, I was terrified and very frightened when it finally happened. My heart started to beat faster and harder. I put on a pair of jeans, a shirt and shoes while they continued knocking harder and harder on the door.

This was a classic example of the belief that horrible things happened only to other people and not to you. In spite of the many stories that I heard of innocent people being arrested in the middle of the night and the systematic torture of prisoners who were perceived to be against the regime or simply not actively in support of it, somewhere in my mind there was the nagging feeling that the victims "must have done something wrong". When my turn came, however, I could not accept it or even think about it objectively. In fact the first few hours went by in a blur, and even today it is difficult to recall exactly what had happened. The most haunting image I remember about the whole episode is the terror I saw in my wife's eyes. We had only been married for four months and somehow she seemed to sense that something terrible was going to happen to me. Her eyes were pools of love but overwhelmed by fright and helplessness.

I could not bear looking at her. She suggested repeatedly that she open the door by herself but in the end we went together. There were four men in civilian clothes with AK47 assault rifles and a vehicle at the ready. A fifth man, obviously their leader, carrying a pistol, asked me to go with them to the secret police N.S.S. (National Security Service) headquarters. I asked them who they were in the first place. This was just to buy time during which I whispered to my wife to go and wake up our neighbour who was an army officer. They tried to stop her but they were too late and the neighbour came out. This upset the leader, because the last thing they wanted was to be seen arresting people in the middle of the night. I asked the neighbour whether he knew the men. He affirmed that they were N.S.S. officers. By then they had lowered their guns and started playing the good guys. I asked the neighbour to come with us and make sure I was taken to N.S.S. headquarters. They reassured my wife, with disarming civility that I was going to be back within the hour. It turned out to be a long hour. It lasted for eight years and six months in prison, mostly in solitary confinement during which I had not able to communicate with my wife or relatives.

The first night I was not taken to the N.S.S. headquarters but to a small police station on the outskirts of town. I was put in a tiny cell with no windows and no light. The fetid suffocating smell of human excrement overwhelmed me. I had to feel my way through a mass of people huddled into a small space. People of different ages, different backgrounds, different outlooks, different in every thing, but united in a kind of inexplicable brotherhood which is instinctive though difficult to articulate. Despite our different beginnings, backgrounds and attainments so far, every one of us realized that we were reduced to the same level, to the basest biological instinct, that for survival.

As is the case in such circumstances, we got acquainted with each other quickly. All reservations were thrown to the wind. Most of my fellow prisoners were petty thieves, drunkards and the like. I could not eat that first night, but my food was hungrily devoured by my cell mates. One of my cell mates gave us a lesson in human relations in the other world. He admitted frankly that he had killed a friend. He told a poignant story. He narrated how under the influence of alcohol he and three others cornered a fifth, a friend of theirs, whom they accused of destroying their lives by introducing alcohol to each of them. One of the groups was then appointed as a judge, another a defence lawyer and a third was the prosecutor. In the end Kangaroo court dissolved into a brawl. The verdict was a summary execution. The sentence was immediately carried out, by throwing the accused into a dry well. A brutal method of getting rid of a friend. Nevertheless, this resembled the chaotic military justice that prevailed in the country at the time. And it may have been a fitting way of introducing me into the equally brutal world of Siyaad Barre's prison system. In fact I expected no better treatment.

4

Interrogation

During the following four months I was transferred from one N.S.S. centre, to another, from security safe-house to torture chamber and then to various military police centres which where all equally equipped for the torture of political prisoners. The torture methods were brutal. There were indiscriminate beatings, of the-whole-body-dipped-in-water beatings, beatings through particularly sensitive or painful body parts. The torturers were military police officers, specially trained for the purpose and supervised by one of the N.S.S. officers leading the investigation of our cases. There was nothing to prevent the N.S.S. officers from taking part in our torture. They usually took part and enjoyed it.

After being held for about a week in the main N.S.S. centre without charges or interrogation and without contact with my family or friends, I was suddenly called to the N.S.S. chief's office. There were five other officers with him. I learned immediately that they were especially sent from Mogadishu, the Somali capital city, for the investigation of the cases of 29 people arrested between the beginning of November and the end of December 1981. The Names of the Interrogation Team:

1. Colonel Ali Hussein
2. Lieutenant Qassim
3. Captain Ali Hussein (Gani)
4. Abdirashid
5. Omer

They were obviously an elite band of interrogators and torturers. They were led by the chief investigating officer of the N.S.S. and organization modelled on the KGB, which also trained many of its officers in the Soviet Union. They were notorious and brutal torturers of detainees.

The NSS was one of the many security groups with their own detention centres which possessed unlimited powers of search, detention without trial, license for torture and confiscation of property. These groups also included the presidential body guards, red berets; *Dhabar Jebinta* (back breakers), a branch of the military police; Hangash, another branch of the military police; *Guulwadayaal* (victory pioneers), a uniformed paramilitary group; the investigative wing of the Somali Revolutionary Socialist Party (SRSP). The first meeting was short. The leader of the group threatened me and bragged about his exploits in the realm. He described in graphic detail how he succeeded, where others had failed, in extracting a confession from Col. Irro (Cirro), the leader of the failed coup attempt of 1978. Walking to and fro in the interrogation room with a heels-first-step and always stopping behind me putting his hands on my shoulders, he finally made a proposition that he would make me a prosecution witness and in return I would be released if I cooperated. I told him that I did not know anything about his allegations which where not even specific enough.

Eventually, he said that my friends and I were members of an illegal organization bent on overthrowing the regime. I denied his accusations. He immediately asked the military police guard waiting outside to take me back to my cell. They took away my mattress and blankets. I was handcuffed hands behind my back. I had no food or water for the following day and was not allowed out of the room even to go to the toilet. Next evening at 7:00 p.m. the lights were extinguished throughout the building. I heard footsteps approaching my cell door. The door was opened; two military police officers and one of the interrogation team entered; they told me to stand up and searched me for the tenth time that week. Then they blind-folded me and put me on the back of a land-cruiser.

I did not know which direction we were going. About 45 minutes later the car stopped. I was made to come down still blind-folded and hand-cuffed, hands behind my back. They tied my feet together. I was made to lie on my stomach. They put a heavy weight on my back while four solders held me down. The weight was held on either side of me by two other soldiers who let it descend gradually while the leader kept asking me if I was ready to confess. I kept silent for a while but then I could not bear it any more. I cried out with the excruciating pain. But there was no let-up and finally I fainted. When I regained consciousness, I was wet throughout. Apparently they had thrown a bucket of water over me to bring me back. As soon as I opened my eyes the leader asked me to sign a prepared statement. I declined. He ordered that I should be given the water treatment. They forced my mouth open and holding my nose shut they poured large amounts of water till I almost suffocated. I vomited everything. They repeated this several times.

By now, I was so weakened that they decided to take me back. At the office they took off the blind-fold. There was a new officer with the original team. Softly he asked me what had happened to me. I explained everything to him and he started cursing the others telling them that it was no way to treat a human-being. They lowered their heads as if in repentance. He told me that it would never happen again. He ordered a sandwich for me, a cup of tea and a cigarette. Before the order arrived, however, he asked me the same questions, which were raised by the others. I told him what I had already told them. Suddenly he was transformed into an animal. He started screaming at me and threatening that he would shoot me on the spot if I did not sign the prepared statement. When the sandwich and tea arrived, he threw them out of the window and assured me that I would follow them if I did not cooperate. I was taken back to my cell.

I lay on the floor for the rest of the night without having eaten or drunk water for more than 30 hours. But I did not feel hungry or thirsty. I could not sleep. I kept thinking about my situation knowing I was innocent of all crimes. I was helpless against these people who did not listen to reason and who were motivated by the single notion of breaking a prisoner and making him confess to having committed some imaginary crime. They seemed to be engaged in a cruel game in which they made all the rules and were allowed to employ all kinds of weapons and techniques. By contrast, the prisoners were stripped of everything. The prisoners could not even use their reason.

Having been through their physical torture, I was not at all concerned by the pain nor by the hunger and thirst but rather by the psychological effects of detention and solitary confinement. I was overwhelmed by a sense of loneliness and being abandoned and forgotten by my family and relatives. I knew this was unreasonable and that they themselves were helpless. All the same, this persisted for most of the day or whenever the interrogators failed to come.

In a sense it was a relief when they came to beat and torture me. The physical pain was easier to cope with than the doubts and fears during lonely days and nights. At exactly 7:00 p.m. the second night they took me away blind-folded. We went through the same routine with the addition of kicks on my shins, cigarette burns on the inner sides of my legs and on my ankles. There were short periods of rest during which they exhorted me to sign their prepared statements.

This continued for about a week when they suddenly stopped coming. I was to learn from one of the military police guards that there were many other prisoners to be interrogated. Two weeks later I was again called to the interrogation room. The chief told me that they had uncovered new incriminating evidence against me. He continued to say that some of my friends were prepared to testify against me and that he did not need my cooperation anymore. He mentioned the names of some familiar people and asked whether I knew them. I admitted that I knew them but no more.

The most incredible accusation came when he asked me why we called ourselves *Barood* (gunpowder), *Olad* (struggle), *Abby* (defence), *Dagal* (war) if we were not involved in a conspiracy. These names were the traditional names of the fathers and grandfathers of my fellow detainees. I countered that some of my other fellow detainees were called *Warsame* (good news), *Dualeh* (blessing), *Madar* (rain) on which he made no comment. During the trial, I found out that some of my fellow detainees went through the same torture. Some of them went through even harsher methods including one whose testicles had to be removed because they were destroyed.

Though the government of Somalia formally recognized certain human rights standards in its constitution and through its ratification of the U.N. Declaration of Human Rights, hundreds and perhaps thousands of prisoners were held throughout the country for years without formal charges, access to their families and lawyers, adequate medical care, and fair trial. Dr. Wendell Block of the Canadian Centre for the Investigation and Prevention of Torture, after examining victims of torture in Somalia, concluded that:

> There is no doubt in my mind detention without trial, under horrendous conditions and accompanied by brutal beatings, exist as a daily reality in Somalia. Further, it seems to be carried out as a means of stamping out political opposition and criticism....... While in detention, these men where interrogated, assaulted, and tortured. Aside from the inhuman [prison] conditions,...there were regular, brutal beatings with kicks, punches, rifle butts...the beatings might be haphazard in some cases, while in others, specific parts of the body, for example the knees or the soles of the feet, would be persistently beaten. One man described being put inside a sack and beaten. Two men described being beaten while tied for one or two hours in what they called "*mig*" (chest on the floor, arms and legs pulled back so that wrists are tied to ankles.

Four months had passed since my arrest and there was no release or even a trial in sight. But on 19th of Feb. we were all served with official indictment papers.

We were officially charged for the first time with high treason. I was charged with two articles. I was charged with section one, article 54 and section one, article 17 for allegedly publishing seditious material and leading a political opposition group. Both of these carried mandatory death penalties under the emergency laws. I was not familiar with these laws. I sent a note through one of the guards to my wife to find out what these articles meant. Her brother contacted a secretary in the security court. He sent back word explaining that each article carried a mandatory death sentence on its own. When I read the note I was floored. I could not think, sleep or eat. That was definitely the worst week of my life. For the first time in my life I was forced to look at the ugly face of death. When I thought about the track record of Siyaad Barre, the way he had executed all his opponents or those perceived to be opponents, the security court's history as his puppet, the inordinate haste with which the accused were executed in the past, all boded ill for me.

5

The Trial

But even worse than my fear of the unpalatable notion of death was my obsession with the manner of death. In his note, the secretary of the court conveyed to my family that both articles carried mandatory death sentences by 'HANGING' – '*DALDALAAD*' in Somali. Somehow my distress, the confinement of the cell, loneliness and my inability to perceive any consolation in this grim picture all added up to make me unable to think clearly. I just concentrated on the horrors of dying by hanging. I spent all my time thinking about the stories I had heard or books I had read on this most terrible of all manners of execution. I was not able to talk to anyone about this and this exacerbated my fears. I was so sure that I was going to be hanged that I even imagined that I could smell death. I had read Hemingway's *For Whom the Bell Tolls* only a few months earlier and I was reminded of one of the central characters "Pillar" talking about the smell of death. I had never understood this before or tried to visualize it, but now I felt sure I smelt death or maybe the fear of death. Suddenly on the morning of 20th Feb.1982, I heard sustained gun fire not far away from where I was being held and there was even some sporadic artillery fire. The shooting seemed to be coming closer and closer and continued until 4:00 in the afternoon. The same thing happened the following day and the following. What in the world was happening? But in solitary confinement you receive no responses. However, one development was that there were no interrogation sessions from the first day of the shooting.

On the third day the interrogation team arrived with two others who they said were judges of the security court. The security, court which was independent of the judiciary, was a military tribunal that heard political cases. It was established in

1970 and was run by military and security forces. Most of these members had no training in legal matters. According to Amnesty International:

> The National Security Court was composed of mainly military and police officers, often without legal training. Legal safeguards for defendants being tried in civil courts are absent. Defendants normally received a summary trial and, although they have no right of appeal, the President must review the sentences. In the past, review of sentence and actual execution had been carried out very quickly after the sentences have been announced.

The security organizations and others of lesser stature had a free reign in oppressing the public and freely carried out extra-judicial executions and arrests on suspected opponents of the government. The German democratic Republic's Development Aid concentrated on funding and building state-of-the-art, efficient prisons throughout the country, or as people preferred to describe it: a pair of hand-cuffs for everyone.

I was charged formally with Law no. 54 and 17 which carried mandatory death sentences:

> *Law NO. 54*
>
> *Chapter 1. Crimes Against the State*
>
> *Article 1*
>
> *Acts against the independence, unity or security of the Somali State:*
>
> *Whoever commits, participates, aids or abets in the commission of, an act which is detrimental to the independence, unity or security of the Somali State shall be punished with death and his properties confiscated.*

When I requested to see a lawyer, they made no response to my request. Two days later I was taken out of my cell. I joined 28 other people most of whom I knew including some friends of mine.

We were put in two buses half of whose seats were taken up by military intelligence (*Dhabar Jebin*) soldiers. For the first time we saw buildings burnt and along the deserted roads, armed soldiers, tanks, armoured vehicles. This route was completely empty of civilian cars and people. Inside the court, most of the seats were taken up by uniformed commandos. Only the last two rows were reserved for the relatives of the detainees – one relative for each prisoner. There was a cordon of commandos around the court and beyond. It was only after the trial when we were taken to the main prison that we found out about the extent of the riots and the death toll.

The trial when it finally came took only 10 hours, from 9:00 a.m. to 19:00 p.m. including a break of one hour for launch. None of us was allowed to say a word other than a brief answer to preliminary questions like "how do you plead to the offence described"? All the 28 defendants pleaded not guilty. Our defence lawyers who arrived from Mogadishu two days earlier had only met us the night before the trial in the presence of the interrogation team and had only 10 minutes interview with each of us to learn our names, ages, professions etc. The lawyers were:

1. Attorney Ismail Jimaale
2. Attorney Faisal Haji Jama
3. Attorney Hussein Bille
4. Attorney Hassan Sheikh
5. Attorney Osman Abdi
6. Attorney Bashir Artan

The prosecutor was Captain Abdulle Ali. The court was chaired by Colonel Sharif Shekhuna Mayow, assisted by Yussuf Abdi Ali and Colonel Ahmed Abdi Awale.

The defence lawyers had no time to prepare their cases. Being veterans of many previous political trials, they knew that it was immaterial whether they presented a case or not because, the final judgment lay not with the court, but with the government and more specifically with Siyaad Barre, the President, himself. The case against us as presented by the prosecution was that we belonged to an illegal organization with intent to over-throw the government and that we published a pamphlet in which we spread pernicious propaganda against the regime. The evidence presented to the court was a list of names in which not all of those accused were included while others on the list were not present at the trial. The list was compiled by an NSS informer called

"Laangadhe" who, earlier on, escaped to Ethiopia after receiving a check for 40,000 Somali shillings, about US$ 4,000, for his services from Major Dahir Cid, head of HANGASH in Hargeisa.

The security police knew about his escape but they made no attempt to stop him because it suited them fine since they did not want him at the trial to be questioned by the defence lawyers. The main prosecution witness, the chief interrogation and torturer, claimed that Laangadhe told him that the accused were plotting to overthrow the regime and that they used to meet and criticize the regime in his presence. When defence lawyers objected that the list of names did not mean anything and that Laangadhe's mercenary allegations could not be considered as evidence since the accused were unable to question him, the judge, a police colonel with NO LEGAL training, overruled them immediately saying that the list could be presented as a genuine piece of evidence to the court.

The other piece of evidence presented by the prosecution alleged that by cleaning up health facilities at Hargeisa Group Hospital and improving educational, cultural and general social services in the region, the accused were trying to portray the government as inept thereby gaining popular support for them. To support this notion the prosecution cited the riots that preceded the trial which in fact occurred because the people were unhappy with detention and torture of prisoners throughout the region. These riots for which we were accused of instigating took place four months after our arrest. They took place during these four months in which we were kept incommunicado and in solitary confinement.

The prosecution, in fact, was not bothered at all by the lack of credible evidence. All it did was recite repeatedly that so and so was accused of such and such a crime. It did not make any effort to convince the court or the audience. It took about 10 hours, including a lunch-hour, for both the prosecution to present its case against 28 people accused of high crimes against the state, punishable by death, and the defence lawyers to rebut. The impossibility of giving so many people a fair trial within such a short span of time does not need any explanation. As a matter of fact, no one expected any fairness from such a court. It seemed that everyone including the judges, the prosecution, the defence lawyers, the audience (which comprise 400 uniformed elite commandos and a relative each of the accused and, in a sense, even us the accused, were all in collusion to let the charade take its course. We all knew that once one was accused of a crime against the state, one was automatically considered guilty of that crime and the only consideration for the accused and his relatives was to find out if the accused was going to be sentenced o death or not!.

There was a sigh of relief from everybody when, as a result of the intensive shuttling between Mogadishu and Hargeisa by two government ministers, one of them a politburo member and a son-in-law of Siyaad Barre, none of us was sentenced to death even though two of us were sentenced to life imprisonment. This was why the defence lawyers, as if admitting our guilt, concentrated on asking leniency from the court since all other requests, including one for examining the wounds and scars left by the torture during the four months of interrogation, had been continually denied by the court. Looking back at the trial proceedings there is no doubt in my mind that the presence of lawyers did not make the slightest impression on the court and did not make any difference on the final sentences. The only thing it did, if any, was lend a stamp of legitimacy to the farce. That was the actual intention of the regime all along. I must hasten to add that the ability and integrity of the lawyers was never in doubt. On the contrary, I respected them and we all appreciated the effort they made in an impossible situation to help the innocent victims of a cruel system.

I believe that we were reprieved, not because of the presence of the lawyers, nor because of the magnanimity of Siyaad Barre as the judge mentioned in his summation and certainly not because of the leniency of the court, but simply because the regime was terrified of the possible consequences of such a course. On Feb. 20th, 21st, 22nd, Hargeisa, Burao and other major towns in the North experienced wild riots in which 43 people, mostly students, were killed by the security forces. Hargeisa was still in turmoil and the slightest provocation was needed to spark off further riots. Testimony to this is the way the final sentences were packaged and wrapped up.

The two ministers promised the families of the accused that we were going to be released soon after the trial ran its course. The court ruling for the 28 detainees was as follows:

A 8 were released for lack of evidence.

1. Hassan Abdillahi Ali (Elgeye)
2. Hassan Abdisalan Aw Ali
3. Mohamed Abdi Ayub
4. Ismail Abdi Hurre (dheg)
5. Ahmed Hassan Madar
6. Lt. colonel Ismail Hashi Madar
7. Mohamed Dagal Hersi
8. Siyaad Mohamed Ibrahim.

B 2 were sentenced to life in prison: -

1. Ahmed Mohamed Yuusuf (Physics Teacher
2. Mohamed Barood Ali (Industrial Chemist)

C 2 were given 30 years imprisonment: -

1. Mohamed Mohamoud Omer (Economist)
2. Abdirahman Abdillahi H. Aden (Civil servant)

D One was sentenced to 25 years in prison

1. Mohamed Ali Ibrahim (Head of self-help at Hargeisa)

E 9 were given 20 years imprison: -

1. Aden Yuusuf Abokor (Medical doctor)
2. Hussein Mohamoud Duale (Biology/Chemistry teacher)
3. Aden Warsame Siyaad (Economist)
4. Yuusuf Abdillahi Kahin (Farmer and businessman)
5. Mohamoud Sh. Hassan Tani (Medical Doctor)
6. Abdillahi Ali Yuusuf (Veterinary Doctor)
7. Osman Abdi Maigag (Medical doctor)
8. Ahmed Hussein Abby (Banker)
9. Bashe Abdi Yussuf (Businessman)

F 3 were sentenced to 8 years each
1. Mohamed Ma'alin Osman (Biology teacher)
2. Mohamed Abdi jiir (Biology teacher)
3. Ahmed Muhumed Madar (Biology teacher

G 3 were sentenced to 3 years each:
1. Ali Eghe Farah (Engineer – Civil
2. Omer Isse Awale (Civil servant)
3. Mohamed Ali Sulub (Medical Doctor)

After the sentences were announced, we were transferred to the main prison in Hargeisa where we were allowed to see our family members and other relatives for the first time in months.

At one time there were 400 school students aged between 11 and 16 years with us before they were transferred to the largest prison in the north at Mandhera. These students participated in the demonstrations for our release. The girls among them were eventually taken to Berbera prison which is reserved for women alcoholics, prostitutes and hardened women criminals.

One of the custodial corps officers, a woman who travelled with the school girls to Berbera, told us when she returned that at one time on the way to Berbera, the soldiers ordered the girls to come down of the lorry. She objected. She was hit by a soldier from the military police with the back of his gun. She believed that the girls were saved when soldiers saw the head lights of an approaching car. The students were released six months later after fresh riots threatened to break out in Hargeisa and Burao.

We remained in Hargeisa prison for the following eight months. In Hargeisa prison, we had relative freedom to do many things within the confines of the prison compound. Our relatives were allowed more visits than the relatives of other prisoners. We were allowed to dig our own pit-latrine so that we would have access to toilet facilities at night which was denied to other prisoners.

During our stay in Hargeisa prison, we often thought of escaping though many of us still believed in Siyaad Barre's promises of release. The late Abdillahi Ali Adar (Olad) was very sociable, what Somalis called "Warraabe la Hadal". He opened doors where there was no obvious door. He spent hours talking to people in the administrative department of the prison. When he came back from talking with his new friends, he always brought us news from the outside world. One day he came back from the prison offices with a bunch of keys. We tried them one by one on the padlocks on our door. After a few trials, we found one that fit all the locks on our door, a master key. We made a copy of the master key by hitting the key very hard on a bar of soap. Olad took the bunch of keys back to the office before they noticed that it was missing. We sent the bar of soap with Mohamed Dagal Hersi(Dayib) who was detained with us but was released by the court. He made two copies of the master key, kept one and brought back one copy to us. We never had an opportunity to make use of Olad's ingenuity because we were transferred to Labaatan Jirow prison soon after this.

Hargeisa prison was run by an Orwellian character by the name of Hassan Jilic. He told us a typical Hassan Jilic story one day when he came back from a conference of the Somali Revolutionary Socialist Party (SRSP) in Mogadishu. This was the end of Siyaad Barre's term of office in 1982 and there was talk of a challenger for office, possibly the party secretary, Ismail Ali Abokor. Hassan related that they we were waiting for the arrival of Siyaad Barre. Suddenly there was commotion at the entrance and Siyaad Barre entered in full uniform. He had not been seen in uniform since the Somali-Ethiopia war in 1977. According to Hassan they started clapping. This continued for sometime without anybody daring to stop clapping first. The front row, then others stood up without stopping clapping. Soon the people in the last were climbing their tables and clapping. Nobody wanted to be seen to stop first. Finally Siyaad Barre himself signalled for an end to the clapping and he was duly elected for a new term.

After the sentence, my father and a relative of one of the other prisoners, Haji Hussein Omer Hashi went with the two ministers on a military plane to Mogadishu. Siyaad Barre himself had earlier on asked for a meeting with a delegation of the relatives before he would grant our release. However, he broke the appointment and left for a 45 days tour of Europe and North America. His plane took off from Mogadishu airport a few minutes before the delegation were due to arrive in Mogadishu. He knew that our relatives and elders were coming to see him in Mogadishu because he invited them. Fresh riots were unlikely to take place in Hargeisa while the elders were still in Mogadishu hopeful of our imminent release by the President. When he returned from his tour abroad, he embarrassed the elders and sent them back empty-handed and with yet another empty promise that he will release us on the then upcoming occasion of the 13th anniversary celebrations of the coup in October 1982.

6

Labaatan Jirrow Prison

On the 24th of October 1982 we were transferred, without any prior notice, from Hargeisa to Labaatan Jirow, the Maximum security prison near Baidoa in the South, about 2000Km away from home and friends. We were moved in the middle of the night and were accompanied by 4 armoured vehicles, 4 personnel carriers and 2 land rovers. We only stopped at 17:00 hours on the second day at Galkaayo, about 700km from Hargeisa (see map fig. 2). We were kept in the main prison for the night. The following three nights we spent in central prison (Carcere) of Mogadishu, the Capital.

The trip from Mogadishu to Labaatan Jiraw took about 18 hours. There were heavy rains and the road from Baidoa to Labaatan Jiraw was impassable. Mogadishu-Baidoa road was better. During these 18 hours between Mogadishu to Labaatan jirow, however, we were not allowed to relieve ourselves, to eat or to drink. There were 20 of us in the lorry, a closed army truck that had space for 8 people at best. We sat crushed against each other. Six of our friends were left in Mogadishu but another six prisoners, who had been held in Mogadishu central prison since 1978 without trial joined us. This group was accused of taking part in the failed coup attempt of 1978 though all of them had been in the provinces at the time. In fact, one of them was in hospital recovering from wounds he received during 1977-78 Somalia-Ethiopia war. Their only crime was that they belonged to the same clan as the leaders of that coup attempt.

We were blind-folded as we left Baidoa to prevent us from knowing where Labaatan Jiraw prison was. We were also blind-folded from Labaatan Jiraw to Baidoa on our release six and half years later. Inside the prison each one of us was taken to a cell and then the blind-folds were removed but not the hand-cuffs. These were taken off a week later. The cell was completely empty. It was 2 X 2 meters with a hole in the right hand corner. This was meant to serve as the toilet since no one would be allowed to go out at all. The walls were un-plastered and made of re-enforced concrete. There were a total of 175 cells in the prison but only 35 cells were occupied during our stay. That was not because there were not enough political prisoners in the country to fill them but because, the other cells did not have toilet facilities and the guards did not want to take the trouble of taking the prisoners outside for the purpose. There were two doors for each cell. The inner door remained looked at all times and consisted of heavy steel bars. The outer door which was opened from 7:00 a.m. to 4:00 p.m. each day was one heavy sheet of iron without even a crack. This door was normally closed during punishment periods which were quite frequent because the slightest sound constituted misbehaviour in the eyes of these guards. There were 20 guards inside the prison and about 150 soldiers outside equipped with heavy artillery and anti-aircraft guns.

Moreover, it must be mentioned that all the guards, both inside and outside the prison, were members of the military police. The guards stationed outside the prison were there to protect the prison from outside attack. There were no custodial guards in Labaatan Jiraw. Administratively, this special prison was run from the President's office in Mogadishu. Furthermore, every single member of the guards including the prison warden colonel Deria Hirsi and male nurse Dheel Deria Yuusuf, was Marrehan- the clan of Siyaad Barre, the President. The membership of the military police in the country was predominantly Marrehans. They had wide powers of search, arrest, interrogation and their own detention centres. They also manned all control posts throughout the country using their powers to extort money and property from the population. The regime denied the existence of a prison called Labaatan Jiraw. In fact the only people who have ever seen it were prisoners or their captors.

On the second day following our arrival, I was given a blanket, an aluminium cup, a plastic plate and a small plastic bucket for water. We were given millet gruel for breakfast and boiled rice for lunch and a glass of powdered milk. This was the usual prison fare for the next six and half years. Only occasionally, perhaps once every three months or once every six months, a goat would be killed, boiled and each prisoner given a tiny piece of meet along with the usual mouldy rice. These were feast days for us and they would be signalled the day before by the bleating of a goat. The feast day itself would be confirmed by the usual movement and number of crows in the prison compound. A bleating goat and increased crow activity definitely meant goat meat. The bleating of a goat, therefore, was beautiful music to our ears. And every time one of us heard bleating of a goat whether in the morning, afternoon or in the middle of the night he would immediately transmit the good news to his neighbours who would also pass it on to their neighbours and so on, until everybody heard and discussed with their neighbour about the delicious part of the goat he would like to get.

One comic incident comes into mind when thinking back about goat meat. A friend, Dr. Osman, dreamt one night, during a particularly meatless period that he heard the bleating of a goat. He woke up to transmit the good news to his neighbours. Everybody woke up and stayed up the rest of the night discussing the good turn of events. The next morning, a group of crows chased another crow holding a piece of red meat on its beak. We all saw this. This was enough confirmation and a reason to lift our spirits. Our moods soared. We watched the lucky crow with hungry eyes. The crows flew back and forth playfully. Suddenly the crow released the piece of meat. We all waited for the piece of meat to fall down to the ground and provide us with full confirmation of the feast. But no the meat stayed up in the air, floating!!. The crows kept it playfully in the air. This was no meat. It was a piece of pink cellophane bag!!!.

Food is, like in all such facilities, the main topic of conversation. Even when you are alone, you find yourself day-dreaming about food. We made many a joke about our yearnings for food. Dr. Osman was asked once by his neighbour through the wall to name his best wish at that particular moment. Without a moment's hesitation, he said "meat!" Freedom definitely came a far second. Only after he asked him about freedom, did he laugh and said "of course". In this type of prison you become obsessed with food. The food was brought in a barrel and pushed on a wheel-barrow. As soon as we heard the noise of the wheel-barrow we literally started to salivate like Pavlov's dogs, even when it was only millet gruel.

We had our greatest problem with food during the Holy month of Ramadan, when Muslims fast from dawn to sunset. We were given food at night; to break our fast at six in the evening and again about 3 o'clock the next morning. The early evening was no problem but at 3 in the morning the soldiers woke you up nosily and violently. If you are not ready at the door with your plate. They just "locked up" the door and that was that. Your next meal? Fifteen hours later at six in the evening. We usually solved this problem by assigning one person to stay awake each night. As soon as he heard the noise of the wheel-barrow he would wake up everybody. We ate in pitch darkness and with the smell of food came the attack from all sides; Cockroaches, mice and ants. We had to cover the plate with one hand and eat with the other. The cockroaches were particularly vicious. They would fly from the walls above the toilet and land on your face or plate and they did not take no for an answer. They were very persistent and if you were squeamish, you went hungry. We were also given a bucket of water every day for all purposes such as cleaning the toilet, washing up the utensils, drinking and having ablutions before prayers. We were not provided with any clothes and our clothes were taken away. I was left with a T-shirt, lungi (macawis) and a pair of sandals cut from an old tyre (*Kabo Shaag* in Somali).

The first few days in Labaatan Jiraw were the most difficult ones. I was confronted with poor food, shortage of water, lack of sanitation facilities, lack of reading material and isolation not only from the rest of the world, but from my fellow prisoners. All contributed to a sense of incomprehension and depression. I tried to get in touch with my friends on either side of me. But as soon as one uttered a word, even *sotto voce*, a guard would be there on one's door step closing the main iron door. There were no warnings given in that prison. Soon we learned that shouting to each other behind the doors would only bring us more punishment. We had to remain content with knocking the wall between the cells when the guards were not looking. At first we did not understand each other but it was good to know that the friends on either side of you were alive.

We were warned of writing anything on the walls. It is a hard job to desist from scratching something, anything on prison walls in solitary confinement because that is about the only way left to express yourself. But we had to be careful. Every day during "lock up" time, three soldiers would enter the cell and tell you to stand against a wall. They would meticulously check for scratches on walls, the floor and the ceiling. As soon as I arrived at my cell, I checked for graffiti but there was none. Obviously my predecessors had taken their warnings seriously and had not dared to write on the walls. Only much later, while I lay on the floor one day and looked at the walls in front of me, I saw something on the wall. At first I could not believe what I saw, but soon I was laughing my head off. I laughed so loudly that my friend next door started knocking on the wall to warn me. At the bottom of the wall, where the soldiers could not possibly see, was EGAL written in capital letters. This was the name of Somalia's last civilian Prime Minister who spent 7 years there. The most powerful man in the country had been reduced to write his name on that obscure corner of the cell to express his protest. But I felt for him at the time. It must have felt great seeing those soldiers checking for signs on the walls and failing every-day. I could imagine him chuckling under his breath.

A grim example of protest graffiti I saw in the large cell I shared with 20 friends in Hargeisa's main prison where we stayed for 8 months before we were transferred to Labaatan Jirrow. On a wall opposite where I slept was clearly written the names of seven male prisoners, every name apparently written by a different person. Every one added a comment after his name. Most of them wrote the names of loved ones. But at the bottom one of them wrote:

> "Siyaad Barre says we die tomorrow on the 28th, April 1981 by firing squad. So says Siyaad Barre but not Allah."

But for those seven prisoners who signed their names on the wall of that grim prison, as for so many Somalis before them, there was no divine intervention. They were promptly shot on the 28th. They were all civilians who belonged to the Majerteen sub-clan. They were accused of belonging to the SSDF, the opposition movement fighting the Siyaad Barre regime.

Looking back at those six and half years, they seem to have passed away in a blur because every one of the 2375 days was exactly the same. I woke up at 6:00 a.m. the outer door was opened at 7:00, millet gruel was served at 7:30, lunch at 11:00 and the outer door was closed again at 4:00 p.m. Nothing in between. Boredom, boredom! And bone-crushing boredom! Time stood still for us. Sometimes it used to occur to me that I was in some kind of an Orwellian zoo in which the humans were in cages with the beasts looking in from outside. The soldiers resembled beasts not only through my bitter view but also because they never said a word. They only made grunts when they disapproved of something or otherwise looking at you scornfully.

One of the cruellest things that happened to us was how they treated detainees in illness. They would think that you were shamming if you told them you were ill. Even on the rare occasion when they believed you, and saw that you were really in pain, they gave you insufficient doses or the wrong medicine. There was only one old male nurse for health care in the prison. We called him Doctor "NO" because his first response was always in the negative. Later on when we learnt how to communicate with each other through the walls between the cells we were able to seek advice from the doctors (four of them) among us in prison. The doctors advised us to keep asking for drugs, particularly aspirins, sedatives, anti-pain medicine, antibiotics and chloroquine against malaria and hoard them even when we were well. This method helped us whenever one of us fell ill and Doctor-No would not come to see him refused to give him any medicine.

We were able to pass medicine from one to the other because we had an exercise period of 10 minutes every three days excluding Thursdays and Fridays. The exercise periods were taken by one person at a time. One would be taken out of his cell and others would be prevented by closing all doors from seeing him walking in front of their cells. If that person had medicine to pass to one of his friends he would inform the person next to him through the walls (more about the wall language later) who would pass it on to the person needing the medicine. The medicine would be dropped at a prearranged place and the ill person would pick it up during his turn of exercise. The walk was between two doors 30 meters apart and with one soldier at each end. We always dropped near a small shrub half-way between the two doors. However, sometimes we were not permitted to exercise for 3 or 4 consecutive months or even longer. This usually coincided with periods of tension in the country as we found out later. For example we did not exercise from May 1988 onwards as a result of the war in the North. I calculated the total number of hours that we came out of the cells during those six and half years to be 72 hours altogether!.

7

Learning a New Alphabet

The major health problems we experienced were mainly connected with immobility, anxiety, fear, depression, and insomnia and poor diet. Most of us suffered from psychosomatic ailments and "Doctor-No" always succeeded in aggravating these conditions. During our imprisonment one man died because of negligence. Warsame Ali Farah, who was in his seventies, was taken to Mogadishu and died there two days later. According to the official pathological report, the cause of death was:

> "Chronic renal insufficiency from multiple bilateral cysts, the seat of supputive pyelonephritis". In simple language he died of kidney failure. But there is no doubt that he died of criminal negligence."

One of the detainees who had been held since the 1978 coup attempt, Mr. Abdillahi Mohamed Nur, fell very ill. Apparently he had been asking for medicine for six months. On 1st May 1985 he started shouting at the top of his voice. The place was normally dead quiet, and we all put our ears against the wall to hear what was happening. He started by reciting his autobiography. Their solution was to close the outer iron door on him. They came at night, took him out and obviously beat him because we could hear him shouting "Allah……..Allah" (God………oh God!"). This continued for about two hours on and off. He never stopped shouting after that until his release in February 1989. They never attempted to treat him for mental disturbance as far as we knew. When we were released, we found out he had been badly maimed that night. Sadly, Adillahi is still mentally disturbed.

We were informed, through the walls by one of those who came before us, that 5 Ethiopian pilots including Col: Wolok were shot dead just before we arrived to make room for us. The pilots had entered Somalia voluntarily seeking political asylum. This was not an isolated incident. The same treatment was given to about 200 young Ethiopians, mostly students, who fled Ethiopia and who were with us in jail in Hargeisa. They were transferred to Mogadishu prisons and shown to foreign journalists as captured Ethiopian soldiers in 1982 when one of the Somali opposition groups, SSDF (Somali Salvation Democratic Front), captured Balanbaleh and Galdogob villages in the South. Afterwards, we were told by a member of the corps who accompanied their transfer to Mogadishu, that the Ethiopian students had all been executed.

When you have so little, you find joy in insignificant things. The most important and useful means of communication between us was through the cell walls. As mentioned earlier. We used to knock on the walls of adjacent cells to inform neighbours that we were still alive. The invention of an alphabet similar to the Morse code started to develop from this. There were two sounds one could make on the walls. A higher frequency rap made with the knuckles of the middle fingers and a low drumming note produced by the side of the closed fist. The high frequency note represented (.) and the low one (0).

THE ALPHABET

a = .	i = . . .	p = o o .	w = o o . .
b = o	j = . . o	q= . . o o	x = o o o .
c = . .	k = . o o	r = . . . o	y = o o o o
d = . o	l = . o .	s = ...	z= . o . o
e = o .	m = o o o	t = . o o o	
f = o o	n = o . . o	u = . . o .	
g = o . o	o = o . o o	v = . o o .	
h = o . .			

For example good morning would be (o.o, o.oo, o.oo, .o; ooo, o.oo, ...o, o..o, ..., o..o, o.o). It took us a few hours to learn this alphabet and since we had nothing else to occupy us, we were able to use it the same day. By the end of the first week one became an expert and understood a word or a sentence even before the other had finished transmitting it. I cannot over-estimate the value of this alphabet to us because it was the only method of human contact left to us. The guards could not see us but even if they saw us, they could not make the mental leap of deducing that we were able to understand each other by "touching the walls" as they called it. They would just tell us to stop touching the wall, if they caught us knocking on it.

Through this tapping of walls, we were able to know who had a cold, who was fine, etc. We were also able to amuse each other through the walls. We could discuss almost anything. As a matter of fact, I was eventually able to learn some German and Italian from two neighbours on either side with the help of the code. The most important use of the code, however, was to seek the advice of one of the doctors. That was the only way we were able to keep our sanity. In this kind of solitary confinement you always imagined the worst. The slightest cough, pain or weakness becomes a terminal illness in your imagination. All you need in this kind of situation is to tell someone about your problem. Then it disappears until the next bout of anxiety. The reassurance was much more effective if it came from a doctor whom you could trust.

Another very important entertainment that kept me busy was bird-watching. There were many of them in the neighbourhood. The area was dry and the birds came to drink from a reserve tank. They usually came to sit on the trees planted in front of the cells to block the view opposite. There is a whole world to learn and behold when you have time to observe these beautiful birds. I had a favourite; small bird which usually travelled in numbers. I called it Ruby for its red under belly. This was the translation of its Somali name (Dahabo uur cas). I liked its antics during play and while singing. They did not sing in one note only. They rather seemed to be a whole orchestra with its winds, pipes, brass and strings. Frequently, they were in session during the afternoons after they had eaten the leftovers of the prisoners. Their concert, I imagined, was a sign of gratitude for our generosity.

The ignorance of the guards was so severe that, in 1987, they put poison in the leftovers. Most of our bird population was brutally exterminated. A few that survived emigrated, perhaps, to a friendlier environment. Apart from these tiny birds, we had ample time to watch other types of animals which came to visit us at certain times of the day. Each type of animal had its peculiarity. The crow that people normally dislike was particularly interesting because it was very playful and gave me enough time to observe its play, method of fighting and mating. There was the hawk, which despite its irregular visits was always a welcome sight. I remember one particular occasion when out of the blue a hawk suddenly dropped right in front of my cell door. I heard the whistling sound of a mouse crying for help. Suddenly the hawk released it because the mouse fought back. The mouse ran for a short distance and halted. The hawk looked everywhere but could not see the mouse whose colour blended with that of the earth. The proverbial vision of the hawk apparently failed him. But at the same time, the cowardice of the mouse took over. It could not remain standing still while the hawk was so close. It darted towards a small shrub but the movement alerted the hawk and it was on top of the mouse within no time. This time there was no escaping the claws of the hawk. It flew away with its prey and with a few powerful strokes of its huge wings, it was away, chased by a gaggle of playful crows, away from my restricted view in the cell. Away, away, majestic, soaring, powerful and FREE.

We played many games across the wall of the cells, but the funniest and at the same time the most serious was the one we called W.H.O. For the World Health Organization's declaration, in the late seventies, to have eradicated malaria in South East Asia only to realize that new and stronger strains had developed. The prison area was a kind of oasis because the surrounding area had no water and the nomads came to drink from the large tank near the prison. Therefore the prison area was the wettest and became a breeding ground for mosquitoes. The drone of mosquitoes in the evening sounded more like the whining of a jet engine than the sound of insects. Apart from the irritation of the sound and bites, there was the fear of being infected with malaria. We used to kill mosquitoes with our hands as we saw them. We had no illusions about our chances of exterminating them but we could not help trying.

The game, W.H.O., consisted of knocking on your neighbour's wall every time you killed a mosquito and he would do the same: a winner would be declared every night, every week, every month and every year. And the winner would be named the Blood Donor of the Day. The greatest number of mosquitoes I killed in a single day and night was 175. We developed a number of techniques to get as many mosquitoes as possible. For example, you have to hold your breath near the mosquitoes because they would feel the slightest change in wind currents. Another technique was to bring your hand as close as possible to the mosquito before trying to kill it. The mosquitoes, while sitting, would lift their hind appendages and use them as radar and they would fly away before you had a chance of reaching them.

The ants which occupied certain corners of the cell I considered a nuisance for the first few weeks. I even tired to get rid of them. But as time went by and the confinement began to weigh on me, I realised that I was exacerbating the effects of the confinement on myself by ignoring all the tiny animals and insects living with me in the cell. Yes I was alone in the cell as far as humans were concerned but there were hundreds and maybe thousands of other beings with me in the cell and to deny their existence would be as foolish and as short-sighted as man denying the presence of the multiplicity of life-forms and the integral pat they play in his world.

There would be a number of ant colonies in the cell at any one time. Each would jealously defend its territory against marauders. The colony seemed to live in perfect social harmony. They took care of their young and the sick, assisted each other in their daily chores. They had a highly developed social organization, with different groups doing particular jobs. The males were large and the queens rarely ventured out of their subterranean tunnels. They mate with the queens and lead short, idle lives. The most active group in any colony are the workers. They are far more numerous than any other group smaller in size and you rarely see them idle. They serve as look-outs, collect food, bring it to the colony and care for eggs, larvae and cocoons.

They do whatever fighting is necessary to protect the colony. A common sight would be one or two workers moving slowly and in zigzag fashion, looking for food. Finding a food particle, a worker would try to carry it or pull it by itself. Failing that, it would start a fast run towards the colony's quarters. This type of running was different from its normal way of running. It was jerkier and more emotional. After it reached the hole there would be a rush of workers towards the food particle. I thought in the beginning that the ants would be guided towards the food particle by the ant that had found it. But no, they would be guided by the trace of odour left by the worker that had found it.

I sometimes moved the food particle from where the ant had left it. They would all come to standstill at exactly where the odour ended, would look around for a while and return to their dwelling slowly as if disappointed. The odour seemed to serve another purpose as well. Different workers from different colonies who looked exactly alike to me would suddenly attack each other. At one time I was able to make a dilute solution of leaves and flowers that fell from a tree in front of the cell. I immersed a worker in this solution and left it among a group of ants from the same colony. After a few moments in which they touched each other with their feelers, they attacked their comrade and carried its corpse into the hole. When I immersed another ant in water, and left it among its friends, they actually helped it to dry its drooping feelers and body. They apparently develop different nest doors.

A different type of ant was the one we called the nomad. It did not live in the small fissures in the cell, but it would travel throughout the prison by means of tunnels through those thick walls. It had a mouth relatively large for its body. The arrival of those nomads was signalled by the evacuation of all the other types of different insects, and animals from their tiny dwellings. The ants and termites and cockroaches would all come out carrying their eggs. The nomads which resembled a plundering army would attack everything in their wake in very large groups and if they found any of these creatures, there would be a massacre, no less. They did not carry their victims like other ants but would devour them on the spot. Once they left, there would be no insects or any other animal left in the cell. There would be the inedible parts of cockroaches on the floors of the cell and the solitary house lizard improbably hanging upside down from the ceiling.

At night, when the doors were closed, the rats came out of the toilet. Of course, I hated these filthy animals that crawled all over me in the darkness of the floors of the cell. When I tried to frighten them away by stomping my feet, they seemed to realize instinctively that I could not see them. They just moved to one side and come back as soon as I sat down. The nights were the worst time in the dark cells because apart from the rats, the cockroaches and mosquitoes, the colonel who ran the prison had a cruel habit of sending his solders to go and get one of the prisoners.

They would come late at night, open the outside steel door noisily, focus a torch on your face and tell you to sand up. They would hand-cuff you, blindfold you and with two of them, each holding one of your arms, they would march you to the colonel's office. He sat there triumphantly smiling with a dozen soldiers standing to attention behind his chair. He would start by asking your name, your profession, how long you had been sentenced to, etc. He would ask if you needed clothes, medicines, and food. Naturally, he could see you needed clothes, he could tell that you needed food and sometimes needed medicines very badly. Whatever you said "Yes" or "No" did not matter. He would just attack you verbally; abuse you, saying that you deserved even worse than what was happening to you.

He played this kind of cat and mouse game until he got bored with you and told the soldiers to take you away. We were lucky that there was bigger fish to fry than us in the prison and of course he enjoyed humiliating ex-vice President Ismail Ali Abokor, ex-Minister Omer Arte Galib more than I or one of my friends. There were ex-ministers, national assembly members, Generals in the prison. But these nocturnal visits left their scars on me. I can now easily understand why captives became brain-washed and cooperated with their captors despite the feeling of hatred towards them. I remember how I felt whenever the soldiers, with their polished high boots and tip-top uniforms, passed in front of my cell. I felt they were superman and I like a mere bantam. I remember thinking as time went by, that every soldier was a giant and their stature increased in my mind. The uniforms, the regular hours they kept, their lack of communications with us, and of course the feeling of abandonment and helplessness all added up to make them look like immortals in my eyes. When I happened to see one of those soldiers in Mogadishu after we were released I was incredulous. He looked so puny that I felt sure he must be a different guy. I am sure this sighting helped to exorcise some the feelings of inferiority that had beset me.

Nights were of course the worst times .The nights were when your fears, real or imagined were heightened. As soon as the outside door was closed at 4pm in the afternoon, the cell would be in total darkness and the fears would come. At the beginning of the solitary confinement, every sound that I heard, I interpreted as a sign that maybe we were going to be released. But as time went by even this coping mechanism of hope was worn out. The night sounds seemed to be more ominous. Every door that was opened or closed during the night would increase the rate of my heart beat. Even the usual antidote to this fear, getting in touch with my next door neighbour through the wall didn't seem to work. The only antidote to this kind of mental state was the flash of dawn. But by this time I would have woken up several times sweating and with my heart beating so fast that it seemed to be in my mouth. The first time I woke up in that way was at the beginning of 1984. I had been having nightmares for a few months. The fear, tension and anxiety reached such a state that my subconscious mind was always on guard. It refused to let me go to sleep even when I had been very tired and badly in need of sleep. I had to sleep in the morning when the outside door had been opened.

Later by discussing the condition with Dr. Aden Yusuf Abokor, who was my next door neighbour, I slept better. But even now I have nightmares occasionally but at a very much reduced rate.

Many friends wondered aloud to us how we were able to survive and keep our sanity in those horrendous conditions. The only answer I was able to give was that people are capable of adjusting to almost any environment however difficult. Furthermore, we have more strength and more resources than we ever use. Only in very trying circumstances are we forced to tap these potentially limitless resources. I feel if we could find a way of tapping these potential resources at normal times we would solve many a seemingly insurmountable problem.

8

Release

The manner of our release was as dramatic as that of our arrest. One morning in mid-march 1989 two soldiers, followed by Dheel, the male nurse, stopped in front of my cell; and for the first time in six and half years called me by name. They wanted to know whether I was called Mohamed Barud Ali. I said "yes". One of the soldiers threw a pair of flip-flops (*Dacas*) through the barred door, took out t-shirt and a *lungi* (*Macawis*) of a cupboard box he was carrying and threw them through the bars of the inner door. They left me without saying another word, open-mouthed. I could hear them stopping in front of my neighbour's door and talking to him even though I could not hear what they were saying. Suddenly, I was overwhelmed by a thousand and one thoughts, all of them incoherent and fantastic.

In a place like Labaatan-jiraw where you never heard anything from the soldiers, and naturally from no one else, you became used to deducing what was happening in the outside world from the slightest changes in the habits of the guards and even the slightest changes in their facial expressions. In this world of half-hints, nuances and winks what happened that day was comparable to a newsreel in Technicolor. And yet it was not easy to extrapolate this and think further than the gate of the prison. I imagined that maybe this meant we were being released, but to believe that needed a great leap of faith, and I always ended up coming back looking through those steel bars as if they were part of my pupils and not a separate entity. As soon as the guards reached a safe distance, I started communicating with my next door neighbour who informed me that he was also given a pair of flip-flops, a t-shirt and a *lungi*. We continued to communicate happily for the next ten minutes concluding in the end that we were definitely going to be released. But as soon as we stopped communicating, I was not sure anymore and the doubts crowded out my fleeting happy mood immediately.

This mood of uncertainty was further reinforced by the fact that my two most powerful indicators of hope for release were both negative. One was the flag-the national flag-which got raised in the morning and which I could see outside the compound when the outside door was opened. The flag was raised punctually that morning. The rationale was that since we believed that we were not going to be released while Siyaad Barre was still in power, we thought his death would be heralded by the flag raised at half mast. Hence my daily checks for the status of the flag. After our release my friends told me they also had looked in the morning for any sign of the flag being lowered. The second indicator was connected with the fact that the soldiers would sing a particular song in praise of Siyaad Barre and his accomplishments without fail every morning. If for any reason, they failed to sing, which was very rare, I would listen all that day for any unusual signs to confirm that Siyaad Barre had been, somehow gotten rid of. That morning they sang and with particular gusto, I thought.

About 2 o'clock in the afternoon that day guards, all of them dressed for parade, stopped in front of my cell, and one of them told me to collect my things and come to the door. There was nothing I wanted to take from that cell and I started towards the door almost running and breathless. They opened the door, hand-cuffed and blind-folded me, which somehow did not succeed to dampen my high spirits, and told me to walk. After a short walk, they took off the blind-fold and I found myself in a cell similar to mine where at a table in the centre sat the male nurse, Dheel, who was also the Assistant Commander of prison.

He told me to sit down on a wooden form. I sat down and lo and behold, through the door came my friends, one by one, everyone blind-folded and in hand-cuffs. They all seemed strangers to me after 6½ years in which we did not see each other. They were all emaciated and aged. Our facial expressions were blank. We said hello to each other as if we had met a few hours before. But then someone started laughing hysterically and we all started hugging each other and laughing. The last time we saw each other was the earlier in October 1982.

We were now at once separated into three different groups hand-cuffed in three's and blind-folded, and put in the back of land-rovers. On our way to Mogadishu, we were never sure where we were going to. We reached Mogadishu after five hours drive. They removed the blind-folds and hand-cuffs on the outskirts of Mogadishu. We were immediately taken to Siyaad Barre palace in the centre of Mogadishu where we saw the fabled cheetah royally kept and looked after by a platoon of guards. While we were waiting to be received at the court of the dictator, we had the first opportunity to speak to each other, because on the way we were separated. For the first time we were shown the scars left by the chains on the feet and arms of one of my friends, Yusuf Abdillahi kahin, who was kept in chains for three months day and night for trying to speak to a soldier. The chains were too short for him to reach the toilet and he had to sleep next to his excrement.

For the first time I saw the amputated big toe of my friend Abdirahman Abdillahi H. Aden, whose toe was injured during torture sessions and was neglected by Doctor No. As a result, it got badly infected until it finally reached the bone and it had to be amputated by Doctor No. who cut if off with a saw without the aid of an-aesthetic, with six soldiers holding the patient. I was shocked by the sight of my friends who were emaciated and all seemed to be survivors of a concentration camp. All of them had aged beyond their years. The effects of anxiety, solitary confinement, were visible on all their faces even to my untutored eyes. Some were unusually withdrawn; others laughed hysterically, and yet others exhibited signs of morbid fear and watched the guards with anxiety as if expecting to be attacked by them at any moment.

General Siyaad Barre kept us waiting for a long time before we were ushered into his chambers. But we were never bored for a moment. We had so much to say to each other and a rising excitement could be felt replacing our usual mood of listlessness and apathy. I had heard many times before that Siyaad Barre usually kept political opponents waiting to consult the old lady who served as his court witch-cum-magician-clairvoyant. It is common knowledge among Somalis that he was superstitious and blissfully ignorant, deceitful and vindictive. There were a lot of anecdotes testifying to his woeful ignorance in the face of circumstances he did not understand.

Finally we were summoned into the presence of Siyaad Barre. We found him seated behind a huge mahogany desk facing the entrance. He was smoking when we entered with a colonel in full uniform standing one step behind him holding a packet of cigarettes and a lighter. Siyaad Barre was mush older than I expected with vacant, tired-looked eyes. There were eight in our group but he ordered Dr. Mohamoud Hassan Tani to remain outside because he was of a different clan than the rest of us.

This was typical of the man; always exploiting the clan divisions in Somali society to remain in power-setting one clan against the other to prevent them from uniting and getting rid of their common enemy. Later, Dr. Tani would tell us that Siyaad Barre, predictably, asked him why he got himself involved in such a group of anti-government subversives. He asked each of us if we were guilty of the offence with which were wrongly convicted in 1982 (Seven and half years before). But he was not listening. He started railing away at us, saying we were traitors that we were responsible for the destruction of the Northern cities, the death of tens of thousands of people, the widowing of so many Somali women and the loss of the property of all Northern Somalis. All this was in fact news to us. It was the first time we had any hint about the destruction of the North and we did not realize the magnitude of this destruction at the time. After this monologue he said we were pardoned but we must refrain from the getting involved in anti-government activities in the future.

He dismissed us by standing up and we were ushered out of his quarters by his of bodyguards who told us that we had been allocated some money by Siyaad Barre to make our reintegration into society easier and handed us a bag full of money. We had all heard stories of Siyaad Barre giving political prisoners large amounts of public money when he decided to release them with his famous refrain:" I don't imprison people, others imprison them and I release them." Some of us imagined building houses, others of establishing their own businesses. But sometime before morning prayers, the soldiers took us into a small café where we had each a cup of coffee and a tiny piece of cake. When we tried to pay for the coffee and cake from the largesse given us by the dictator, the café proprietor told us it was not even enough to pay for the coffee and cakes. We were incredulous. But this, more than anything, made us understand the failing state of affairs in the country. The rate of the dollar against the Somali shilling was 1dollar against 7 shillings when we last used money; now 1 dollar equalled 400 shillings.

We were taken to a hotel on the Mecca Al-Mukarama road. In the hotel, we met other people (Isaaqs who had also been released from prison). Early in the morning, the first of our relatives found us, Nourine and Catherine Michael Mariano, who were members of one of the two or three Christian families in the country. Apparently they had been expecting us and they had been checking all hotels. One of the prisoners, colonel Mohamed Jama Galal, a close cousin of the Michaels, fervently kissed both girls on the head saying: "you are both great girls. You are well-educated, you are well respected in our community, you have charisma, you have everything, if only you converted to Islam......." Before he finished, Catherine stopped him by saying, Look, I want you to imagine a situation where my religion is proven the correct one after all and I tell the angels at the gate to Heaven to let you in because you were my cousin....."

Within no time the hotel was flooded with relatives, friends and other well-wishers. We found we were heroes. This was a kind of testimony to how the country desperately needed heroes. We had been put on a pedestal and it was frightening to think about the daunting task awaiting us to fulfil those expectations. We were welcomed so heartily by so many people we wondered what we had really done to deserve so much adulation. Even this sort of welcome, however, was threatening to Siyaad Barre's regime. Three men who invited us for the first three days were promptly arrested by the Security (NSS) and held for a week before they were released as a result of the intervention of a group of elders who went to see Siyaad Barre. He told them he was not aware of the arrests of those men and ordered their release, but he also told them not to continue with celebration for the criminals. This showed that he personally ordered their arrest in the first place.

The first day of reunion with our families and friends was both happy and traumatic. It was happy because seeing them and speaking to them, holding them after six and half years of solitary confinement was exhilarating. But it was also traumatic because apart from the fact that we passed from solitary confinement into large, ebullient crowds with no transition, we were told the shocking details of what had happened in the North for the first time. These planes donated by the Government of the United Arab Emirates, piloted by South African and Rhodesian mercenaries, had caused so much trauma to the children who survived that bombing – most of them still involuntarily dive under the nearest cover every time they hear the sound of an aircraft, a year after the war.

We heard reports of so mach cruelty and inhumane behaviour of the regime, so much suffering by our people that were we were made to forget our own experiences. These atrocities are well-documented by neutral observers such as Amnesty International and other Human rights group. It served as a kind of shock therapy to help us not to dwell too long on our prison experience.

9

Escape

Immediately after our release, and arrival in Mogadishu, the Somali capital, we realised that it would be foolish to stay in Mogadishu and risk being arrested again. We knew they needed no other excuse other than the fact that we had been in jail to arrest us and imprison us again. Remembering the conditions and given the extent of the atrocities committed against the whole Isaaq clan, we decided to waste no time in leaving. There were two options open to us. Either we had to go through the usual channels, get passports and fly out of Mogadishu Airport, risking detection; or by land. Either way there were risks. We weighed the pros and cons and in the end decided to try the air route. The risks here were higher but we were encouraged by the corruption and confusion of the whole system. We applied for passports using our names. But we did not go to the immigration authorities ourselves. Instead we gave US$300 to a go-between who would share the money with his contact in the immigration department. Within two weeks we all had new passports. They only scary moment came when the name of one of my friend's name was discovered among a group of people who were listed as undesirable and ineligible for a passport. Later they found out that it was a completely different person.

After receiving our passports, we decided to leave in small groups rather than altogether. Timing was crucial. There was an Amnesty International delegation visiting Somalia at the time and we knew the authorities would do everything to placate this delegation and that they might crack down after the delegation had left. Most of us left while they were still there. On the night before I left Mogadishu, I was approached by Gen. Jama Mohamed Qalib, ex-commander of the Somali Police and probably the most active resistance leader inside the country. He told me about the need of the Amnesty International team for one of our group to be interviewed. It was prudent that I was chosen because I was leaving the next day. Jama took me in his car and drove me around Mogadishu for sometime before finally bringing me to a compound with all lights extinguished. I was taken to a small room lit by a table lamp; there was a table in the middle of the room and two men sat facing the door. There were two empty chairs on the near side. I was invited to sit down. The two gentlemen introduced themselves as a delegation from Amnesty International in London, which had been one of the international organisations campaigning for our release. They talked to me four two hours, taking turns and gently asking about the conditions in prisons we were in: if we were tortured inside Labaatan Jiraw, if we knew how many other people were still in there, what kind of food we were given and many other similar questions. In fact one of the people who talked to me that night is a life-long friend and we have collaborated on human rights activities on may occasions.

Two weeks after the Amnesty International delegation left, on July 14th, there were demonstrations, after a group of religious elders were detained, the regime responded with the usual brutality, killing over a thousand people the first day. According to eye-witness reports, most of the deaths were not caused by regular army units but by goon squad belonging to Siyaad Barre's "Marrehan" clan who shot demonstrators on sight.

A dawn to dusk curfew was declared and during the curfew hours, on the night of the 17th, death squads, led by Maslah Siyaad Barre, the president's son and heir-apparent and another Marehan Colonel called Anjeh, went in search of young Issak men. They went to the predominantly Issaq neighbourhoods of Madina and Hodan. They knocked only on Issaq households and they picked up only Issaq young men which seems to confirm the suspicion of many people that the operation was pre-planned and for this purpose. Forty seven (48) young men were taken in two closed military lorries. They were taken to Jezira beach 12kms east of Mogadishu and extra-judicially executed. A single youth, Mohamed Arab, escaped unhurt by stumbling to the ground with those killed as hails of bullets rained on them. He escaped because the killers had to leave in a hurry when agro-pastoralists who were bringing their produce to the city started appearing in numbers. They threw earth over the bodies of those killed perfunctorily to bury them. The Issaq community in Mogadishu managed to spirit him out of Somalia and he lived to tell about this harrowing tale.

A number of those killed at the beach were regular visitors to our home while we were in Mogadishu. It was particularly distressing to us to find out about their brutal death. At least four of my friends were still in Mogadishu and they had to change houses every night until they left on the 18th with, the group called "Parliamentarians." They were stopped at the airport on the way to Mecca, to make their pilgrimage. They had their passports taken and they still remain in Mogadishu, not in prison but unable to travel or to work.

I left with Hussein Mohamed Dualleh on June 27th. We had our luggage taken to the airport by friends who told us to come to the airport only at the last possible moment. The NSS were everywhere at the airport when we arrived. When I reached the window where I had to have my passport stamped, and officer took my passport. He handed it to another sitting at a desk that looked at me. Then at a list of names in front of him. And finally, he gestured to the first officer and whispered to him for what seemed ages. Many thoughts passed through my mind. Should I run? But then he stamped in the passport, called my name and gave it to me. I breathed again and went to sit in the waiting hall. I had to sit as far away as possible from my friend Hussein.

We sat there not looking at each other and trying not to look frightened whenever someone came to look brazenly into the faces of the passengers. When finally our flight was announced and we went to the runway, there were NSS officers standing next to the plane to have a last look at the passengers. In fact more of them were aboard the plane and asked for our passports. The plane took off and as soon as we were able to untie our seat belts we both stood up, left our places and hugged each other in the middle of the passenger way. The passengers and the crew thought we were crazy and it was not far from the truth. We were mad with happiness.

When the plane landed at Djibouti we had to quickly reign in our enthusiasm and come down to earth. The immigration people here were notorious for the arbitrary nature of their decisions of whether to grant visas or not. Many people with bonafide documents had been denied admittance into the country and returned to Somalia, even when they knew that those people might be in danger for their lives in Somalia.

10

Djibouti

In Djibouti, we were welcomed with open arms especially by the large prosperous Issak community in the country. We were showered with gifts in the many banquets held in our benefit. The people of Djibouti opened their doors to us, competed to invite us to their homes and what is more listened to our stories with compassion and understanding. They embraced our cause and made it easier for us to integrate into society. But the people of Djibouti are also emotional, fickle and fleetingly generous and it is never advisable to overstay your welcome. It is the nature of the setting.

Djibouti is one of the hottest places on earth, rocky and dry with no natural resources of its own. It owes its existence to a series of accidents culminating in the French occupation of this tiny bleak territory to bury their disappointment for being denied other prized colonies in East Africa by the British. The French had constructed the railway between Ethiopia and Djibouti which carries the bulk of land-locked Ethiopia's goods. Djibouti's geographic location between two powerful and feuding neighbours and its anointment as the seat of the Igadd (Intergovernmental Authority on Drought and Development) made its position, between a rock and a hard place, almost untenable. But Djibouti seems to have, not only benefited but, thrived in this tough neighbourhood. The near destruction of the former Ethiopia, and secession of Eritrea, and the total disintegration of Somalia made Djibouti a political power player in the region. Somali businessmen set up their operations in Djibouti and artists and other cultural groups enriched the otherwise impoverished cultural scene of Djibouti.

When we had been in Djibouti for a few weeks, we got word from the American Embassy inviting us to go to the UNHCR office and give our personal details to them to expedite our resettlement in the US. But UNHCR refused to meet us citing Djibouti government policy on Somali refugees which stipulated that Somalis may stay in Djibouti but may not be accepted as refugees or seek third country resettlement. This apparently would have reflected badly on Siyaad Barre, who was a patron of many of the powerful in Djibouti and a close ally of Hassan Gulaid, the President. Hassan Gualid also hosted the meeting between Siyaad Barre and Mengistu Haile Merriam reached a peace accord which included an agreement that neither government would support rebels against the other. This peace accord forced the SNM into swift attacks on the major towns of Hargeisa and Burao. As a result, The Somali Armed Forces unleashed heavy artillery and aerial bombardment on population centres.

Finally, UNHCR were forced to recognise those fleeing the war as genuine refugees. According to Roger Winter, Director of the US Committee Refugees, whom we met in Djibouti in August1989, and who was detained for four days in Djibouti before being released without charge.

> In May 1989, massive violence between the forces of Siyaad Barre's government and the Somali National movement broke out all over northern Somalia. Refugees poured into Ethiopia (of all places) and into Djibouti. They reported widespread indiscriminate killing of civilians, especially of the Issaq clan, which supplies the vast majority of the S.N.M fighters. This is not to suggest that the S.N.M is without blemish. There almost never are totally innocent parties in today's Third World third civil wars. But the refugees I have talked to are universally clear on who the victimizer is. They talk convincingly of the shooting of children, the strafing of civilian refugee columns, the destruction of major portions of northern cities along with many of those caught within.
>
> These 10 (UFFO group, released from Labaatan Jirow Prison), of all the Somali refugees in Djibouti, are exceptions because their cases are well known to the human rights community internationally. A few weeks

> ago they were in danger of forced repatriation. Because of interventions by human rights activists and the US government, however, they won't be forced out of Djibouti.
>
> What about the other 30,000 here at the end of the earth-real refugees who have not been "blessed" with official designation? One hopes the world will not just forget them, the human burden Djibouti now grudgingly bears.

While I was in Djibouti, my wife who had been in Germany since 1986 came to visit me. Time usually stops still for prisoners, particularly in places like Labaatan Jiraw, while people outside were able to grow, develop and mature. Talking to my friends, I realized that there were no lines even on our faces like other people of our age who have been experiencing life in its full.

This was brought home to me when a lawyer friend, with whom I was staying in Djibouti, and I went to meet my wife at Djibouti airport. I had been yearning to see my wife for the last eight years. She had been through a harrowing experience during my imprisonment. The regime wanted them to repudiate their husbands, some religious leaders even finding Quranic verses to sanction the divorcing of prisoners by their wives. But they refused to budge. These wives were the unsung heroes of the struggle. When she came out of the airport, I did not immediately recognize her. Then suddenly, she was there in front of me. But to my horror, like my father before me, I did not hug her. I just shook hands with her like we were perfect strangers. We got in the car and we tried to say something to each other, but there were very awkward silences during the trip to Jama's house. We groped for the old shared experiences, but the gap in our lives was obvious. Like other people outside, she had grown and matured while my experience remained frozen to that of our wedding. It would need a great leap forward on my part to catch up. In spite of all that, life must go on and we had to live with all the difficulties. The main problem was that we did not understand all this and deep in our hearts we blamed each other.

11

Refugee Camps

We stayed a few months in Djibouti. We were not able to go to Ethiopia because of the difficulty of getting a visa. Finally when we went to Ethiopia (Diredawa, Jijiga and the refugee camps), I was not prepared for what I saw. In Hargeisa, 1980-1981, I had seen refugees around the city (there were 14 camps in the northern Somalia with an estimated population of two million.) I had heard about the problems those refugees were facing, but their lives did not touch mine directly. The great numbers quoted were somehow more statistics than human to me.

But now I was faced with a totally different situation. These people living in the wretched camps, trying to preserve some semblance of dignity in this dehumanizing situation were my own father, brothers, sisters, cousins, nephews, uncles, aunts, neighbours, ex-school mates and colleagues. I know that refugees all over the world suffered incalculable difficulties, faced all manner of diseases, hunger, thirst and indignity to their humanity. What I saw in those camps was, however, more personal than the humane pity one feels for others in these circumstances.

Here was Hassan, a well-off businessman in Hargeisa, squatting in front of a tent wearing a filthy *lungi* and a shirt with more holes than material, flies sitting on his eyes and unable to shoo the flies away, not knowing what had hit him. There was Hussein, a Doctor at Hargeisa Regional Hospital almost bare-footed trying to visit the sick in his neighbourhood but knowing that he could not be of much help without the equipment to examine them and even if he knew their ailments there ware no drugs with which to treat them.

And here was aunt Halimo who had a well-ordered house in Hargeisa with maids administering to her every whim.

Now reduced to carry a pail of water from the reservoir thirty (30) kms away. Worst of all were the kids drifting aimlessly through the camp, big heads and bellies, no school, adequate food, games except war games and worse of all no apparent future.

I had no problem finding my family. As soon as I got to Kamabokor (camp abokor), I was directed to a small tent, where my father shared with three of my brothers, nine nephews, a niece and two of my brother's wives. My father had aged considerably since I last saw him nine years ago. None of my family members cried when I first met them after nine years. I was the only one who cried; they were all emaciated and had fixed stares in their eyes. Only the children were curious. I had known three of my nephews and they were very young when I had seen them last. Only the two older ones, Mohamed and Abdirahman, remembered me. The others wanted to touch me but were wary of me at first. However, after I gave them some sweets they opened up and started smiling and recounting their harrowing tales to me. Yusuf, who was seven years old, was the most articulate. He told me how he had heard the shooting in Hargeisa, how they had to abandon their house, how he and his mother, father, grandfather, brothers and sisters walked to Geddeble (North of Hargeisa) and later towards the Ethiopian border; how his mother had a miscarriage and delivered a dead baby, how they buried the stillborn girl; how they had hidden themselves under the trees when Somali Air Force planes bombed them; how the Barre's Air Force planes had hit a young girl who was with them, whom they had to leave without burying her.

I heard all of this in Mogadishu and Djibouti, but to hear this from the impressionable innocent view of a seven year old child was particularly heart-wrenching. I had to try and ask him to tell me about his sisters and brothers, and how their time went by playing now; he was adamant and wanted to tell more about his harrowing experience. My brother had a trucking business when I was detained and sent to jail. However, I was told that soon after they transferred us to the maximum security prison in the south (Labaatan Jiraw), the National Security Service (NSS) began visiting him, and demanded of him to get a permit for the movement for his trucks and for himself as well when he wanted to go to Berbera only about 110 miles away, which also was part of the North-West region. Nevertheless, when he had asked for those permits, he had been invariably refused. Thus, he had to get rid of his business. In addition every member of his family had to report their whereabouts every night even that of the newly-born. I asked the whereabouts of the rest of the family. Some were in Europe, Arabian Gulf and others were displaced within Somalia. Life in the refugee camps was terrible; food was the least of their problems. They were overcrowded, lacked all forms of sanitation. Medicine was chronically short. There were epidemics. There were no schools whatsoever for the kids. During my short stay of two weeks, the Doctor at the two camps told me that at least forty people died of hepatitis within the first few months.

12

USA

When we came back from the refugee camps, we went to Djibouti where our visas to the US where waiting. We went through some perfunctory medical check-up and we were allowed to proceed. It was the turn of Ahmed Jabane, with his four member family and me to go first. We went through Nairobi and Frankfurt, carrying handbags with the logo IOM showing that we were refugees, before we arrived at Washington's Dallas Airport. We were welcome by Somali friends who were told about our impending arrival. Ahmed and his family were taken by friends to Alexandria, Virginia, and I went with an old school friend from Sheikh, Dr. Ahmed Husein Esa, to his magnificent house in suburban Maryland, in Silver Springs. There I was welcomed by his vivacious diplomat wife, Terry and his son, Roble, who was conversant with the multiplicity of relations in Somali society and accepted me as one of his many uncles. After a few weeks, I moved to an apartment with my friend and his family across the Potomac River in Alexandria, Virginia. While we were here, our friends helped us to establish the Somali Relief and Rehabilitation Association (SORRA), a humanitarian NGO, to help in the reconstruction of Somaliland. We were helped by many Somalis in this endeavour, including the Somali National Movement (SNM) representative, Mohamed Hussein Esa, brother of Ahmed and his staff, and later by the Somaliland representative, Harir and Dan Quayle, Abdi Dayur. But we were also supported in this by Americans, including Susan R. Benda, a lawyer for the Washington firm of Arnold and Porter. Susan was instrumental in the incorporation of SORRA and obtaining a tax-exempt status in the US. Others

I left the US after six months in May,1991 to join my wife in Konigswinter, near Bonn in Germany. There in the Children's Hospital in Bonn was born my first son in February 2nd, 1992. It was an incredible journey from where I was born at the Mourning Tree (Weerane) near Aware town, in Ethiopia. But that is the nature of nomadic society, the most conservative, yet the most adventurous people in the world, moving without consideration for international borders.

My life came to a full circle since the day I was arrested in Hargeisa in November 4th, 1981.I went back to Hargeisa in 1993 and became a parliamentarian, then made the Minister for Rehabilitation, Resettlement and Reconstruction. But the more important and rewarding thing was that I was given the same office that the National Security Service interrogated me in the first night I was arrested. What can I say? All the demons have been exorcised from my life.

Appendix I

General Morgan's Letter of Death

The Letter That Set The Stage For The 1988 Genocide Of The Isaaqs

In the year 1987 the northern regions of Somalia (present day Somaliland) were still part of a wider country called the Somali Democratic Republic and ruled by Siyaad Barre, a military-General-turned president who came to power some 18 years earlier through a coup detach. Or so it seemed, theoretically at least, to the outside world then. In reality however, those so-called northern regions were being treated at the time as forcibly annexed and occupied territories. In 1986 Siyaad Barre appointed his son-in-law General Mohamed Saeed Morgan as the new military ruler of the north, a former British protectorate that after gaining independence merged voluntarily with Somalia, a former Italian colony, to form together the Somali republic on July 1, 1960.

Morgan's appointment came after his predecessor Gen. Mohamed Hashi Gani, a ruthless man who was Siyaad Barre's cousin, failed to put down an armed rebellion that was being waged essentially in rural areas by fighters of the outlawed opposition group, the Somali National Movement (SNM). The SNM drew its recruits from the Isaaq, the dominant clan in the north that was singled out for repression by the Siyaad Barre regime.

By turning Isaaq inhabited territories into concentration camps, Gani had actually alienated the majority of the local population.

After his arrival in the north as Gani's successor, Morgan was quick to boast of anti-insurgency courses he had recently taken at military and civilian institutions in the United States. But Morgan's military tactics failed miserably. And within less than one year on his new assignment, Morgan was already showing signs of growing frustration that was born out of his inability to score not even a one single military victory in the war against the SNM.

In February 1987, Morgan wrote to Siyaad Barre asking him for permission to launch a programme for the obliteration of Isaaq villages and towns and the substitution of the Isaaq population with Somalis from Ethiopia's Ogaden clan whom the Siyaad Barre government encouraged to leave their settlements and portrayed to the world that they were refugees fleeing Abyssinian repression.

Although the letter was marked strictly secret, however a copy of the original was filed in the archives of the ministry of Interior in Mogadishu. An Abgal man who worked there had shown it to Ahmed Mohamed Tukale (Berberawi), at the time an employee of Mogadishu's Electricity Power Supply Station. A few days later Berberawi met a friend of his called Jama Ali Osman, who taught at the Lafoole University near Mogadishu. Berberawi decided to share the information he learnt from reading Morgan's letter of death with Jama. Jama convinced Berberawi that he should ask his friend, the archivist, to allow him photocopy the document. The Abgal man agreed. Jama made several copies of it at different photocopy shops in Mogadishu, translated it into English and then after a risky adventure managed to smuggle it outside Somalia. Later in that year some of the world's major newspapers were already reporting on the horrifying details contained in General Morgan's plan for the extermination of the Isaaq people. But it wasn't until mid 1988 when Morgan's plan had been put into implementation.

Before the end of 1988, at least one hundred thousand innocent Isaaq civilians were massacred by Siyaad Barre's occupying Southern army while close to 2.5 million either sought refuge in SNM-controlled "liberated zones" or in the Ethiopian side of the border. In January 1991 the SNM drove the last remnants of Siyaad Barre's army out of the north and with that brought the entire territories of the former British Protectorate of Somaliland under its firm control. The victorious SNM declared peace and general amnesty. No clan was to be collectively held responsible for the atrocities and crimes against humanity that took place in Somaliland during the reign of Siyaad Barre. Those who perpetrated acts of genocide were to be held accountable as individuals in front of a court of law.

However Morgan and his many other associates in the Somaliland genocide are yet to be made accountable for the crimes that they have been accused of committing. Morgan was not only able to escape justice but also visited foreign countries such as Kuwait in his capacity as Advisor to Abdillahi Yusuf, president of Somalia's Transitional Federal Government. His former boss during the 1988/1989 bombing of urban and rural centres in Somaliland, General Ali Samater, now lives in the Virginia, USA.

Jama Ali Osman who after braving Siyaad Barre's dreadful secret police smuggled Morgan's shameful letter out of Somalia, is now living in Norway with his family. The present whereabouts of Berberawi are not known. The identity of the Abgal man still remains a mystery.

Full text of Morgan's letter of death translated by Mohamoud Sheikh Ahmed Musa is re-published in the *Somaliland Times*.

The Final Solution to Somalia's Isaaq Problem
(*Translated into English from the original Somali, with footnotes and Translator's Note*)

THE MORGAN REPORT: AN OFFICIAL SECRET REPORT ON IMPLEMENTED AND RECOMMENDED MEASURES FOR A FINAL SOLUTION TO SOMALIA'S " ISAAQ PROBLEM"

The Somali Democratic Republic
The Ministry of Defence
26th Sector G.H.Q.
TQ 826/XKT/28-56/87

Date: 23/01/87 TOP SECRET

Report (1)
: The President of the SDR Mogadishu
: The Minister of Defence, SDR Mogadishu
: The Minister of Interior, SDR Mogadishu

Please refer to the report on the state of the defence and security of the 26th Sector's area of control which I transmitted on 17.1.87. (2)

The security of the North West and Togdheer Regions has deteriorated. The Ethiopians brought additional troops to the area with the objective of securing a foothold similar to [those of] Balan Balle and Galdogob. (3) As you gathered from my previous report, they did not succeed in their joint incursion. Subsequently we took punitive measures against the positions jointly occupied by Qurmis (4) and the Ethiopians resulting in loss to both of them and in the obliteration of villages, including Dibiile, Rabaso, Raamaale, and Garanuugle.(5) All our measures were implemented at night and, except for some light injuries, all the troops returned safely to base.

Following their incursions and their consequent losses, Qurmis resorted to appealing to clan sentiment and began to sound a clarion call to action under [the slogan] "On Isaaq clans!" (6) Their objective is to present the curfew (7) as a persecution of their own people. Similarly, they directed a propaganda campaign at the people to the effect that they were about to capture the North West Region and Togdheer.

This much can be gathered from the expressions written on the walls of buildings and from the leaflets distributed in Gabiley District, and at Allaybaday village, Lughaya District. (8) All this is an indication of a resurgence of anti-State clan sentiment. They have appealed to their various sections to recruit 2000 persons for Qurmis to be trained in Awaare (9). So far, 400 individuals have joined. Similarly, 60 Sa'ad Muuse members of the Faraweyne Front (10) and a lieutenant who was their commanding officer gave themselves up to the Ethiopians and the Qurmis following the capture of the State-wreckers. The rest stole into the bush out of fear, but they have now started to return to the village.

COMRADE PRESIDENT, COMRADES:
It has been demonstrated to us that, unless Qurmis and its supporters are subjected to a campaign of obliteration, there will come a time when they will raise their heads again. But, today, we possess the right remedy for the virus in the [body of the] Somali State. It consists of:

1. Balancing the well-to-do to eliminate the concentration of wealth [in the hands of the SNM supporters].

2. The reconstruction of the Local Council in such a way as to balance its present membership which is exclusively from a particular people; as well as the dilution of the school population with an infusion of children from the Refugee Camps in the vicinity of Hargeisa (11).

3. Rendering uninhabitable the territory between the army and the enemy, which can be done by destroying the water tanks and the villages lying across the territory used by them for infiltration.

4. Removing from the membership of the armed forces and the civil service all those who are open to suspicion of aiding the enemy — especially those holding sensitive posts.

We set out below for your information those steps of the planned action already implemented:

i) Before now the number of buses used as public transport were 337, two-thirds of which were owned by members of one clan (the Sa'ad Muuse). However, when, on investigation, it became clear that most of the buses were not operating in accordance with security procedures, due to defects in their registration and circulation documents; and when information received revealed that they were sometimes used to carry drugs (12) or persons open to suspicion, in

secrecy and without notification to the security organisations; and since the number of buses greatly exceed the needs of the city, the following decisions were adopted and implemented:
(a) the number of the buses must not exceed 80;
(b) every bus must have a serial number for identification purposes;
(c) the buses must be evenly distributed amongst the districts of the city, with each bus limited to a particular route and departure and finishing points;
(d) a just and balance redistribution of licences regulating bus ownership in such a way as to give preference to persons relating to the Revolution, and to deny those politically opposed to it; six four-wheel drive vehicles were confiscated at Berbera harbour, and similarly, the removal of vehicles in the city is in progress; those found to be serviceable will be mounted with weapons and the others used as transport for reconnaissance purposes and for officers in command of forces in forward positions; we are also engaged in a process of reclassifying transport.

ii) Of the persons detained as suspected supporters of Qurmis, 45 are from Hargeisa, 30 from Burao, while seven are officers. Most of them are businessmen and well-to-do people, while some are headmen (Nabadoons) (13). They are held in Mandhera prison. However, it is hereby requested that they be transported urgently to Laanta Buur prison, or Bari prison, etc.(14) in order to ensure their continued incarceration during the reorganisation of the local prisons which show many defects from a security standpoint.

iii) The Western Somali Liberation Front (WSLF) (15) has been remobilized, and 300 men have been stationed at a place near Geed-Deeble (16). According to plan, they will be re-armed and then put amidst those brigades and battalions considered to be capable of furthering the fight against Qurmis. At the same time they can implement operations inside [Ethiopia] whenever required.

iv) Since it has become evident that the Isaaq were, by act and intent, with the SNM; and since we could not see them giving up the line they have pursued so deceptively for some time; and in order to forestall them; we arranged for the other inhabitants of the North continuous meetings and a mobilization campaign designed to rouse them to action and to raise their level of awareness. This was intended to strengthen their unity and to surround Somali unity with a defensive wall. Among those inhabitants are: the Awdal people, the various sections of Western Somalis, the Las Qorey people, and the

Daami people, etc. (16) There is no doubt that the unity of these people will restore the balance of the scales which are now tipped in favour of the Isaaq. If they attack their tasks energetically, their unity will also undoubtedly humble those who arrogantly maintain that they own the North when the reality is otherwise.

v) We are still engaged in identifying the positions of those people who maintain current accounts at banks in the North West and Togdheer Regions. The accounts of those recognised as Qurmis supporters will continue to be frozen; the rest will be unfrozen in the near future.

We see the economic strangulation of the people who work for the enemy as serving a useful purpose. However, it is absolutely essential that this should be accompanied by the strengthening of the economic positions of non-Northerners, with a view to raising the level of their capabilities and their interests in these Regions. This will enable them to put under pressure those who have grown fat on the opportunities offered by the Government banks, but have revolted against the State, having persuaded themselves to use their acquired capabilities against the State and it Revolutionary Government.

Undoubtedly, those successive steps, taken to cripple Qurmis, will instil anxiety in those in Mogadishu who are related to it. We hope that these will not be listened to or heeded so that the impetus of the war being waged against it would not drop.

An investigation into the action of Qurmis against the Burao base revealed that a lieutenant and five asakaris (all police) and some civilians had been behind it. It was implemented by the Habar Je'lo Qurmis (17). When the inquiry is completed, the culprits will be court-martialled.

Comrade President, in order to implement the above-mentioned matters, we need to:

1. (a) purge the Somali Police Force, the Security Force, and the Hangash Force, (18) the members of all of which are largely recruited locally; this can be done by finding a force to dilute them and by transferring the present members; and
   (b) replace the present members of the Custodial Corps, who — having assumed the distinctive character of being exclusively from the North — cannot be entrusted with the task of guarding the prisons, with a force composed of other Somalis.

2. We also need up to a Division to reinforce the 3rd Division's zone if it is possible to withdraw units from sectors whose areas of control are stable, since the quality of a force in a state of mobilization cannot achieve very much.

3. We also need the power of the Commercial Bank to give loans and to determine who shall receive them to be transferred to us, so that the past mistakes relating to the economic strengthening of the anti-State people may be rectified and those worthy of it be given a chance.

We propose that those of our forces we consider to be unsatisfactory should send representatives to discuss urgent corrective action. The reason is that the reaction to the measures we have already taken or will take must be met in advance. Since the intelligence-gathering organisations are suspect, and since some of them have committed clear offences, it is prudent to take precautionary measures before it is too late. Up to now we have been walking on ground deliberately strewn with broken glass in an attempt to reduce the momentum of [our] efforts. It is essential to sweep away the broken glass without leaving a single piece behind. There is a Somali proverb: "Oh hyena, you cannot drag away hides without making a sound." (20)

We are awaiting your guidance and directives.
(signed)
Major General Mohamed Saeed Hirsi (Morgan)
The Commander of the 26th Sector, North West
—— End of text ——

Footnotes

1 Introductory Note: The Report purports to be signed by Major-General Mohamed Saeed Hirsi, President Mohamed Siyaad Barre's son-in-law and commander of the 26th Sector, North-western Somalia; the Sector covers the Togdheer, North West and Awdal Regions — the major part of what used to be British Somaliland before it merged on July 1, 1960 with former Italian Somaliland to the south, to form the Republic of Somalia. This name was changed to Somali Democratic Republic (SDR) following the seizure of power by General Mohamed Siyaad Barre on October 21, 1969.
The report is addressed to the President of the SDR, the Minister of Defence, and the Minister of Interior. The latter, Major-General Ahmed Suleiman Abdalla, is also a son-in-law of the President, and Third Deputy Prime Minister. Since President Barre is also the Minister of Defence — the

previous holder of that portfolio, General Mohamed Ali Samatar, having been promoted Prime Minister on January 30, 1987 — the report is seemingly confined to family members. This would explain its extreme frankness in specifying certain clans as targets for implemented and recommended punitive action.

The target is the Isaaq Clan Family. The term "clan family" was first coined by Professor I.M. Lewis, Professor Social Anthropology at the London School Economics, to describe the collective name for each of the several major divisions to which Somali clans traditionally divide themselves. The Isaaq clan family sub-divides into four main clans.

2 Regular secret security reports from a range of top officials in the North West and Togdheer Regions are sent to President Barre and to designated senior ministers and Party chiefs. Delivered by special couriers, the reports are submitted by General Morgan, Sector Command, the Regional Governors, and regional Party Secretaries of the ruling Somali Revolutionary Socialist Party (SRSP); the latter also report to Present Barre in his capacity as SRSP Secretary General.

3 Two small settlements near the disputed border with Ethiopia — Balan Balle to the south and Galdogob in Mudug Region — which were captured in mid-July 1982 (and are still under occupation). The Somali Salvation Democratic Front (SSDF), one of the two main guerrilla groups, claimed credit for the capture, but the Somali Government alleged that it was the Ethiopians.

4 *Qurmis*, meaning "the rotten", is a derogatory term for the SSDF and the other guerrilla group, the Somali National Movement (SNM) founded in 1981. The reference here is to the SNM, which operates in the area covered by the report. The reference to "jointly occupied" implies the SNM and the Ethiopians.

5 These are very small villages to the south of Hargeisa running parallel to the border from west to east and 40 - 50 miles inside the Ethiopian border.

6 See note 1 above.

7 Curfews are familiar to the inhabitants of the North West and Togdheer Regions The current one has been in force since January 1, 1987.

8 Allaybaday village is about 30 miles south of Hargeisa.

9 Awaare, south of Hargeisa, is deep in Somali-populated eastern Ethiopia, in the area commonly known as the Ogaden.

10 The Faraweyne Front is a Somali Government-sponsored clan militia organised in 1983 to counter expected Ethiopian invasion. The Sa'ad Muuse is one of the sub- divisions of the Isaaq clans; see note 1.

11 The children in the refugee camps are either non-Somalis (e.g. Oromo tribes from Ethiopia) or else from Somali clans other than those to which the local school children to be diluted belong. Refugees are cared for by international aid agencies whose work is coordinated by the UNHCR and Somalia's National Refugee Commission.

12 The "drugs" referred to here is the *Khat* or *Chat* leaves, a mild stimulant, chewed in East Africa and the two Yemens. It was banned in Somalia in March 1983. The anti-khat law was further tightened and penalties increased in May 1984, but a black market is known to be flourishing.
13 Tribal elders:during British rule they were known as *Akils* and *Sultans*. When President Barre's regime passed a law outlawing tribalism in 1970, the titles of tribal elders where changed to *Nabadoons* (peace-seekers).
14 Laanta Buur Prison is in the south of the country, about 50 km from Mogadishu. It is a maximum security prison and accommodates many of the political detainees. Bari is in eastern Somalia. The idea is to move prisoners from Mandhera prison, between Hargeisa and Berbera, so that the SNM or its supporters do not arrange a jail-break as they did twice before.
15 The WSLF (Western Somali Liberation Front) which fought the Ethiopians in 1977-78, during the Ogaden War, was an all Somali multi-clan force. The new WSLF referred to here does not embrace clans considered even potentially sympathetic to the SNM and its supporters.
16 Geed-Deeble is in the vicinity of Hargeisa.
17 The "*Awdal* people" and the "*Las Qoray* people" are euphemisms for the Somali clans that are predominant in the areas of Awdal in the extreme northwest and adjacent to Djibouti, and Las Qoray in the extreme northeast of Somalia. "*Daami*" is a collective name, apparently used only in the North for certain groups of Somali clans.
18 *Habar Je'lo* is one of the four main divisions of the Isaaq, see note 1.
19 The " Hangash Force" (an acronym) is the military police.
20 The proverb means that if you have to do a particular task, it is no use trying to be discreet or squeamish if that is going to prejudice the results. Here, General Morgan seems to be recommending an all out campaign that puts aside caution, in implementing the punitive measures he is proposing.

Translator's Note:

The translation of the text of the above report is from Somali — the original language of the report. The footnotes are not part of the report and have been added by me to enhance the clarity of the document. Accuracy, rather than elegance of style, has been my principal aim in this translation.

I am persuaded, on investigation, that the signature to the report which purports to be that of Major-General Mohamed Saeed Hirsi (Morgan) (Commander of the 26th Sector and de facto governor of the regions covered by the report) is in fact his own, and that the report is genuine. My aim in translating this remarkable document is to make it available to researchers, lawyers, and human rights officials. I am not a member or sympathiser of the SNM or SSDF, although I am opposed to the present regime in Somalia.

In my years in Somalia as a legal practitioner, or member and then President of the Supreme Court, I never saw an official document with recommendations so frank in their departure from legality or accepted norms. Such a document ought not to be allowed to be confined to dissident circles that are privately circulating copies of the original.

This translation was done by me, ***Mohamoud Sheikh Ahmed Musa***, in London on ***April 27, 1987***.

(signed)
Mohamoud Sheikh Ahmed Musa
Signed before me this 27th day of April 1987 by the above mentioned

(signed)
R. Barnett
113-116 Strand
London WC2

Appendix II

Translation to English of the Verdict of the Hargeisa National Security Court that tried *"My Teachers' Group"* in February 1982. by Dr. Ahmed Hussein Esa, 1987.
(Reprinted with permission)

The document was translated by Dr. Ahmed Hussein Esa in 1987 to publicize the case of UFFO. It was intended to be used by Human Rights Organizations, particularly the US National Academy of Sciences who, in collaboration with the Institute of Medicine's Committee on Health and Human Rights (USA), co-sponsored a mission to gather reliable information and to express concerns of the two institutions regarding the case of UFFO group and the cases of other scientists and engineers arrested in Somalia at that time. The Academy delegation included Nobel Prize laureate Lawrence Klein; Francisco Ayala, Distinguished Professor of Biological Sciences at the University of California; M. Alfred Hayes, former president and dean; Charles Drew, Postgraduate Medical School and Carol Corillion, director of the two committees.

These pages were previousely published in "A note on my Teachers' Group: News report of an injustice" by Jama Musse Jama.

The publisher is thankful to Dr. Ahmed Hussein Esa for the permission to reprint this document and to the Institute for Practical Research and Training in Hargeisa to have kept this document in its archives.

Bx 10/82 Bg 18/82

SEAL OF THE COURT

Somali Democratic Republic

Security Court

Northwest Region

Hargeisa

Sentence of Mohamed Baruud Ali

and 27 Other Defendants

Hargeisa

4-3-1982

Security Court - Hargeisa Region

Nineteen Eighty-Two, 4th March, Hargeisa

Security Court of the Northwest Region

1. Colonel Shariif Sheekhuna Maye – President
2. Attorney Yusuf Haji Abdi Ali – Advisor
3. Major Ahmed Abdi Arrale - Advisor

in which Public Prosecutor Captain Abdulle Ali participated and was assisted by Mohamed Ali Abdi (Arab),

announced the following Judgement concerning the case against the accused:

1. Engineer Mohamed Baruud Ali, 31 years, Mother: Udbi Ali, Employed at the Pepsi Cola Factory, Hargeisa Defended by Attorney Ismail Jumaale
2. Ahmed Mohamed Yusuf "Jabane", 33 years, Mother: Awo Elmi, Teacher, university graduate Defended by Attorney Faysal Haji
3. Dr. Mohamed H. Mahamoud Omer, 33 years, Mother: Basra Ismail, Businessman Defended by attorney Faysal Haji
4. Dr. Aadan Yusuf Aboker, 34 years, Mother: Haali Yuusuf, Director, Hargeisa General Hospital Defended by attorney Faysal Haji
5. Abdirahman Abdilahi H. Aadan, 26 years, Mother: Dahabo Mahamoud, Employed at the Transportation Office of the Northwest Regional Government Defended by attorney Faysal Haji

6. Ahmed Hussein Aabi, 33 years, Mother: Faadumo Mee'aad, Employed at the Hargeisa Branch of the Commercial and Savings Bank Defended by attorney [not indicated]
7. Hussein Mohamed Duale "Berberaawi", 33 years, Mother: Mako Ibrahim, Teacher, university graduate Defended by attorney Ismail Jumale
8. Dr. Mohamoud Sheikh Hassan Tani, 32 years, Doctor at Hargeisa General Hospital Defended by attorney Ismail Jumaale
9. Dr. Abdillahi Ali Yusuf (Olad), 34 years, Mother Asha Abdillahi Employed at the National Rangeland Management Defended by attorney Hassan Sheikh Ibrahim
10. Mohamed Dagal Hirsi, 32 years, Mother: Muumina Mohamed, Former teacher, university graduate, unemployed Defended by attorney Hassan Sheikh Ibrahim
11. Ali Egeh Farah "Ali Biid", 29 years, Mother: Ardo Kaba Director of Hargeisa Building Agency Defended by attorney Hassan Sheikh Ibrahim
12. Yusuf Abdillahi Ibrahim, 29 years, Mother: Ibado Warsame, Farmer Defended by attorney Bashir Artan
13. Dr. Osman Abdi Megag, Mother: Kaha Farah, Unemployed medical doctor Defended by attorney Osman Abdi
14. Mohamed Abdi Duale "Ayuub", 35 years, Mother: Khadija Haji, Works in Saudi Arabia Defended by attorney Hussein Bille
15. Aadan Warsama Saeed, 33 years, Mother: Awa Ismail, Businessman Defended by attorney Ismail Jumale
16. Mohamed Ali Ibrahim, 35 years, Mother: Idumo Duale, Employed at Communications Office of the Northwest Region Defended by attorney Hussein Bille
17. Ahmed Mohamed Madar, 28 years, Mother: Asha Ali, Teacher, university graduate Defended by attorney Hussein Bille
18. Omar Isse Awale, 33 years, Mother: Amina Nur, Accountant, Agency for Labor Affairs, Defended by attorney Osman Abdi
19. Dr. Mohamoud Ali Sulub, 30 years, Mother: Fadumo Mohamud, Doctor at the Hargeisa General Hospital Defended by attorney Bashir Artan
20. Bashe Abdi Yusuf, 29 years, Mother: Amina Ibrahim, Businessman Defended by attorney Faysal Haji
21. Ismail Abdi Hurre, 26 years, Mother: Habiba Moge, Employed at the Haji Ali Business Establishment Defended by attorney Bashir Artan

22. Hassan Abdillahi Sh. Ali, 23 years, Mother: Ibado Haji Employed at the Pepsi Cola Factory, Hargeisa Defended by attorney Bashir Artan
23. Ahmed Hassan Madar, 29 years, Mother: Fadumo Aabi, Unemployed Defended by attorney Ismail Jumale
24. Mohamed Abdi Je'er, 34 years, Mother; Khadija Barud, Teacher, university graduate Defended by attorney Hussein Bille
25. Mohamed Ma'allin Osman, 32 years, Mother: Shukri Jama Teacher, university graduate Defended by attorney Hussein Bille
26. Saeed Mohamed Ibrahim, 33 years, Mother: Mako Khaiyre, Teacher, university graduate Defended by attorney Hussein Bille
27. Major Ismail Hashi Madar, age---, Chief, technical Department of the 26th Army of the Somali Armed Forces, Defended by attorney Hussein Bille
28. Hassan Abdillahi Ali "Eelgeeye", 36 years, Mother: Fadumo Mohamoud Unemployed Defended by attorney Ismail Jumale

Dates of arrest:

Accused No.1: 4.11.81; No. 2: 2.11.81; Nos. 10 & 19: 11.11.81; Nos 3, 4,5, 7, 8, & 9: 19.11.81; Nos. 11, 12, 14, 15, 16 & 18: 11.12.81; No. 28: 4.12.81; No. 6: 5.12.81; No. 17: 14.12.81, No. 20: 29.12.81; Nos. 24 & 25: 30.12.81; Nos 21 & 22: 9.1.82; No: 20: 29.12.81; No. 26: 6.2.82; No. 27 not in detention.

Indictment

A. Accused No. 1 (Engineer Mohamed Baruud Ali) No. 2 (Ahmed Mohamed Yusuf "Jabane") No. 3 (Dr. Mohamed H. Mohamoud Omer)

You stand collectively accused of the crime of forming an illegal association incompatible with the Somali National unity as referred to in article 3, section 1 of Law No. 54 of 10.9.1970, and article 71 of the Somali Criminal Code (SCC), the reason being that you have organized in Hargeisa an organization injurious to the unity of the Somali Nation, which you named RUDM, which means "Ragga U Dhashay Magalada"-Native Sons of the City.

B. Accused Nos. 1 and 2, you are also separately charged with the crime of writing anti-state propaganda as referred to Article 18 section one of Law No. 54 of 10.9.1970 as related to article 71 of SCC, the reason being that you, as leaders of RUDM further caused, printed, produced and distributed a journal "UFFO",meaning the storm that precedes rainfall.

You intended the RUDM organization and its journal as a prelude to undermining the policies of the Revolution and its overthrow with the backing of external forces opposed to the integrity of the Somali Nation.

C. Accused No. 3, you are also separately accused of the crime of possesing counterrevolutionary written material, as referred to in article 19 of the same law No. 54 of 10.9.1970, the reason being that one copy of the journal UFFO was found in your house, a journal published by accused Nos. 1 and 2, with whom you form the leadership of the illegal association RUDM.

D. Accused

Nos.4. Dr. Adan Yusuf Abokor
5. Abdirahman Abdillahi H. Adan
6. Ahmed Hussein Aabi
7. Hussein Mohamed Duale "Berberawi"
8. Dr. Mohamoud Sheikh Hassan Tani
9. Dr. Abdillahi Ali Yusuf "Olad"
10. Mohamed Dagal Hirsi
11. Ali Egeh Farah
12. Yusuf Abdillahi Ibrahim
13. Dr. osman Abdi Megag
14. Mohamed Abdi Duale "Ayub"
15. Adan Warsama Saeed
16. Mohamed Ali Ibrahim
17. Ahmed Mohamed Madar
18. Omer Issa Awale
19. Dr. Mohamed Ali Sulub
20. Bashe Abdi Yusuf
21. Ismail Abdi Hurre
22. Hassan Abdisalam Sh. Ali
23. Ahmed Hassan Madar
24. Mohamoud Abdi Je'er
25. Mohamed Ma'aalin Osman
26. Said Mohamed Ibrahim
27. Major Ismail Hashi Madar

(Page 4 of the record containing the charges against Nos. 4 through 27 is missing, but they can be derived from the verdict [pp. 56-60]. The charges are:

- membership in an illegal organization; and

- setting explosives in the homes of government officials and members of the community [accused Nos. 17, 20, 24, 25, 26, and 27]).

?(sh) (i) Accused No. 28, you are charged with the crime of rumor-mongering as specified in Article 21 of Law No. 54 of 10.9.1970, the reason being when the above accused were arrested for some of the crimes they committed, you started and spread propaganda against the leadership of the government of the Northwest Region and the investigating agencies, in which you stated that the accused were innocent and had been framed and that the journal UFFO was in fact published by the government officials of the Northwest Region. These crimes were committed in the city of Hargeisa in the last six months of 1981.

Pleading to the charges

The presiding judge upon their appearance read to the accused the charges against them and asked them in accordance with articles 103 and 104 of the SCC how they pleaded to the charges. All of the accused pleaded innocent. Accused No. 16, Mohamed Ali Ibrahim, who was charged with membership in an illegal organization and possession of weapons without a legal permit, admitted to the possession of a weapon, but pleaded innocent to the charge of membership in an illegal organization.

Following this, the court ordered the Public Prosecutor to prove that crimes have occurred and if so, to prove in accordance with articles 110 and 163, that the crimes were committed by the accused.

Introduction

The Public Prosecutor proposed to the court, pursuant to Article 114 of the SCC, and stated that some Somalis opposed to the integrity of the nation returned in 1981 to the country from overseas areas and met with the accused, consisting of university graduates and their acquaintances, who formed an illegal organization and published counterrevolutionary publications. More crimes occurred after their detention. "I shall present the witnesses for the prosecution":

First witness:

Captain Dahir Id Elmi stated under oath: "I am the head of the Security Office of the 26th Division of the Somali Army. At the end of October,

1981, we were informed that a publication was produced by some Somalis. We assigned credible informers. A man by the name of Abdi Langare brought to me a copy of the journal UFFO published by an organization called RUDM. I read the journal and took it to General Gani, the Commander of the 26th Division. We decided to refer the matter for further investigation to the Regional Commander of the National Security Services."

Public Prosecutor and the First Witness:

A. It consisted of five typed pages. I do not remember the format of the journal, but I will recognize it if I see it.
A. (Witness shown a journal): Yes, it is the same journal.
A. That Adan visited me at the office once before in the company of Abdi Langare. He told me that he came from Mogadisho and that he had met with General Mohamed Samater, Commander of the Mogadishu National Security Services. He [Aadan] expressed a desire to work with me.
A. I asked Abdi Langare to find and bring me a copy of that journal. He informed me that Adan was able to secure the journal.
A. I did not ask Adan whether he gave the journal to Abdi Langare. I took the journal to the Commander of the 26th Division, but he [the Commander], Abdi Langare and Aadan met separately without me.

Attorney Faysal Cross-Examining the First Witness:

A. A journal is a printed statement with an objective.
A. The title UFFO and the organization producing it are written in the journal.
A. I did not see anyone producing it or where it was produced.
Q. Is any false statement contained in the journal? The court ordered the witness not to answer that questions.
Q. Is there anything attesting to the names of individual authors?
A. The words UFFO and RUDM prove its anti-government stances, because it is an association unknown to the government.
A. I gave money to Aadan and Abdi Langare after they delivered the journal to me.

Attorney Hassan Sheikh Cross-Examining the First Witness:

A. My testimony is limited to the journal.

Attorney:

No further questions.

Attorney Hassan Sheikh Cross-Examination of the First Witness:

A. I gave them [Abdi Langare and Aadan] and the money after they delivered, not when I sent them to find the journal.
A. I understand UFFO in the sense it was written.
A. Adan left the Police Force, and he is now unemployed.

Public Prosecutor and the First Witness:

A. To me UFFO is a hot wind.
Q. Does it have another meaning?
A. Its meaning is just that. [Translator's note: "UFFO" is the cool moist breeze that precedes rainstorms].

Court's Cross-Examination of the First Witness:

A. I did not undertake any investigation as to who produced the journal.
A. Abdi Langare said that Aadan told him that there were some young men showing signs of dissent and that he [Adan] would inform the Commander of the 26th Division.
A. I forwarded the journal to General Gani who in turn forwarded it to the office of the NSS.
A. I asked Abdi Langare, and he told me that Mohamed Baruud Ali (accused No. 1), Jabane (accused No. 2), and Dr. Tani (accused No. 8), wrote the journal and it was typed on the Pepsi-Cola factory premises.

Proposal by Attorney Ismail

The Court has introduced new questions pertaining to the defendants I am representing. Since this changes the matter, I move that the witness repeat his testimony.

Courts Response:

The court is searching for a just prosecution. You may state the new point that came out of the cross-examination.

First Witness

Abdi Langare told me that Dr. Tani (accused No. 8), Baruud (accused No. 1), and Jabane (accused No. 2), wrote the journal UFFO and had it typed at the Pepsi-Cola Factory.

Attorney Ismail to the Court

The witness earlier testified in reply to attorney Hassan Sheikh that he did not investigate the production of the journal, or whether the accused had any organization. He now tells the court that the first, second and 8th defendants wrote the journal. Which of his two testimonies is true?

First Witness

I replied to two questions.

Proposal by Attorney Ismail

The witness is a liar. He replied differently to the same question and should be prosecuted under article 291 of SCC.

Reply by the Assistant Public Prosecutor

The witness did not lie. He was not asked the second question before.

Attorney Ismail

He should be prosecuted under the said article and it is not proper for the Prosecutor to defend his witness. The witness took an oath, the charges carry the death penalty, it is not a simple matter. This trial is being watched by the whole world and the proceedings are being transcribed by three assistants.

THE COURT'S REPLY:

Three assistants are transcribing the proceedings, the listeners in the room heard the two questions and their answers. The court after hearing attorney Ismail and the reply of the Public Prosecutor, rejects the proposal of attorney Ismail to charge the witness with untruthful testimony.

Second Prosecution Witness, Colonel Hassan Mohamed Nur, Commander of the NSS, Nothwest Regional Government, after taking the oath said:
Information reached us in October, 1981 that a journal was being published at Hargeisa, and that copies of the SNM (Somali National Movement) journal were in circulation in the town, and that SNM propaganda leaflets were placed in various parts of the city. We did not get these publications at the Office, but the Commander of the 26th Division of the Army forwaded to us a copy of a journal entitled *UFFO* and one issue of the SNM journal. Jaalle (Comrade) Omer Jees of the

Supreme Revolutionary Council (SRC) was advised of these developments and we sent copies of the publications to NSS Headquarters in Mogadisho. After that we received directives from Mogadishu to investigate. The informant told us that a copy of the *UFFO* was brought from the house of accused No. 2. We arrested accused No. 2, who confessed that he and accused No. 1 alone wrote the journal. When I returned to the office in the same afternoon a statement written by accused No. 2 was brought to me by the officer on duty. In this statement he, accused No. 2, wrote that his earlier statement was false, but that work of the journal was based on the "efforts of twenty of us". He listed some of the names, but while he knew some of the people by sight, he did not know their names. We then arrested accused No. 1. Following this an *Investigative Committee* was sent from Mogadishu, to which we transferred custody of accused Nos. 1 and 2, and all the documents related to the case.

DIRECT EXAMINATION OF THE SECOND WITNESS BY THE PUBLIC PROSECUTOR:

The witness read the text of the material on top of the journal.

A. I don't recall the date accused No. 2 was arrested.

A. There was a 2-day gap between the arrest of the first and second accused.

A. Accused No. 2 stated in his written confession that twenty people were involved.

A. Accused No. 1 was arrested on the basis of Accused No. 2's account.

A. Accused No. 2 wrote a handwritten statement addressed to me.

A. (exhibit) Yes, this letter is the one he sent me.

A. On it was written:

To: Colonel Hassan Mohamed. I remember (and I cannot readily recollect all of the names) that the names were as follows:

Adan Ali Farah

Adan Aw Warsama Saeed

Mohamed Baruud Ali

Dr. Sulub

Dr. Bashiir

Dr. Haddi

Dahir Farah Jireh

accused No. 2 himself, and many others.

It (the letter) also said that the readers of the journal are many, although the printed copies are very few. It is circulated among the readers. The defendant [accused No. 2] wrote that [the statement]in his own hand and he signed it.

A. I asked the accused only one question to which he replied that he was certain that these were his associates.
A. I do not know anything about accused No. 2.
A. I transferred the testimony of the accused, and the custody of accused Nos. 1 and 2, to the Committee headed by Colonel Ali Hussein.

Cross-Examination of the Second Witness by Attorney Faysal.

Q. Who sent you the SNM publication?
A. General Gani sent it to me.
Q. Do you know who brought the journals to General Gani?
A. No, I do not know who brought the journals to General Gani.
Q. Did Abdi Langare tell you that it was Aadan who obtained the journals?
A. No, Abdi Langare told me that he removed the journal from the home of accused No. 2.
Q. Was accused No. 2 threatened or tortured?
A. As far as I know nobody tortured him.
Q. (Exhibition). In this letter is the writing of the name SULUB different from the others?
A. The answer is no, it is simply written with a different pen.
Q. In this letter written by accused No. 2 [above statement], is Abdi Langare included?
A. Yes.
Q. Do you know from whose possession the SNM journal was removed?
A. No, I do not.
Q. Did you arrest all of the people on this list [list contained in the above mentioned statement written by accused No. 2]?
A. Some are in detention, but others are not.

Cross-Examination of the Second Witness by Attorney Ismail

Q. Was this journal formally sent to you or was it informally passed on to you?
A. It was hand-carried to me.
A. Two different statements were taken from accused No. 2; which one did he give freely?
A. He made both statements freely.

Q. Were the methods in which the two statements were taken in conformity with conditions specified in article 201 of the SCC?
A. Both statements are with the Public Prosecutor.
Q. When was accused No. 1 arrested?
A. Towards the end of October and after the confession of accused No. 2.
Q. Did accused No. 1 make a written statement?
A. No.

Cross-Examination of the Second Witness by Attorney Hassan Sheikh

Q. Was the statement of accused No. 2 written in your presence or was the signed statement brought to you?
A. This signed statement was brought to me.
Q. Is the pen used to sign the statement different from the one used to write the statement?
A. I cannot tell whether it is the same pen or a different one.
Q. Did you investigate?
A. No, I did not.
Q. Wasn't it your responsibility to verify?
A. I did not investigate because I transferred responsibility for the matter to the Committee.

Cross-Examination of the Second Witness by Attorney Osman

Q. Was the report on the publication submitted to you by the individuals who provided the journal?
A. No, but I was aware of who provided the journal.
Q. Did you call for the individuals who provided the journal?
A. Abdi Langare told me that he provided the journal.
Q. Did the association RUDM exist? and do you know of it?
A. I did not testify about the existence of the association. My testimony concerns the journal and the arrest of accused Nos.1 and 2.

Cross-Examination of the Second Witness by Attorney Bashir

Q. Did you take a statement from Abdi Langare?
A. Yes, he informed me that he brought the journal UFFO from the home of accused No. 2 after he found it under his bed.
Q. Do you know the present whereabouts of Abdi Langare?
A. No.
Q. Do you know anything about his background and character?
A. I do not know anything about his background.

Q. How many of the accused were in detention at the time you transferred the investigation to the Committee?
A. Accused Nos. 1 and 2.

Cross-Examination of the Second Witness by Attorney Bille

Q. Did you see any other copies of this journal UFFO?
A. Only the copy referred to before and another shown to me by the Committee.
Q. Did you investigate and did you find where the journal originated from?
A. We had information about the existence of the journals and copies were later submitted to us.
Q. Did you investigate where UFFO was actually printed?
A. No, but I arrested the reported publisher.
Q. Was accused No. 2 physically abused during the interrogation and statement?
A. Another officer was present when I was taking the statement from him [accused No. 2]. He was not harmed then, and he did not report to me any harm to him. Furthermore, he was being held just outside the offices of the NSS for two days.
Q. Were you told who provided the journal?
A. Many were reported to have provided it, but I only met Abdi Langare.
Q. Do you know the whereabouts of Abdi Langare?
A. I don't know his whereabouts.

Cross-Examination of the Second Witness by the Court

Q. Did you ask the accused whether he wrote the Second Statement?
A. Yes, and he told me he wrote the Second Statement.

Attorney Osman: Would the court ask the witness:

Q. From where did Abdi Langare obtain the journal?
A. Abdi Langare told me that he had qat with accused No. 2 in his home, and that he found the journal under his pillow. [translator's note: qat is a mild stimulant that in Somalia is consumed with close friends, it serves as a form of entertainment]

Attorney Bille: Would the court ask the witness:

Q. Were there other statements made by the accused?
A. There were no other statements apart from the two.

Third Witness, Lt. Qaasim Yuusuf Cali, after taking the oath stated:

I am from the National Security Office in Mogadishu. On 8.11.81, a combined Committee of the Police and the NSS - of which I was a member - went to Hargeisa in order to investigate an incident. The Committee was headed by General Ali Hussein Dinle. On 11.11.81, we were given documents reporting the existence of a secret association in Hargeisa with the objective of promoting regional and tribal division. The documetns further stated that the secret association was a front for associations in Western Europe, the Gulf States and Ethiopia. The two detainees transferred to us were accused No. 2 (Jabane), a former teacher, and No. 1 (Eng. Baruud), an employee at the Pepsi-Cola factory. We were told that these two were the only ones in detention among the organizers of the association. We interviewed accused No. 2 and also received his two previous statements. The accused told us that he and accused No. 1 wrote the journal UFFO. He also listed the names of his associates for us. We asked him about the two previous statements, to which he replied in the following way:

Some Ida-Geli clansmen and I jointly undertook these activities. They abandoned me when I was exposed. When I found out that I alone was trapped, and two of our associates from the Ida-Geli clan had betrayed us for money, I told about our other secret activities.

He further stated that:

The activities of the group started in 1977, after the Soviet influence was eliminated, an influence which kept Somalia isolated from the world. But we were disappointed by the failure to repudiate Soviet ideology and the appointment of a Governor to Hargeisa who was nicknamed "Afar Jeeble", "The one with four pockets." This Governor introduced pervasive corruption which crippled the local economy. He was replaced as Governor by General Abdirahman, locally known as "the one that beheads", who wanted local taxes on the construction of a monument. The wasted revenue was needed for improving local services. The administration kept on worsening.

Accused No. 2 also said in his statement to us:

The Group became aware of the formation of SNM headed by DUQSI, an organization which advocated the restoration of democratic government; we worked to support the new organization. At the wedding of accused No. 1, held at his brother's home, we agreed to undertake community improvement activities without waiting for government help. In the second day, we adopted a resolution to form a community development and welfare association - URUR SAMAFAL. Our activities demonstrated our intentions to the public in order to gain their support. We held our meeting at a house rented to accused No. 5, and used the home of accused No. 4 as our operational base. In a meeting at the home of accused No. 4, accused No. 1 proposed that we start a publication. We asked him to prepare the material for the first issue. Accused No. 1 gave me two copies of the first issue.

Accused No. 2 further stated:

I contributed to the writing of the second issue. A typewriter at the Pepsi-Cola factory was used to type the first issue. We typed the second issue on a typewriter belonging to Mahamud Qalib. It was brought from his home. The third issue of the journal was prepared by accused No. 1, who typed it at the Pepsi-Cola factory. I gave a copy to accused No. 3 and another copy to a man by the name of Aadan Walli. I also distributed all other copies.

Accused No. 2, in his statement to us, also said that he had a meeting with a man by the name of Mahamed Nur Handulle, together with accused Nos. 5, 11, 10, and 7. He related a message to us from DUQSI and ina-Wadaad Diid, who held a meeting with the members of the Isaaq clan working in Saudi Arabia. He told us that the informed and educated members pledged their support to SNM. He referred to those who refused to oppose their country [join SNM] as "Reer Sablaale". Accused No. 2 told the Committee that:

Mahamed Nur Handulle urged us during the meetings not to be like "Reer Sablaale" and told us that Aadan Walli had direct communication with DUQSI, leader of the SNM. Mahamed Nur Handulle (Arab) told the group that every Somali clan formed a movement, and we should work to consolidate the support of the Isaaq clan to SNM, and especially work on unifying the Ida-Geli members to the rest of the Isaaq clan. The Ida-Geli clan should disarm the leadership of collaborators like Abdi Warraabe. That was the message that Handulle related to us. We decided to affiliate our group with the WUHDADDA - the Brotherhood - to give a religious mass appeal. We held a meeting to exchange information on the WUHDADDA. We wondered why their members wear their watches on the right hand and refrain from meat in their diet. The WUHDADDA were three in our group, of which accused Nos. 22 and 23, former primary school teachers in Burao, were the leaders.

Accused No. 2 stated that the WUHDADDA leaders told them they were an association opposed to the Government, and:
They asked us who we were. We told them that we were a network of schoolmates who graduated at about the same time. They asked us what our objectives were. We gave ambiguous answers. In the end we agreed to cooperate, and we advised them to refrain from any display of open personal rebellion.

Direct Examination of the Third Witness by the Assistant to the Legal Counselor

A. Accused No. 2 met with Mr. Arab (Handulle) together with accused Nos. 5, 7, 9, 10, and 11.
A. As far as I can remember, accused Nos. 1, 2, 3, 5, 6, 7, 8, 9, 10, 11, 12, 14, 15, 22, 17, and 20 met with the Brotherhood group.
A. I don't recall who asked him the specific questions.
A. The meeting was at the home of accused No. 22. He was also among the conveners of the meeting. The meeting was chaired by accused No. 21, who was the leader of the Brotherhood group. Two others took part in another meeting at the home of accused No. 1.
A. Accused Nos. 21 and 23 represented the Brotherhood at the meeting.
A. Accused No. 22 stated that the Brotherhood group was informed of the meeting, following which he [No. 22] decided to take part in the meetings with the group.
A. Accused No. 23 (sic) asked the Brotherhood group what form of government they desired, to which they replied "an Islamic government". Accused No. 3 asked them whether it was of the Khomeini type. They replied "no", but of the Caliphate Islamic form. Accused No. 3 asked whether that was compatible with conditions of the modern world. They replied that Islamic scholars in Pakistan and Egypt had analyzed the issue and concluded that it was possible to establish and run modern governments on Islamic principles.
A. The Brotherhood group asked accused No. 3 about his impression of the country after his return from overseas studies. He [No. 3] said, "The girls have been reduced to prostitution, boys to drug addiction, older women to qat merchants, and old men to exile". Accused No. 1 told the Committee that he initiated the first issue of the newsletter UFFO. He used a typewriter at the Pepsi-Cola factory and gave three copies to Jabane (accused No. 2). He said:
Myself and [accused No. 2] wrote the second issue at my home. We planned its distribution for 21.10.1981. I produced the third issue using the typewriter at the Pepsi-Cola factory.

Accused No. 1 also stated that copies of the newsletter were often taken to the homes of accused Nos. 4 and 2, and a copy was given to accused No. 7. He [No. 7] organized the meetigns with the Brotherhood group by contacting accused Nos. 21 and 22, who worked with him. Accused No. 1 told the Committee that he and accused No.4 proposed that they should send credible anti-government propaganda to the editor of SNM journal and suggest to him the use of the Somali language instead of English in writing the journal.

A. (Exhibition)-Yes, it is the SNM journal which used to be read at the meetings of the group. Accused No. 1 proposed the use of the Somali language and the inclusion of credible propaganda information.

Reading from the Journal UFFO

Item 1. "Tension increases in Berbera". "Colonel Abdilaziz Bilad qualified as a hero after he shipped the Marehan merchants livestock". Item 2: "Nationalization of the government--the Marehan head all government offices: list of offices headed by members of the Marehan clan (NMS, the local militia, and so forth).

Q/A. Accused No. 1 stated that he alone wrote the newsletter UFFO. We found at his office at the Pepsi-Cola Factory a notebook containing items published in the second and third issue of UFFO. I only recall: "General Gani transfers the husband of.....". Accused No. 1 said that those were predictions. We found the typewriter at the home of Mohamud Qalib. Accused Nos. 1 and 2 idenitified the typewriter. The wife of Mohamud Qalib confirmed that accused No.2, a former teacher of hers, borrowed the typewriter. We did not find other copies of UFFO.

Accused No. 3

According to the statement of No. 2, accused No. 3 played a prominent role at the meeting held at the home of accused No. 1. We found at the home of the accused [No. 3] a copy of UFFO. He told us that he acquired the copy from accused No. 2, after it had been read by accused Nos. 8, 15 and 6, and after accused No. 6 took it to the home of No. 2. The accused spent a long time in England, where he studied development economics. He joined the staff of the Islamic Development Bank in Saudi Arabia. He later returned to Somalia. He told the group in one of their meetings that while he was at the Islamic Bank

the bank agreed to finance a scheme for replacing and expanding Hargeisa electric power supply, following a request by the government.

But the city remains without electricity, causing hardship to the people. This is indicative of government mismanagement.

He claimed not to have seen or met any political activists in the trips he made to the United States, United Kingdom and Saudi Arabia. [Translators note: this defendant studied economics in the U.K; he briefly worked for the Islamic Bank in Jeddah. He visited the United States once, in 1980, for his sister's wedding in California].

Accused No. 4

About 18 of the accused confirmed in their confessions that the home of accused No. 4 was the regular venue of their meetings. The accused is a government employee and lives in government-provided residence. Second, the meetings and activities in his residence were of organizational nature. The accused stated to us that meetings were held in his residence and concerns discussed. He told us that he had heard of the journal UFFO, but did not recall anyone who had the journal. He also said that he read the SNM journal, as did the other accused: Nos. 1, 2, 5, 6, 7, 8, 9, 11, 13, 15, and 17.

Accused No. 5

His arrest was prompted by the statement of accused No. 2, to the effect that the accused [No.5] was a member of RUDM. He and accused No. 2 live in two houses directly opposite each other. He was a regular visitor at the home of accused No. 4. He also frequently attended the sessions with the Brotherhood, but did not take part in the discussions. We found in his residence a text of a poem, copied in his own handwriting, which was offensive to the President of the Somali Democratic Republic. Accused No. 5 met in his residence with Mohamed Nur Handulle and Adan Ali Farah (Adan Waali), who were carrying a message from DUQSI (then the Secretary General of the SNM). He stated that some of the group liked the message, but others did not get involved. He stated that accused No. 2 brought two copies of UFFO to his residence, where it was read, as was the SNM journal. (The witness read the text of the handwritten poem found at the residence).

The accused told the Committee that the poem was composed by a former teacher, whom the Hargeisa National Security Court sentenced to 10 years in prison on account of this poem. The witness said that he did not recall who dictated the poem. [Translator's note: in Somalia, poems are first recited by the composer, then memorized by the listeners, who often recite the entire poem at gatherings].

Public Prosecutor and Witness No. 3

Q. What interpretation did you give to the poem?

A. An anti-government propaganda which was a sequel to the "Deelay" [a series of poems with the "D" alliteration that were critical of the government. In Somali poetry every major word of the poem must start with the same letter]. Accused No. 5 stated that he was not a member of any organization, but that he often sat in group discussions.

Accused No. 6

Some members of the organization were regular visitors to his house. One day accused No. 3 brought a copy of UFFO to the home of accused No. 6. Accused No. 6 was with [having qat with] accused Nos. 8 and 15, and together they read the journal there. When accused No. 4 was arrested, he [accused No. 6] urged that they help him [accused no. 4].

Accused No. 7

Q. On what grounds did you arrest the accused? and what prompted it in the first place?

A. Accused No. 2 told us that he gave a copy of UFFO to accused No. 1 and No. 7. Accused No. 1 stated that he did not recall. The accused [No.7] took part in the meetings, particularly the meeting at the wedding of Mohamed Baruud Ali and that with the Brotherhood. According to accused No. 5, the accused also attended the meeting with Mohamed Nur Handulle. Accused No. 7 denied this, but he told us that he had qat at the home of accused No. 4, with accused Nos. 4 and 5. Accused No. 2 did not tell us anything in particular about accused No. 7 except his presence at the meetings.

Accused No. 8

According to the statement of accused No. 2, accused No. 8 was a member of the organization. He [No. 8] confessed to all the information we had on him. He admitted attending the meetings at the homes of accused Nos. 4, 5, and 6, and the meeting with the Brotherhood, and having privately met with Mohamed Nur Handulle, the visitor from overseas. He took part in the discussion of group activities relating to community health problems at the home of accused No. 1. He copied a letter directed to the Regional Government, dictated to him by others who had other objectives, that was prepared by accused Nos. 7, 15, and 17. The letter was prepared for accused No. 28 who had said that he wanted to release his friends from prison by any means. Previously, they met with accused No. 28 at Bar Hargeisa, and accused No. 28 told them [7,15,&17] that he had met with the Assistant Minister for Marine Transportation, Comrade Jama Gas Ma'aawiya, who asked them to prepare a letter about their concerns and grievances. Accused No 8 said the reason accused No. 28 wanted to take the letter was that the Assistant Minister was his cousin. I am not sure but I think accused No. 28 worked at the Commerce Agency. Dr. Tani [accused 8] told us that his father used to be a judge in this region and that he himself went to schools here and that he has many friends in the region, although he is only related to some people through his mother. Accused No. 8 confessed to the above and his confession is in agreement with that of accused No. 2.

Accused No. 9

We followed the confession of No. 2. According to the confession of No. 2, before the NSS committee arrived, accused No. 9, accompanied by Nos. 7, 8, and 9 (sic), came to where he [accused No. 2] was detained. They asked him the reason for his detention. Accused No. 2 told them that they were responsible for his detention, that when he was caught, they abandoned him-" nobody did anything for me". Accused No. 2 further stated that No. 7 and 9 came back after few days, and told him that the rest of the youth said and wanted them to convey to him, that everything will be done for him. They told him to increase the number of the people on the list that he had submitted so that investigations would become difficult, and to make sure that every clan was affected. Accused No. 9 gave this [similar account] in his confession. He also stated that he [No. 9], accused No. 28, Abdi Langare and Adan Ali Guhad talked about how to make sure that Ida-Geli clan stops supporting the Marehan and to make them ally with the SNM. He was also among the men who met with ARAB at the home of No. 5, and after most of the accused were detained he [accused No. 9] was among the men appointed to talk with the elders.

Accused No. 10

Accused No. 10 confessed to most of the crimes of which he is being accused: that he was a member of the organization. He used to have "qat" with [with whom?], but he also told us that he took part in writing the letter of accused No. 28 [translator's note: this is the letter of grievances No. 28 is said to have delivered to the Assistant Minister of

Marine Transportation]. He was also among the men who decided that Jabane [accused No. 2] should increase the names on his statement to the NSS.

Accused No. 11

As accused No. 2 confessed, No. 11 took part in the meetings but did not tell us that he [accused No. 11] was a member of the organization. He [accused No. 11] confessed that he took part in some meetings and that he read the journals UFFO and SNM.

Accused No. 12

First, accused No. 2 in his confession told us that he [accused No. 12] read the journal UFFO and that he took part in some meetings, but did not know what the real purpose of these meetings was. The other men did not tell us anything more relating to him. This man [accused No. 12] is a farmer and he said he did not have any extra time, and that the discussions did not alarm him. After the detentions of these men [the other defendants], he was among the people who were appointed to see the authorities about their case.

Accused No. 13

He was educated overseas. Accused No. 2 told us this in his confession. It is mentioned in the confessions of the accused that he took part in the meetings at the house of accused No. 4, his housemate. He confessed that he read UFFO and SNM. According to the statement of Bashe Abdi Yusuf (accused No. 20), he [accused No. 13] inquired about the response of the elders at one of the meetings. He was told that they said "we will not get involved in the affairs of youngsters who would not keep their mouths' shut". To which he replied "they are criminals we should kill the authorities". The accused told us that he did not participate in the meetings, but that he read a copy of the journal brought to his house.

Accused No. 14

Jabane (accused No. 2) said in his confession, and several of the other defendants confirmed, that he was a member of the organization [RUDM]. He [accused No. 14] told us that he used to visit the house of accused No. 13, who was his physician, because he [accused no. 14] has a heart ailment. Accused No. 14 did not attend the meeting with the Brotherhood.

Accused No. 15

Accused No. 2 told us in his confession that accused No. 15 participated in the meeting with the Brotherhood and the meeting at Guraysamo [a section of the city] and that he read the journal at the houses of accused Nos.6 and 8. He [accused No. 15] also confessed to that.

Accused No. 16

In his confession, accused No. 2 made it clear that accused No. 16 took part in the meetings at the house of accused No. 5, but that he [accused No. 16] did not speak at these meetings. When we searched his house, we found a Makarof pistol. None of the others told us that he participated or spoke at the meetings.

Accused No. 17

Jabane (accused No. 2) confirmed that he [No. 17] took part in all the meetings. We did not find any clear evidence so we delayed his arrest. He did not give opinions at the meetings. He had met with accused No. 20. About 13 others confessed that he [No. 17] was a member of the organization. While we were waiting to arrest him, an explosion ocurred at the house of the 1st Assistant of the Somali Socialist Revolutionary Party of the Northwest Region. A second time, another bomb was thrown at the house of Tindeere, a private businessman. At about the same time, 2 bombs were thrown at the house of the Commander of the 26th Army Division, but they did not explode. Leaflets were dropped at the Immigrations Office, the office of the "Guulwadayaal" victory pioneers, and other places. In these leaflets were written "victory to SNM, death to Afweyne" (Translators note:"Afweyne" is a pejorative name for Siyad Barre that literaly means "big mouthed"). The rumors circulating in the town indicated to us that members of the organization that had not been arrested yet were behind these explosions. The accused fled between Hargeisa/Berbera/Hargeisa between 9.12.81 and 14.12.81. After that we arrested him. After we arrested him, we immediately asked him about the explosions, and he confessed to the fact that he was behind their distribution and planning, and that he and accused Nos. 20, 24 and 25 met together about it and reached agreement. Those meetings took place at Bar Hargeisa [translators note: Bar Hargeisa, a small cafe in the middle of town, belongs to the father of accused No. 17], the house of accused No. 4 and near the Regional Headquarters. Their aim was not to kill anybody but to terrorize those responsible for arresting their friends, after mediations were fruitless. Accused No. 17 told us that he met with accused No. 27, who is his cousin, and the Chief of the Technical Unit of the 26th Army Division, and asked for 10 explosive devices, to scare away wild animals that were destroying a friend's farm. Accused No. 27 refused [according to the statement of accused No. 17], saying that it did not make any sense and that it was not something one can ask a person like him.

I then asked him a second time. This time he became angry. After I pleaded with him a third time, he [accused No. 27] brought the explosives to my house and told me not to add to my troubles if I was not going to use them on the farm. I left the explosives at the house of No. 24, I also met him there. He [accused No. 24] took them to the house of accused Nos. 25, 20 and 26. I caused the explosion at the house of the 1st Assistant of the Party on 9th December, 1981. I made accused No. 20 responsible for the house of the commander of the 26th division of XDS and accused No. 24 to bomb the house of Tindeere.

He [accused No. 17] did not tell us who went with him, but he himself confessed. He said they all fulfilled their objectives.

Accused No. 18

Jabane (accused No. 2) first mentioned him. According to accused No. 20, at one meeting at the house of accused No. 18, it was decided that they should organize as a region to struggle against the government. He took part in the meeting at the wedding [the wedding of accused No. 1]. He told us that he read a copy of the SNM journal brought in by a man from Jeddah. He denied that there was a meeting at his house or the house of Dr. Aaden (accused No. 4).

Accused No. 19

At first Jabane (accused No. 2) mentioned him [No. 19] in his confession. He [No. 19] took part in the meeting at Guraysamo at the wedding of accused No. 1. He [No. 19] had been a housemate of accused No. 4 except for the last two months. He [No. 19] did not take part in the meeting with the Brotherhood. He took part in the self-help project meeting. He [No. 19] confessed to that.

Accused No. 20

We have followed the confession of accused No. 2. At first we could not find him [No. 20], and we issued "Baadi Goob" [All Points Bulletin?].

After we caught him, he confessed that he was a member of the organization and took part in the discussions and read all the journals. He told us that during the detention of the defendants, he met with accused Nos. 24 and 25, and had good contacts with accused No. 17, who was his friend. They used to meet at the house of accused No. 4. He told us that one day he was given a lift in a car driven by accused No. 17, accompanied by accused No. 24, to the construction site of his new house. He said that accused No. 17 asked him whether they should do something for the youth that were in detention, since "we are the ones on the outside [free]". I told him that I was not part of that. He [accused No. 20] said that he did not want to take part in the earlier decision proposed by accused No. 13 to kill the leaders of the regional government. He [accused No. 20] said that accused No. 24 agreed with him on that point.

Accused Nos. 21, 22, and 23

They were members of the Brotherhood who took part in the meeting with RUDM. Accused No. 1 organized that meeting, and accused Nos. 21 and 23 first took part and later contacted accused No. 22, who organized the other meeting. All three confessed and made statements that their meetings were concerned with "learning about each other, collaboration and exchange of ideas".

Accused No. 24

Jabane (accused No. 2) at first confirmed that he [accused No. 24] was a member of the organization. He [accused No. 24] did not discuss matters with him [accused No. 2] or carry functions. After accused No. 17 told us that he made them [accused Nos. 24 and 25] responsible for the attack on the house of Tindeere, we asked him [No. 24] about accused Nos. 17, 20, and 25, and he said he did not know them. After we brought them to his face, he said "I know these as Johny, Bashe-yere [young Bashe] and Ma'allin Osman" [all of these are nicknames]. He said:

We met near the headquarters of the region, myself, accused Nos. 20 and 17, in the car of No. 17, and he [No. 17] asked us whether we should do something for those that had been arrested and explode bombs. Bashe Abdi, accused No. 20, said he is not part of it. After a few days, having refused it the first day, I agreed. Accused No. 17 distributed among us explosive devices and I was given the responsibility for the house of Tindeere at Guraysamo, and accused No. 25 helped me and threw the bomb with his own hand. At the same time accused No. 17, accompanied by accused No. 26, caused the explosion at the house of the 1st Assistant. Accused No. 20 was responsible for the house of the commander of the 26th Division, but at the specified night no news of explosion reached the city. In the morning we found out that an extra device, different from the ones we had, was found at the house. Then we confronted accused No. 20 who was responsible for that house. He said that the extra bomb was given to him by accused No. 17, and that once he threw the bomb it was not his responsibility. The wall of Tindeere's house was 1.8m tall and Mohamed Ma'aalin Osman threw the bomb. Mohamed then walked to his house and I took the bus.

Accused No. 25

He [accused No. 25] said that he is acquainted with these [probably Nos. 17, 20, and 24] and that they used to meet, but that he did not know anything about explosives, but he told us that he and accused No. 24 took the pay check of accused No. 17 to No. 17's wife who works at the Tax Office in Hargeisa. He told us that No. 17's wife told them that he [No. 17] was in prison for the explosives. When we were looking for accused No. 17, we used the name Ahmed Mohamed Madar, but we found out that he uses another name, which I do not remember now, that he used in drawing a salary from the government.

Accused No. 26

In his confession, accused No. 24 said that he was accompanied by accused No. 26. Accused No. 17 did not say who was with him. This accused [accused No. 26] also denied he knows anything about it [explosives].

Accused No. 27

Accused No. 24 told us that accused No. 17 told him that he would get explosives from Ina Hashi Madar, and accused No. 24 said that he found out that that man was Major Ismail Hashi Madar, who is the cousin of accused No. 17. This defendent [accused No. 27] denied any knowledge about the explosives and said that he is not responsible for explosives. He also said that he only gave accused No. 17 a ride home after work one day.

Accused No. 28

He [accused No. 28] is not a member of an organization. His cousin (accused No. 1) was in prison. This accused contacted Jama Gaas

[Assistant Minister for Marine Transportation], who was on his way to Mogadishu, and gave him a letter written by his friends and typed by him. In the letter were lies about the leaders of the region and the on-going investigation. In the letter they said that the authorities of the region were behind the publication of UFFO and Qurmis (Translator's note: Qurmis is a pejorative name for the SSDF, an external opposition movement).

Defense Lawyer Ismail and Prosecution Witness No. 3

Q. What evidence did you have for the existence of the organization that No. 1 is accused of?

A. In the beginning of our investigation, our conversation with accused No. 2 pointed to the existence of RUDM and indicated that accused No. 1 was a member.

Q. Did you find physical evidence and an office of the organization?

A. We did not find an office or material used by the organization.

Q. Is there any evidence, besides the information of accused No. 2 that proves the existence of the organization?

A. We based it on two things: 1) the information of accused No. 2, and 2) the journal UFFO.

Q. Under article 199 of the Somali Criminal Code (SCC), incriminating statements by one defendant against another can only be used if corroborating evidence is found. Do you have other evidence?

A. [Translator's note: the answer to this question is missing from the original Somali, but the same question is repeated several more times and the answer seems to be "no"].

Q. What brought in the typewriter?

A. Accused No. 1 told us that he wrote the journal using a typewriter in his office. We took him to the office, and he said it is the same typewriter. When we checked the journal against the typewriter, there was no difference between the letters.

Q. Per article 161 of SCC, did you use an expert's opinion to check whether the typewriter was the one used to write the journal?

A. No.

Q. Is this paper (a paper is shown to the witness) typed with the typewriter at Pepsi-Cola or another?

A. If I do not compare it with the other typewriter I cannot tell.

Q. Was Abdi Langare brought before a court previously?

A. I heard that during the war with the enemy, he aided the enemy and was prosecuted.

Q. Do you know where he, Abdi Langare, is now?
A. No, I did not know where he was before either.
Q. Did you tell Abdi Langare that his testimony was necessary and that he should not leave the country?
A. No, I did not order him.
Q. Did you ask the court to order Abdi Langare to stay because his testimony was needed?
A. No, I did not ask.
Q. Did you meet with Aaden Ali Guhad, and did you know that he was involved in bringing the journal?
A. I did not meet with Aaden, but Abdi Langare told me that he sat with (had Qat with) a man called Sare Geye, accused No. 2, and another man, and that he found the journal at the house of accused No. 2.
Q. Did you ask Abdi Langare whether he was told to find the journal?
A. No, I am not sure whether he was told to find the journal, but he told me that a man called Faysal Ali Waraabe advised him [Aadan Ali Guhad] to help the government.
Q. If there is no evidence that a crime is committed, was a crime committed?
A. We did not find proof.
Q. Was there a crime?
A. Yes, there is.
Q. But did you find any witness outside the accused?
A. We have the confessions only.
Q. Do you know that the confessions of the accused alone are not enough to show crime?
A. Yes, I know that.
Q. How is accused No. 3 different from No. 1 and 2?
A. No difference.
Q. The journal found in his home, what about it, and did you have a warrant for the search?
A. No, I did not see a warrant. I was not a member of the search team and I do not know whether he [No. 3] permitted it or not.
Q. Accused No. 23, how is he different from the others?
A. No difference, No. 8 is also the same, and also Aadan Warsama Nur.
Q. Did not accused No. 28 ask to speak with the Assistant Minister?
A. I do not remember.
Q. Did you ask him that the Assistant Minister told him to put it in writing? (translator's note: the meaning of this question is not clear from the Somali text)

A. As the accused told me.
Q. Did you ascertain whether the Assistant Minister said that?
A. I did not ascertain whether that was the case.
Q. Did it appear to you that it was a grievance submitted to leadership, and how did it [the letter accused No. 28 is alleged to have carried to the Assistant Minister] appear to you?
A. No, I did not see it as a grievance, it appeared to me as slander, criticism and false libel of the leaders.
Q. Why did you refuse to believe that the journal UFFO was put out by Kulmis (translator's note: Kulmis is the name of the external opposition movement), since Abdi Langare, the enemy-helper, is now with them.
A. That is a reasonable point.
Q. Did that not warrant further investigation?
A. Yes, but I did not see how he [Abdi Langare] was different from the rest of the public.
Q. Did accused No. 28 tell you that others wrote the letter?
A. Yes, he told me so.
Q. Why is he then accused of propaganda?
A. The reason was that he had specific motives.
Q. Do you know whether he is literate or not?
A. No.
Q. Do you have the letter?
A. As far as I know, no.
Q. Did he have physical contact with the letter?
A. No, we found about it from the men who wrote it and him; there was no other evidence.

Defense Lawyer Hassan Sheikh and Prosecution Witness No. 3

Q. Tell the court where accused No. 9 works, since you have been investigating him for a long time.
A. He works for the Livestock Development Agency. He came to Hargeisa on leave, so that he could marry, and he did marry.
Q. Did you ask him anything about the writing of UFFO and SNM?
A. He took part in the reading of the two journals.
Q. Is the accusation based only on the statement of accused No. 2?
A. Yes, that is so.
Q. Is it because he was among the group that proposed talks with the government that he has been imprisoned?

A. Being a member of the committee is not a crime. All the members of the committee were not arrested.
Q. Did you harm him while he was in prison, and do you know that torture is against the law?
A. Yes, torture is forbidden, and I do not know that he was tortured.
Q. What was accused No. 10 doing when you arrested him, and where was he working?
A. He had been a teacher but he had resigned and he was not doing anything in Hargeisa.
Q. Where was he when you arrested him?
A. He broke into the camp of the "guulwadayaal" [victory pioneers militia] where accused No. 1 was jailed, and they were caught while they were with him.
Q. Do you have any evidence?
A. He has confessed and given a statement.
Q. It says in my notes that he has not confessed.
A. That is possible.
Q. Is it true that accused No. 10 has complained of injuries?
A. I do not remember, but on 20.11.81, I ordered him tied with cuffs.

DEFENSE LAWYER HASSAN: I wish to ask the court to examine the body of accused No. 10, so that justice can be served, because we have *FLESH* that broke off of his skin.

PUBLIC PROSECUTOR: We object to this matter, since the accused did not show who inflicted these injuries, he is responsible for his body, this matter creates disturbances.... and the court should not allow it.

DEFENSE LAWYER HASSAN: Per article 150 of the SCC, confessions extracted by threats and the like, promises, money are invalid. Jaalle (Comrade) Chairman, what stronger proof is there than to show the flesh that broke from his back and the wounds, is there? The court should allow us. I was appointed by the government to represent him.

THE COURT: After listening to both sides of the argument, the court decides not to undress the accused in the court room, and not to allow the request of the defense lawyer, but for the court to check that in a private place if it is necessary for the justice.

DEFENSE LAWYER HASSAN AND PROSECUTION WITNESS No. 3

Q. Did you come across any written document naming the divisions, the leadership and posts for this organization, either secret or regular?
A. No, we did not find it.

DEFENSE LAWYER OSMAN AND PROSECUTION WITNESS No. 3

Q. Show me where the name of accused No. 13 appears on this document.
A. We did not mention accused No. 13 in this document; it is the confession of accused No. 2 that says something about him.
Q. What did you mean by "accused No. 13 entered the country recently"?
A. That he returned from overseas not long ago, but when he came back I do not remember.
Q. What evidence do you have against him?
A. Confession and a statement he gave in the presence of a lawyer, that he read the journals UFFO and SNM.
Q. Can you tell where, besides his house, he went?
A. The house of accused No. 4, who was his housemate.
Q. Was that a regular meeting or an occasion for qat?
A. He did not mention a regular meeting, but it was a qat occasion, where the journal was read, gossip exchanged, and news told.
Q. What date was the meeting where accused No. 13 is supposed to have proposed the killings?
A. It was between 4.12.1981 and 19.12.81.
Q. When was accused No. 13 arrested?
A. He was arrested on 4.12.81.
Q. Did he say that [propose the killings] while he was in prison?
A. No, I mixed that date with the other. The man who told us about that meeting was being sought during that period.
Q. Were any injuries inflicted on accused No. 13?
A. No, he was not harmed.
Q. Accused No. 18, how did you find him, and did any witness tell you that he was a member of the organization?
A. Accused No. 2 alone told us. We did not base it on any other evidence.
Q. How did you prove,(when you say) that a man from overseas showed him the SNM journal and he read it?
A. Whether that is even so, I do not know, though he himself told us.
Q. Why did not you conclude or ascertain that Abdi Langare could be an indispensable witness.

PUBLIC PROSECUTOR: I have an objection about this point. He was asked this question before

Q. Is there any evidence, besides the confession of accused No. 2, that implicates accused Nos. 13 and 18?
A. No.

DEFENSE LAWYER BASHIR ARTAN AND PROSECUTION WITNESS No. 3

Q. Since evidence could not be found about the existence of the organization, material and the like, what implicates the defendants that I am representing (12, 19, 21 and 22)?
A. We did not find material.
Q. Do you have evidence against the defendants that I am representing, that is proof, besides the confession of accused No. 2?
A. No, we do not.
Q. The brotherhood that I heard about several times, why did you.... [the rest of the question is missing from this copy]
A. Since they are not accused, why ask me about them?

DEFENSE LAWYER FAYSAL HAJI AND PROSECUTION WITNESS NO. 3

Q. How many statements did you obtain from accused No. 2?
A. Up to 5 reports were obtained.
Q. On which of those 5 statements did you base your investigation?
A. The first one that we wrote from him was used as a base.Q.Were all the men named on that statement arrested?
A. No.
Q. Did you tell us anything other than the statement of accused No. 2 that was used to arrest them?
A. The satement of No. 2 was used as a base.
Q. Why did you not arrest the rest of the men on that list?

Public Prosecutor: I have an objection about this question. He said it was a base for the detention of the accused. The witness told us that they found all the events that each person participated in and for which they were arrested. The witness had been on the stand for a long time. Jaalle [comrade] chairman, I object to that question.

Defense Lawyer Faysal Haji: Rebuttal: Honorable court, the witness had repeatedly stated that the confession of accused No. 2 was used as a basis for the accusation, especially to the question that attorney Ismail asked him. The witness should not evade the question. He should tell the court.

The Court:

After listening to the question that had been asked of the witness, the argument of the Public Prosecutor and the rebuttal of attorney Faysal, the court orders the witness to answer the question of the lawyer, that is: If you followed the confession of accused No. 2, why were only some of the men he mentioned arrested?.

The Witness:

A. The detentions were not my decision. Any man against whom there was no evidence besides the news of Jabane was not arrested.
Q. That an organization was formed at accused No.1's wedding, if I say is not reasonable, how would you respond?
A. I did not say that the organization was formed there, I previously said there issues relating to the organization were started.
Q. When was the organization that you mentioned formed?
A. Jabane accused No. 2 told us that the organization was formed in 1977.
Q. Did he tell you who started it?
A. No, accused No. 2 did not tell us who started the organization.
Q. Accused Nos. 1, 2 and 3 are accused of starting the organization. Why did you accuse them if he [accused No. 2] did not mention anybody?
A. The organization was started in 1977, who started it he did not tell.
Q. In the accusation it says that it took place in the last six months of 1981, can you tell us the number of meetings it [the organization] had?
A. Nobody told us the number of meetings.
Q. How many times were meetings held at the house of accused No. 5?
A. 3 times.
Q. How many times were meetings held at the house of No. 3?
A. I do not remember.
Q. During your investigation did you find out that accused No. 2 was a member of the "self-help project"?
A. I did not find out that he was a member.
Q. The meetings that these defendants allegedly had, can you tell the court how they diminish the power of the government?
A. Yes, at the meeting at the house of accused No. 18, they discussed whether the organization should be based on clan, region or nation.

Q. Can you tell us anything they did that will diminish the power of the government?
A. At a house in Guraysamo [section of the city], they resolved to start a self-help committee, but the government did not know that.
Q. Who told you they did that?
A. The statement of accused No. 2.
Q. Did they take steps to usurp the power of the government?
A. That they formed a self-help committee, collected money, material, cleaned, organized the Hargeisa Hospital, and secured it. The authorities of the region did not know about that self help scheme.
Q. Are you sure that the authorities did not know that?
A. It became known later.
Q. That accused No. 2 was starved for 5 days and at the same time threatened with a pistol?
A. I do not know that. He was not asked to write a statement at a time when I was not there.
Q. Was it creating a gulf in the relationship between the government and the people?
A. That shows their independence, since the authorities of the region did not know about that [the self-help project].
Q. From whom [defendant] did you get the SNM journal?
A. We did not get it from anybody. We showed it [this copy of the SNM journal] to the accused and asked if it was among the ones they read.
Q. As you told us, accused No. 4 did not take part in the meeting......?
A. He told us that he took part in the meeting held at his house. Mohamed Sh. Hassan Tani [accused No. 8] told us that he gave an opinion at one point.
Q. Is there anybody besides the ones arrested with him who could attest to his guilt?
A. No.
Q. Were you there when the house of accused No. 5 was searched?
A. No, a man called Abdirashid represented us in that task.
Q. That accused No. 20 is a memeber of the organization, is it the statement of accused No.2 alone that you base that on?
A. Yes, but he [accused No. 20] also confessed to it.
Q. You said before that the Brotherhood and the self-help committee could not name the objectives of the organization, and now you say it is an established organization, are those two statements in conflict?
A. Yes, they conflict.
Q. the....[original missing]..

A. No, we do not have other evidence.

DEFENSE LAWYER HUSSEIN BILLE:

Accused Nos. 26, 27 and 28 asked that I defend them, I ask the court to allow me.

THE COURT allowed the request of the lawyer.

DEFENSE LAWYER HUSSEIN BILE AND PROSECUTION WITNESS NO. 3

Q. Did accused No. 2 tell you the time of the day they used to hold meetings?
A. I do not know the times, but accused No. 2 suggested that it was after lunch.
Q. Can you tell us anything about the divisions of the organization, how functions were divided, who the leaders were and how many people were in the organization?
A. No, I do not know any of that, and he did not tell me.
Q. Did Abdi Langare and Adan Waali (Translator's note: Aadan Waali is also referred to as "Adan Ali Guhad" elsewhere in this transcript) take part in the meetings?
A. Abdi Langare went to (had qat at) a meeting held at the house of accused No. 2.
Q. Did Adan Ali Guhad ever sit with them?
A. One day he had qat with accused No. 9.
Q. Are you aware that Aadan has now escaped; and what is his status?
A. We were outside of Hargeisa when he escaped, we would have arrested him, he is accused in absentia.
Q. Would you have arrested Abdi Langare?
A. No, he did not do anything illegal.
Q. Why did not you arrest him for the meeting in which he took part?
A. That is because he was always doing a job that he was told to do.
Q. Did Abdi Langare tell you that he had obtained the Journal UFFO?
A. Yes, he said he removed it.
Q. If I were to tell you that he [Abdi Langare] had in fact said he did not obtain the journal for you, what would you say?
A. I have a statement that I wrote from him.
Q. Is there any evidence besides the statements of the accused that prove the existence of this crime?
A. No.

Q. Why could you not find something in your investigation?
A. That they wrote the journal was told by them (accused Nos. 1 and 2).
Q. Accused No. 6, do you know how many times they used his house?
A. No, I do not know.
Q. The two meetings with the authorities, which one did he take part in?
A. The second one.
Q. Accused No. 14, does he have a heart problem as he told you?
A. Yes, we saw that several times during his imprisonment.
Q. Did he give speeches or opinions?
A. No.
Q. Did accused No. 16 tell you that he bought the pistol for a specific reason?
A. There is nothing to prove that money was brought from the border, and he did not tell us that.
Q. The illegality of the organization, what proves it?
A. Their confession only, we do not have anything else.
Q. Do you know that accused No. 17 was tortured?
A. Not as far as I know.
Q. Was accused No. 17 limping when you arrested him?
A. No, he was not limping.
Q. Is he limping now?
A. I do not know.
Q. Is there any evidence implicating them in the explosions?
A. Their verbal statements only, nothing else.
Q. Accused No. 24, is there anything against him except his statement?
A. No.
Q. Did you torture him too?
A. I do not know.
Q. Accused No. 25, do you have anything on him besides his statement?
A. No, his confession only, but we have nothing else.
Q. Accused No. 27, who told you something about him?
A. Nobody told us anything about him; he did not confess to anything, except the story of accused No. 17.
Q. Does accused No. 17 have two names?
A. We used the name of Ahmed Mohamed Madar when were searching for him. [translator's note: I have known accused No. 17 for at least 25 years, including preschool, and that is his real name.]
Q. When did you find accused No. 17?
A. When he came back from Berbera, where he was bidding farewell to his brother, who was leaving for overseas.

REQUEST BY DEFENSE LAWYER FAYSAL HAJI:

I request that the body of accused No. 20 be examined in front of the court.

PUBLIC PROSECUTOR: If he cannot tell who inflicted harm on him, he is responsible for his body. If the defendants and their lawyers do not prove this harm, they will be prosecuted. This story was there before. Some irresponsible people have spread it through the town so that the government and people confront each other. The riots that took place in the city were part of this issue. Because of that, the body of the accused should not be checked in front of the court. The request should be denied. The proceedings should go on as they were.

---------------*and Witness NO. 3*

Q. Accused No. 26, you did not tell us anything about him, and the Prosecution did not ask you anything about him. Tell us why he was arrested?

A. Accused No. 24 said that he [accused 26] was with accused No. 17 the night the explosives were distributed.

Q. What statements do you have from him?

A. He told us that he did not know anything about that, and accused No. 17 did not tell us anything about him [accused 26] either.

Q. This SNM journal, is it the one that you said was read at the houses of accused 4, 5, 6 and 7?

A. The SNM journal that we have, we did not find it on anybody, it is only an example.

Q. Who told you about the names RUDM and UFFO?

A. Accused Nos. 1 and 2.

Q. Did you find out whether other members knew of its publication?

A. No, we did not find that out, they told us they read it.

Q. Where did you find the SNM journal?

A. I do not know. It was brought by General Ali Hussein who can be contacted about it.

WITNESS NO. 4 MOHAMED AHMED WELI: After taking oath he said:

I know accused No. 1 (Mohamed Baruud) he used to work at the Pepsi-Cola factory. One day some NSS officers came to me for a typewriter that belongs to the factory. They said it was needed in connection with an investigation involving accused No. 1. I gave them a typewriter that belonged to the factory.

DEFENSE LAWYER ISMAIL AND WITNESS No. 4:

Q. Who used to work with that typewriter?

A. A girl and a young man are employed to use it. They use it to type for the management.

Q. Have you ever seen Mohamed Baruud come back to the office in the evenings or at night?

A. No, I have never seen him do that.

WITNESS NO. 5 ABDIRASHID YASIN MOHAMED:

After taking oath he said: This poem of the DEELAY TYPE was among papers we took from the house of accused No. 5 when we searched it. I found the poem and realized it was a poem critical of the nation, written in the handwriting of accused No. 5. After I read it and concluded it [the poem] was illegal, I typed it so this one is the one I typed. When we asked him about this matter, accused No. 5 told us that he wrote it down in his handwriting, but that another person dictated it. He said it was composed by a former teacher who had been sentenced by the court. While going on with our search we found a Makarof pistol of the Russian type. The way we found the pistol was: we asked him whether he had any weapons and he [accused No. 5] answered that he has this pistol that he bought a long time ago, but had not yet obtained a permit for it. That is how we took the pistol from him.

DEFENSE LAWYER FAYSAL AND THE 5TH WITNESS:

Q, Who gave you the order to search the house, and did you have a court warrant?

A. Only our officers told us to arrest him, and to search the house.

Q. Was accused No. 5 with you while you were searching the house?

A. Yes, he was with us.

Q. How did you know that this peom was anti-nation?

A The name AFWEYENE, that is meant to be the President, and its type, that is the "D" alliteration.

DEFENSE LAWYER HUSSEIN BILLE AND THE 5TH WITNESS:

Q. Did the accused [No. 5] tell you that he takes government money to an area near the so-called border [between Somalia and Ethopia], and that he alone guards that money?

A. No, he did not tell me that.

WITNESS NO 6 CAPTAIN ALI GANI AHMED: After taking oath he said:
I was a member of the Committee appointed to investigate the accused. We forwarded two copies of UFFO to the Prosecutor. They were a copy submitted to us by the Hargeisa NSS after we arrived, and the other we found during our investigation, and we took it from the house of accused No. 3 the night we arrested him.

DEFENSE LAWYER ISMAIL AND THE 6TH PROSECUTION WITNESS:
Q. What hour did you go to the house [of accused No. 3]?
A. 1:30 a.m.
Q. Did you have a warrant for the search?

A. Although we did not have a warrant, it was permitted under article 58 of the SCC.

SEVENTH WITNESS KHADRA ISMAIL NUR: After taking oath she said: We live in the 26th June section. Late one night, accused No. 2, accompanied by soldiers, came to my house, where a typewriter belonging to my husband was removed. Accused No. 2 and my husband used to work together and whether my husband was there or not he [accused No. 2] used to borrow the typewriter whenever he wished. Although I do not know anything about typing, its cover is the one that is in front of the court.

WITNESS No. 8 MOHAMOUD SHEIKH ABDILLAHI JIBRIL: After taking oath he said: I am the security guard at the hosue of the 1st Assistant of the Somali Socialist Revolutionary Party of the Northwest Region. One night, while I was sitting under the verenda, about evening time, an explosion occured at the cement driveway leading to the garage. Both inside or outside the house nobody besides me was there. I stood up and I looked towards the area I thought the explosive was thrown from. I did not see anybody. After that I was afraid to check around to see if anybody was about, I went inside and turned the lights off both inside and outside. I then went to the house of Saido who lives nearby and is the niece of the 1st Assistant. She telephoned the NSS. They came and investigated it and took photographs. There was not much damage except a crack in the cement. There was no loss from the explosion.

WITNESS No. 9 FADUMO MOHAMED HIRSI: After taking oath she said: I live in the Guraysamo section. At a time when I just went to bed, I heard an explosion, I stood up to check it. I was met by dust coming from the veranda of the house. I opened the outside door, but I did not see anybody and I did not hear anybody. There was no damage from the explosion. The people in the house were sleeping in their rooms.

WITNESS No.10 SUB/LEUT. MOHAMED AHMED DHOORE: After taking oath he said: I am the leader of the 18th Technical Unit of the 26th Division of the Armed Forces of which accused No. 27 is the Chief. While I was in my office, L/X Abdillahi Sharub accompanied by M/le came to me and told me that they brought a grenade found in the house of General Gani. The grenade's safety was almost out. This grenade was the "C.Q. Sida" attack type. It has two safeties, one over the other. We showed the explosives to the Criminal Investigation Division, who photographed it, and then for safety reasons, I detonated it in a safe area. Later, I went to Gen. Gani and Major Ismail Hashi Madar, accused No. 27, and while we were with the commander of the 26th Division [Gen. Gani] another grenade was brought to us and that one was found outside the house of General Gani where it did not detonate. The two bombs were the same kind, RBG from Russia. It was like the other one. If it had fallen on a hard surface it would have exploded, where it fell the ground was soft. It was placed outside, and as the other was given to the Criminal Investigation Division officers, and when they were finished with it, I and accused No. 27 took it and detonated it.

WITNESS NO 11 AHMED ALI JAMA: After taking oath he said: I am the accountant of the Ministry of Education of the Northwest Region, I know accused No. 17, he is a teacher who draws salary as Abdirahman Abdillahi Madar. He teachs at Farah Omar School. While he was in jail, I gave his pay check to accused No. 24 and 25. We allow the practice of teachers picking up each other's salary.

DEFENSE LAWYER HUSSEIN BILLE AND WITNESS NO.11

Q. When do you let teachers pick each other's salaries, and do you know that he has another name?

A. The name he used in his employment for the government is that one. It is on the top of his file. We do that when we cannot reach the teachers.

PUBLIC PROSECUTOR: The prosecution's case is complete. We request under article 155 of the SCC to submit to the court the statement obtained from Abdi Langare, who is absent now; the reason is that it is impossible to find this witness, and we could not serve him the summons.

OBJECTION: DEFENSE LAWYER ISMAIL:

This does not follow article 155 of the SCC. We request the court not to accept the request of the Public Prosecutor so that justice can be observed.

OBJECTION: DEFENSE LAWYER HASSAN SHEIKH:

"Bi-maslax caddala" To serve Justice- I object to the prosecution's request. It breaks articles 184 and 188 of the SCC that deal with the procedure for witnesses. Article 155 of the SCC provides for the proper procedure for obtaining statements from an absent witness......[the rest of the statements cannot be translated; meaning is not clear]

OBJECTION: DEFENSE LAWYER OSMAN:

The statement that Abdi Langare wrote, as per article 197, because of his bad character, cannot be accepted as evidence. If that statement is related to someone who had been promised favors or given money, he cannot be a witness. The Public Prosecutor's request must be denied.

OBJECTION: DEFENSE LAWYER HUSSEIN BILLE:

Section A/B of Article 155 of the SCC invalidates the statements of the witness that dies. The article does not address a witness who is alive who refuses to testify. Because of that, the request of the Public Prosecutor should be denied.

REBUTTAL BY THE PUBLIC PROSECUTOR:

As indicated by article 155 of the SCC that I referred to before, the witness cannot be found. The issue that the defense lawyers are objecting, it has been told that he escaped to Ethiopia, people in the city were behind that. The reward that he was given was before these defendants were arrested. He [Abdi Laangare, in his statement] does not talk about the accused in detention. Because of that we should be allowed to submit his statement, and the objections of the defense lawyers should be overruled.

DEFENSE LAWYER ISMAIL:

Since the investigators and the prosecutors did not see the importance of Abdi Laangare's testimony before, I do not see why Abdi Langare's statement is being forced on us now. Therefore, I request the Court not to allow the introduction of Abdi Langare's statement as evidence.

THE COURT:

After listening to the request of the Prosecutor relating to the introduction of Abdi Langare's statement and to the objections of the defense, and having seen Articles 155, 184, 188, and 197 of the SCC, the Court has agreed to accept the statements of Abdi Langare.

PUBLIC PROSECUTOR:

I submit to the Court exhibits and statements as follows: 2 (two) typewriters, a Makarof pistol and 6 rounds of ammunition, the letter from the Pepsi-Cola Co. indicating that they own that typewriter, one SNM journal, one block note "Victor" on which is written the titles of the articles that were printed in UFFO, the letter that the NSS Director wrote about the explosions that took place in the city, a leaflet on which is written "Victory to SNM, Death to Afweyne", a telegram, and the statement of Abdi Langare. I also submit to the Court:

1 (one) envelope specific to accused No. 1, containing 5 (five) statements, 2 (two) Court confessions, his fingerprints and his picture;

Accused No. 2's file, containing 5 (five) statements, one of which he wrote with his own hand, and 2 (two) Court confessions;

Accused No. 3's file, containing a confession and two statements;

Accused No. 4's file, containing a confession and two statements;

Accused No. 5's file, containing a confession, a statement, and a poem written in his own hand;

Accused No. 6's file, containing a confession and a statement;

Accused No. 7's file, containing a confession and a statement;

Accused No. 8's file, containing a confession and a statement;

Accused No. 9's file, containing a confession and a statement;

Accused No. 10's file, containing a confession and a statement;

Accused No. 11's file, containing a confession and a statement;

Accused No. 12's file, containing a confession and a statement;

Accused No. 13's file, containing a confession and a statement;
Accused No. 14's file, containing a confession and a statement;
Accused No. 15's file, containing a confession and a statement;
Accused No. 16's file, containing a confession and a statement;
Accused No. 17's file, containing a confession and a statement;
Accused No. 18's file, containing a confession and a statement;
Accused No. 19's file, containing a confession and a statement;
Accused No. 20's file, containing a confession and a statement;
Accused No. 21's file, containing a confession and a statement;
Accused No. 22's file, containing a confession and a statement;
Accused No. 23's file, containing a confession and a statement;
Accused No. 24's file, containing a confession and a statement;
Accused No. 25's file, containing a confession and a statement;
and two copies of UFFO, one of which was taken from the house of accused No. 3 when it was searched, and the other which was transmitted to the Prosecutor by the NSS.

REQUEST BY DEFENSE LAWYER ISMAIL:

So that we can study the documents introduced to the Court, I request that the Court recess for 30 minutes.

THE COURT:

After listening to the request of Attorney Ismail, the Court agrees to recess for 1 hour to allow them to study the matter.

ARGUMENT: *ATTORNEY ISMAIL:*

For Six of the seven accused that I represent, 1, 3, 7, 8, 15 and 23, the exhibits in their files do not indicate their involvement in UFFO or RUDM, and at the same time, accused No. 3 is accused of having a copy of UFFO. His house was searched illegally, since there was no warrant for the search of his house and there was no other reason for the search.

ARGUMENT: *ATTORNEY HASSAN SHEIKH:*

The prosecution is governed by article 114 of the SCC and the defense is governed by article 116 of SCC. Article 115 of SCC is between us. The court should observe the relevant articles. Also as related to the three defendants that I represent: There was no statement in the File of accused No. 10, Mohamed Dagal Hirsi, and there is nothing he had confessed to. Therefore, I do not think its proper to forward his file to the court. Accused Nos. 9 and 11, their statements and their accusations are not related. Another point, when we speak of a confession, it must be one written in front of an attorney, we do not have anything indicating that this is so, even if it was one stamp alone or a signature of an attorney showing that these were obtained in his presence. The prosecution also introduced a letter from the director of the NSS, a leaflet, a copy of the SNM journal and various other papers. Under article 172, an exhibit submitted to the court must be specific to an individual's case. I want to know WHETHER THESE RELATE TO MY DEFENDANTS OR NOT. If they do not relate to them specifically or generally, all of the accused, I request that they should be returned to the Prosecutor.

ARGUMENT: *ATTORNEY OSMAN*:

The prosecution has submitted exhibits that do not relate to the accusation. The statement of Abdi Langare is 12 pages and only the last page is signed. There is not even a stamp to indicate who wrote it. That shows that only the last page of Abdi Langare's statement can be accepted. In his statement, on page 5, Abdi Langare says "after I was told to search for it, I said that I knew of two copies of UFFO that were with Adan". We can understand from that he [Abdi Langare] was responsible for the journal UFFO and he should have been accused of its writing.

ARGUMENT: *ATTORNEY HUSSEIN BILLE*:

As we all know, article 149 of SCC indicates what constitutes a confession. It appears that 3 confessions and 3 statements were introduced relating to my defendants. But it is clear that the first three are not confessions at all, and the three statements are not even statements, and neither of them fulfill article 172 of the SCC, but are only verbal statements. I therefore request that the ocurt return these exhibits to the prosecution, and I am sure that even these were obtained by coercion.

REBUTTAL: *PUBLIC PROSECUTOR*:

Jaalle (comrade) chairman, as is clear from article 10 of XLY 8 that was issued on 26.1.70, if the accusation is related to national security, it is not neccessary that confessions be taken in front of an attorney. I am surprised that attorney Hussein Bille is not willing to believe the signatures on these statements, and why he talks about coercion. If I come back to article 172 of the SCC, it is possible to introduce to the court any exhibit that relates to the accusation. I mean by that and I want the court and the public to fully understand that the organization RUDM is tied to SNM, and I want to show true examples that are the SNM journal and the leaflet. Therefore, I request the court to allow me to submit these and to present my concluding remarks.

THE COURT:

After listening to the arguments of the attorneys and the rebuttal by the public prosecutor of the National Security Court of the Northwest Region that related to the submission of exhibits, and after studying article 10 of XLY 8 of 26.1.70 and article 151 of SCC, the court decides to accept the exhibits and to use them.

As for the presence of an attorney when confessions are obtained, as argued by attorney Hussein Bille, the court after reading article 68 of SCC, believes that these [confessions and statements] were obtained properly and legally.

The third point that related to the SNM journal, the letter of the Director of the NSS of the Northwest Region, the court, after reading article 172 of of the SCC, decides to return them to the prosecution as these are not directly tied with the accusation that these defendants were arrested for.

REQUEST BY PUBLIC PROSECUTOR:

As per article 112 of SCC, I wish to tell the court that I dropped the charges against accused No. 26, Mohamed Said Nur, as his membership in RUDM organization or involvement in the explosions could not be proven. I also wish to drop the charges against No. 27, Major Ismail Hashi Madar; it could not be proven that he was a member of an illegal organization and chrages specific to the explosions could not be substantiated. And also accused No. 28, Hassan Ali "Ceelgeeye", the charges of rumor-mongering could not be proven against him. These should be released.

THE COURT:

The court after listening to the prosecutor about the charges against accused Nos. 26, 27, and 28, and after seeing article 112 (2) of the SCC, accepts the request of the prosecutor and allows that charges be dropped.

CONCLUDING REMARKS OF THE PUBLIC PROSECUTOR:

Jaalle (comrade) chairman, attorneys and the honorable court, accused Nos. 1, 2 and 3, together established the illegal organization so-called RUDM, and took steps to publish the journal UFFO that their organization produced. While this investigation was underway, it was also found that they [accused 1,2 and 3] had contacts with the illegal SNM organization that is based in London. Abdi Langare is a man who was previously charged with spying for the enemy, and the National Security Court of the Northwest Region had sentenced him to death, but later the same court released him from that punishment. That should suffice to show us that we can honor the statement of this absent witness, since when releasing him from the death sentence the court did not sentence him to life or a similarly long imprisonment; and it is important that the attorneys understand the appropriateness of his statement. As written in Abdi Langare's statement, he tells us that RUDM was not limited to the city and that Adan [Adan Waali] wanted to ally himself with the government since he knew of the illegal objectives of RUDM. Accused No. 1,2 and 3 were the men who met with Mohamed Nur Handulle (ARAB) who had met with DUQSI and Ina-Waddaad Diid in Jeddah, these men are the leaders of the so called SNM. They [accused 1, 2 and 3] said "these two men recently met the Isaaq clan in Saudi Arabia, execpt most of the knowledgable who are now among Reer Sablaale." By "Reer Sablaale" they mean the Somalis who were hurt by the "Dabadheer" Famine [famine of 1974], who were subsequently aided by their government, and later some of them went to Saudi Arabia for economic reasons. These people [reer sablaale] are now returning the favor to their government and have refused to join DUQSI and Ina-waddaad Diid to weaken the Somali Nation. They added [accused 1, 2, and 3] that it was necessary to bring the Ida-Gele clan back to the rest of Isaaq and to free them from the Marehan clan [Siyad Barre's ruling clan]. That has no basis. The ways they attempted to achieve this can be seen simply from the articles written in UFFO that were read in the court, such as "Nationalization of the region", "Berbera was captured" and "La socoto". "La Socoto" [those with] it is clear is to mean anybody who completely fulfils his responsibility for his country and his flag. "La Socoto" means those who kow-tow to the Marehan, and its objective is to demoralize and to begin ways of breaking the ties of the nation and to hurt those who are ready to fulfill their responsibilities. In order to fulfil their objectives, the so called organization realized that the Somali people are susceptible to religion, and that they needed to use religion as a cover, and it happened that accused No. 1 met with the youth of the Brotherhood that he thought were opposed to the government. In that same meeting accused No. 3, Mohamed Haji Mohamoud said things like " Girls have now become prostitutes, boys have become drug and alcohol addicts, the men have become emigres and the women have become sellers of qat." And he suggested that the government was responsible for this state of affairs. His intentions were to create problems between the governemnt and the public. I am sure the result of that has been seen. The riots that took place in Hargeisa lately, the detention of the accused was only a cover. False news was spread through town that the detainess were sentenced to death or life terms. We were all present for the results [riots]. These things show you the existence of the organization of which Dr. Adan, Jabane, Abdurahman and Aabi were members. Accused Nos. 4 to 20 together are accused of also being members of RUDM. Accused No. 21, 22, and 23, their charges are different. They were the members of the Brotherhood who illegally met and decided to cooperate with the RUDM organization. Specific charges: Accused No. 16 has confessed to the crime of having an illegal weapon. As for the explosions, their planning, we charge accused No. 17 and 20, at the same time they themselves tell us that accused No. 24 and 25 helped them. I remind you that the manner these explosions took place can suggest that it was related to the publication of the UFFO journal. Because the houses of the three men that were mentioned in UFFO, and who were thought to be behind the detentions, were attacked. If I estimate, these men are between 28 and 38 years in age. The one with the least education has a secondary school diploma. It would have been good if their intentions were good and they were honestly aiding their people. But we find that they were men who wanted to establish a clan-based government, and they were set to create problems between the government and the people. Because of that, we strongly urge that accused 1, 2 and 3 be found guilty. We request that accused No. 4 to 20 be sentenced each to 30 years in prison. We leave the court to decide the punishment of 21, 22, and 23. We also leave the punishment of accused No. 24 and 25 to the court.

DEFENSE OF ATTORNEY ISMAIL

As indicated by the prosecution these are young men who today are very dear to our country with respect to their educational qualifications and professions. We can understand that by the fact they include doctors, engineers, and educated businessmen. They are people who have held responsibilities for our nation previously and are now helping in the development of our country. The existence of an organization was mentioned but the accusation does not fulfil article 322 of the SCC and article 3 of XLY 54, because up to now we do not have an existing organization. The prosecution also speaks about confessions, but article 66[?] of the SCC, I believe that these have no importance as they were obtained by threats, terrorization and the like, and are diminished by the sloppy investigation that shows many faults. There are many defendants accused of belonging to the organization. Let us ask ourselves, how can someone be accused of membership in a nonexistent organization? The charges against accused No. 3 are not proper and his house was searched illegally. That invalidates the finding of the journal. But were was the journal originally brought from? Dahir Id [Witness No. 1] told us that after hearing news about it, he asked some people to find the journal. When it was brought to him he improperly forwarded it to the Commander of the 26th Division of the Army, who repeated the mistake by forwarding it to the office of the NSS. The management of Pepsi Cola indicated that the typewriter is theirs, but as is legally required under article 161 of SCC, an expert was not consulted to show that this is the typewriter used to write the journal. When it is said that the accused complained about the lack of water and electricity and other problems pertaining to the government, is it possible to say that the group was anti-nation? That is not correct because these criticisms and the problems they have spoken about are true. Wasn't it just last night when the court was completely dark? and Isn't it unfortunate that the small village of Wanla Weyn [town in the south of Somalia] gets electricity regularly while the second capital of the nation, Hargeisa, does not get electricity after lunch each day and that it [electricity] goes out at any time as it did last night; especially since we are so close to the so-called border. The third prosecution witness testified that the youth (accused) established the self-help project that was later recognized by the authorities of the region. The purpose of the leaflets was to create chaos and it did. I request the court to release the 6 defendants I am representing as none of them was shown to have been a member of RUDM.

DEFENSE OF ATTORNEY FAYSAL

I am representing accused Nos. 2, 4, 5, and 20. The prosecution's case was not sufficient. It is also true that the statements of accused No. 2 cannot be a basis for the accusation. Accused No. 2 is charged under article 3 XLY 54 and writing the journal UFFO. Why then did the prosecution ask for the death penalty? The confessions, the statement of

Langare and the thrid witness all stated that accused No. 2 established the organization. But later it was found that the organization was started in 1977 and that they [prosecution] did not know who started it. The witness [witness No. 3] also told us that he did not have any other trail to follow except the statements of Langare. There are other people who have not been arrested who have been listed in the statement of No. 2 that was used as a basis for these charges, and why these others were not arrested we have not been told. I, therefore, request that the court ignore the statement of No.2. Accused No. 2 said that they established a self-help organization, but Langare who wanted money, and Aadan [Waali], who was advised by a man called Faysal in Mogadisho to work with the government, created these problems. Langare stated that he was "chewing" qat with the Commander of the 26th Division one day when the commander asked him to bring him the journal UFFO and that he, Langare told the Commander that he [Langare] himself had two copies that he would bring to the Commander. Abdi Langare also mentions in his statement that there is a self-help organization in Hargeisa, at no time did he mention RUDM or antything like that. I believe that this matter is meant to bring the people and government in conflict. The third witness lied about the the fact that accused No.2 confessed to RUDM, and up to now we do not have the RUDM organization or its objectives. That shows there is no proof against accused No. 2 with respect to RUDM, and the charges are not appropriate. There is no evidence against accused No.4 except the confession of accused No. 2 and I do not know why the prosecution did not drop the charges against him. There is no evidence against accused No. 5 except the statement of witness No. 3, that he read or had the journal UFFO as he is charged with. Accused No. 20 is charged with the explosives but there is nobody except accused No. 17 that these charges relate to as under articles 322, 325 or 332. The placement of the bombs at the house of Gani cannot be accused of any one except accused No. 17. He [accused No. 20] does not know anything about weapons as stated by witness No. 3. All these points should be respected by the court. It also appears that the prosecution did not fulfil its proper role and, therefore, I urge the court to release the defendants I represent No. 2, 4, 5, and 20.

DEFENSE OF ATTORNEY HUSSEIN BILLE

The name RUDM cannot apply here because Dr. Tani was born in Aware [a town in the Ogaden Region of Ethopia] and Jabane (accused No. 2) was born in Odweyne [a small village some distance away from Hargeisa].

The 3rd witness testified that Langare brought them the journal, and he also testified that there are no other witnesses except the defendants. This shows that the prosecution has no case. Because of that I urge the court to reexamine the charges. There is no evidence against accused No. 6. Accused No. 14 is sick and used to go to the house of Dr. Aadan [accused no. 4] for that reason. Even while he was in prison he required treatment. Accused No. 16 is the same as the others, and there is no evidence against him, except the possesion of the pistol and that relates to "ordinamento pubblico e sicurezza". There are no statements by accused No. 17 that indicate his membership in the organization, and where did the explosives come from? Accused No. 24 was tortured, and there is no evidence against him or accused No. 25. They should all be released. I am particularly surprised why the prosecution wishes to believe the guilt of some while disregarding that of others, as charges were dropped against accused No. 26 and 27. Accused No. 27 was charged with bringing the explosives and No. 26 was said to have taken part in the execution. Yet, the charges remain for others.

DEFENSE OF LAWYER HASSAN SHEIKH

The following articles should be studied for the fulfillment of justice. Somali Criminal Code articles 1, 16 and 20, and the court should base its judgments on them. Let us ask ourselves--what can be a crime? Human Rights laws relate to the individual's honor and his freedom, and both crime and punishment are specified. The articles of law cannot by themselves speak but the person can. Are the charges based on these articles? the answer is no. When the action causes harm isn't the guilty person the one who ties himself with chains in front of the court (rapporto di causalita)? To show that they [defendants] were active members of RUDM we must find material and office as the article of accusation mentions. It should be shown how the objectives of the organization diminish the unity of the nation and compromise the ability of the government. It is a wrong interpretation to say the unity of the nation is being destroyed by Hargeisa. Such conspiracies can take place in other cities. The problems created by Abdi Langare, wherever he is now, have forced the army to besiege the city and waste its efforts; and the intellectuals we were all waiting for are now accused of nonexistant charges. Under article 149, the alleged confessions do not prove the accusations. It is not necessary to sign all statements in front of an attorney, but those statements that incriminate the accused himself must be witnessed by an attorney. Mohamed Dagal Hersi (accused No.

10) was brought in front of an attorney but the other 3 [defendants] were not. As per article 146 SCC, we did not see any statement proving the charges that fulfill the requirements specified under article 199 of SCC, we are ignorant of these. Thus our defense is incompetent. The accused did not confess to anything, and charges against them were not proven. The Public Prosecutor himself was invited to the wedding [the wedding of accused No. 1 where an illegal meeting to start RUDM was allegedly held]. There is no crime, they should be released.

DEFENSE OF ATTORNEY OSMAN ABDI

The court should be pursuaded by the arguments presented by the previous lawyers with whom I am defending these accused. The charges brought by the prosecution belong to another department. We are here for justice. Abdi Langare is now a member of an illegal organization that is against our nation and he now broadcasts from enemy radios and people hear him every day. It is amazing that we are asked to believe a person of that character. Pursuant to articel 197 of SCC, if two statements contradict each other, the defendants statement is followed. In his statement accused No. 13, Dr. Osman, said that he used to have qat with these individuals. That is not a crime. The defendants I represent (accused No. 13 and 18) must be released.

DEFENSE OF ATTORNEY BASHIR ARTAN

The four defendants I am representing (accused No. 19, 12, 21 and 22) have not been asked whether they belonged to an organization, and they did not confess to anything. Their cases should have been dropped. The existence of the organization has not been established. The prosecution did not fulfill the requirements of articles 110 and 163 of the SCC. The prosecution was afraid to drop the charges and left them to the court. The investigator's testimony was only about verbal statements that he himself wrote down, and there are no other witnesses that were brought before the court. Since there is no crime committed by the defendants I represent, they should be released and returned to their places of employment.

THE COURT'S ANALYSIS AND VERDICT

The following conclusions have been reached by the court after listening to the witnesses and hearing the arguments of all sides:

1) That between 1977 and 1978 some of the accused who thought of themselves as "intellectuals" held meetings at places of qat, discussed and exchanged opinions about the government; in particular, the regional government. They used as a cover the dissent that already existed in the region of Hargeisa.....................................

While still continuing with their secret meetings, they started to educate the public about the problems present in the region. At all times the presented the government in a bad light. Finally, in June of 1981, they strengthened their meetings, they held several consecutive meetings and they contacted members of the illegal organization SNM based in London and headed by DUQSI who lives in Saudi Arabia. Those members of SNM had managed to illegally enter the country and informed them about how the "Isaaq' clan in the Gulf States are now members of SNM. The members of SNM who came from Saudi Arabia were Adan Ali Farah (Adan Waali) and Mohamed Nur Handulle (ARAB) and they fled after the NSS began investigating this case. They [SNM members] were made responsible to start in Hargeisa an illegal organization opposed to the government and to start matters that are against the peace and security of the region and at the same time opposed to the unity of the nation. Afterwards, they [the SNM members] held many meetings with some of the accused telling them that all of the "Isaaq" clan except the Ida-Geli have joined the illegal SNM. They [the SNM members] indicated that every Somali clan has satarted their own force and that it was neccessary for them to strengthen SNM and to stop serving the Marehan as the Ida-Geli does. After the two ("accused" Adan and Handulle) who were emissaries from the DUQSI-lead SNM, were successful in their efforts, they started an illegal organization they named RUDM which means "men born in the city". The following accused joined that organization:

accused 1 Mohamed Barud Ali
" 2 Ahmed Mohamed Yusuf
" 3 Mohamed Haji Mohamud
" 4 Adan Yusuf Abokor
" 5 Abdirahman Abdillahi Haji Adan
" 6 Ahmed Hussein Aabi
" 7 Hussein Mohamed Duale
" 8 Mohamoud Sheikh Hassan Tani
" 9 Abdillahi Ali Yusuf
" 12 Yusuf Abdillahi Kahin

" 13 Osman Abdi Megag
" 20 Bashe Abdi Yusuf
" 16 Moahmed Ali Ibrahim
" 15 Adan Warsama Said

In their initial meetings the defandants and the founders of RUDM (Adan Waali and Handulle) reminded each other of the injustice of the regional government and its lack of concern for the region, and they resolved at the same time to soley rely on the public and not to wait for government action, and also to scede from the rest of the Republic. They then began a committee called "SAMAFAL" [philanthropy, good samaritan] that collected money, material, medicine for the Hargeisa Hospital. Their objective was to make the citizens and the government confront each other so that they could gain the suport of the public who would then join their illegal organization. It is also true that they met some of the public on the occasion of the wedding of accused No. 1 (Mohamed Barud Ali) held at the house in Guraysamo owned by accused No. 28 (Hassan Abdillahi Eelgeeye). Some of the defendants gave speeches there [at the wedding] that were intended to inflame the public. Among those speeches were some that related to injustices and the problems in the region and the fact that "boys are now becoming drug addicts, girls are becoming prostitutes, mothers are becoming qat sellers and the old men emigres". It was mentioned at the same time that "soldiers are shooting people in the streets for no reason, schools have all decayed and that nobody cares about the roads and the hospitals"...........................

Thus when the court carefully evaluated how these actions took place, and considering the confessions they gave in front of the court attorney, the court has decided that without doubt these defendants are guilty of wilfully committing these ugly actions that are anti-unity of the Somali nation, and that they violated article 3 (2) XLY 54 issued on 10.9.1970.
2. That accused No. 1 (Mohamed Barrud Ali) and No. 2 (Mohamed Ahmed Yusuf) were active members of the illegal RUDM that they started in Hargeisa. In September 1981, they together printed a journal called UFFO. They meant by UFFO "the wind that precedes rainfall". In that journal they printed propaganda and lies against the leaders of the region, intended to inflame the people. They wanted the people to realize that the leaders were not honestly concerned about the problems of the region. These actions were meant to create anti-revolutionary sentiment.

In addition, accused Nos. 1&2 distributed the journal UFFO to all the members of the RUDM organization, and some copies were left in places around town, especially at busy locations such as Bar Hargeisa and Bar Kulmiye etc..

Therefore, the court considering the confessions that these defendants wrote before the court attorneys and the exhibits (issue 1 of UFFO) and having seen how these crimes took place, finds accused No. 1 Mohamed Barud Ali and accused No. 2 Ahmed Mohamed Yusuf, guilty without doubt, and that they willingly violated article 19 of XLY of 10.9.1970.

3. It is also clear to the court that accused No. 3, Mohamed Haji Mohamud Omer and accused No. 5, Abdirahman Abdillahi Haji Adan, were active members of the illegal organization RUDM. In their houses one copy each of UFFO and a anti-revolutionary poem were found. Therefore, they are guilty of the charges of possession of articles criticizing the government and they violated article 19 XLY 54 of 10.9.1970.

4. Accused No. 16, Mohamed Ali Ibrahim, was also a member of the illegal organization RUDM that had been established inside the country. In addition a Makarof Pistol and six rounds of ammunition were found in his house. He had no permit for these. Thus the court considering his confessions in front of the court and having listened to the presentation of the evidence, without doubt concludes that Mohamed Ali Ibrahim, is guilty of possession of an ilegal weapon under article 1 of XLY 65 3.11.77.

5. The following defendants; Omer Issa Awale (accused No. 18), Mohamed Ali Sulub (accused No. 19) and Ali Egeh Farah (accused No. 18) were accused of belonging to an illegal organization. After listening to the witnesses, the court concludes that these defendants were not guilty of these crimes; they are however, guilty of the crime of NOT REPORTING A CRIME under article 22 XLY 54 10.9.1970. That is because they did not tell the NSS about the existence of the illegal journal that accused Nos. 1 and 2 published and that they themselves read several times.

6. It is also clear to the court that after accused No. 1 & 2 were arrested, several others: Ahmed Mohamed Madar (accused No. 17), Mohamed Abdi Je'er (accused No. 24) and Mohamed Ma'allin Osman (accused No. 25) started a campaign of terrorism to focus the attention of the public on

this case. They decided to target the people they thought were behind the detentions and to drop explosives at their houses. After that, the above-mentioned defendants threw three bombs at the houses of the 1st Assistant of the Party of the Northwest Region, the house of businessman Tindeer and the house of the Commander of the 26th Division of the Army.............

Therefore, the court after considering their confessions and having seen the actions that they took, especially the houses they attacked, concludes without doubt that the defendants are guilty under articles 322, 325 and 332 of the SCC.

7. The following defendants: Mohamed Dagal Hirsi (accsued No. 10), Mohamed Abdi Duale (accused No. 14), Ismail Abdi Huree (accused No. 21), Hassan Abdillahi Sh. Ali (accused No. 22) and Ahmed Hassan Madar (accused No. 23) were accused of the crime of membership in an illegal organization. The charges against these defendants were not proven

THEREFORE

THE COURT:
After seeing: Articles 3 (sec. 1/2). 18, 19 and 22 XLY 54 of 10.9.1970. Article 1 XLY 65 of 3.11.77, artcles 322 (sec. 1/2), 325 and 332 SCC that are related to article 71 SCC--
After seeing: Articles 68, 108, 109, 110, 112, 163,146, 155, 172 and 202 SCC---
After seeing: Articles 40, 44, 109, 110, 119, 127, 128 (sec1/2) and 158 SCC---
After seeing: Article 10 XLY 8 of 26.1.70 and the related article 151 SCC--
After seeing: Articles 120. 121, 122, 123, 124 SCC---------------------

IT IS CLEAR

THAT:

1. Accused 1 and 2 are guilty of the crime of "*MEMBERSHIP IN AN ILLEGAL ORGANIZATION AND THE WRITING OF ANTI-NATION PROPAGANDA*".............

2. Accused 3 is guilty of the crime of "*MEMBERSHIP IN AN ILLEGAL ORGANIZATION AND POSSESION OF WRITTEN MATERIAL ANTAGONISTIC TO THE POLICIES OF THE REVOLUTION*" ....

3. Accused No. 5 is guilty of the charges that are "*MEMBERSHIP IN AN ILLEGAL ORGANIZATION AND POSSESSION OF A WRITTEN MATERIAL ANTAGONISTIC TO THE POLICIES OF THE REVOLUTION*"..

4. Accused 4, 6, 7, 8, 12, 13, 15 and 20 are accused of the charges that are *MEMBERSHIP IN AN ILLEGAL ORGANIZATION* and are guilty............

5. Accused 16 is guilty of the charges that are "*MEMBERSHIP IN AN ILLEGAL ORGANIZATION AND POSSESSION OF A WEAPON WITHOUT PERMIT*"............

6. Accused 17, 14 and 25 are guilty of the charges they are accused of that are "*PARTICIPATION IN A CRIMINAL GROUP AND DISTURBING THE PUBLIC SECURITY*"..

7. Accused 18, 19 and 11 are not guilty of the charge of *MEMBERSHIP IN AN ILLEGAL ORGANIZATION* the court replaces those charges with the crime of *NOT INFORMING SECURITY ABOUT A CRIME* under article 22 XLY 54 of 10.9.70.

THE COURT SENTENCES

B. Accused Mohamed Barud Ali and Accused Ahmed Mohamed Yusuf: LIFE TERM. THE COURT observed the rules that allow leniency.
I. Accused Mohamed Haji Mohamoud and accused Abdirahman Abdillahi Haji Adan on the count of *MEMBERSHIP IN AN ILLEGAL ORGANIZATION* each to 20 years, on the count of *POSSESSION OF WRITTEN MATERIAL ANTAGONISTIC TO THE POLICIES OF THE REVOLUTION* each to 10 years of imprisonment; the court has followed the rules of leniency.

J. Accused Mohamed Ali Ibrahim for the crime of *MEMBERSHIP IN AN ILLEGAL ORGANIZATION* to 20 years of imprisonment, on the count of *POSSESSION* of a *WEAPON WITHOUT A PERMIT* 5 years in prison and 10,000 shillings in fines; the court has followed the rules of leniency.

X. Accused Adan Yusuf Abokor, Ahmed Hussein Aabi, Hussein Mohamed Duale,Mohamoud Sheikh Hassan Tani. Abdillahi Ali Yusuf, Yusuf Abdillahi Kahin, Osman Abdi Megag, Bashi Abdi yusuf and Adan Warsama Said, each to 20 (twenty) years of imprisonment. The court has followed the rules of leniency.

KH. Accused Ahmed Mohamed Madar, Mohamed Abdi Je'er, and Mohamed Ma'alin Osman, for the crime of *PARTICIPATION IN A CRIMINAL ORGANIZATION* each to 3 years of imprisonment, for the crime of *TERRORISM BY THROWING HAND GRENADES* each to 2 years of imprisonment, for the crime of *ENDANGERING THE GENERAL SECURITY* each to 3 years of imprisonment. In total the punishment for each is 8 (eight) years in jail.

D. Accused Omer Issa Awale, Mohamed Ali Ibrahim and Ali Egeh Farah each to three years in prison.

The court releases accused: Said Mohamed Ibrahim, Ismail Hashi Madar, and Adan Abdillahi Ali "Eelgeye", after the Assistant public Prosecutor of the National Security Court of Hargeisa dropped the charges against them. Since the charges have been dropped, they should be released as per article 112 of SCC.

At the same time, the court releases from imprisonment the following defendants: Ismail Abdi Hurre, Hassan Abdisalam Sh. Ali, Ahmed Hassan Madar, Mohamed Abdi Duale, and Mohamed Dagal Hirsi, after the charges against them could not be proven. The court orders their quick release from prison if they are not in jail for other crimes.
The court orders the return of the typewriters: OLIIVETTI LMM 4445733 to the Pepsi-Cola factory and CITIZEN K3 SER No. 3008567 to the owner, Mohamoud Qalib. The court also orders that the MAKAROF DAM 3138 and 6 rounds of ammunition be confiscated.

Hargeisa, March 4, 1982

Chairman
Sharif Sheekhuna Maye, Colonel
(signed)
Senior Assistant
Mohamed Ali Abdi

ADVISORS:

1. Attorney Yusuf Abdi Haji
2. Colonel Ahmed Abdi Awale

STAMP OF THE SECURITY
COURT OF THE NORTHWEST REGION

Appendix III

Original document of the Verdict of the Hargeisa National Security Court in Somali language. by Hargeisa National Security Court, 1982.

Few days after the verdict of the Court that tried UFFO group, copies of the transcript of the Court decision were distributed to their relatives. The publisher is thankfull to those people who fled to Ethiopia during the Hargeisa destruction in 1988, taking with them this copy of the transcript and preserved this important document for future references.

The last page of the document are missing from this copy, but the reader can refer to the transalation of the same document in appendix II.

These pages were previousely published in "A note on my Teachers' Group: News report of an injustice" by Jama Musse Jama.

SX. 10/82
SG. 18/82

Jam. D Somali

Maxkammad Badbadada
G W G

HARGEYSA

Xukun lid **Ku Ah** Maxamed Baaruud Cali & 27 Eedaysan oo Kale

Hargeysa 4 3 82

JAMHUURIYADDA DIMUQRAADIGA SOOMAALIYEED
MAGACA DADKA SOOMAALIYEED
MAXKAMADDA BADBAADADA G. W. GALBEED

Sannadka Kun Sagaal Bogol iyo Siddeetan iyo Laba, maalinta 4aad Bisha Maarso, Magaalada Hargeysa.-

MAXKAMADDA BADBAADADA GOBOLKA WAQOYI GALBEED

1. G/Dhexe Shariif Sheekhuna Maye .... GUDDOOMIYE
2. Gars. Yuusuf Xaaji Cabdi Cali .... LA TALIYE
3. G/le Axmed Cabdi Cawaale .... LA TALIYE

oo uu ka soo qayb galay Dadweyne U Doode Dhamme Cabdulle Cali. Kaaliyena uu ka ahaa Maxamed Cali Cabdi (Carab)

WAXAY KU DHAWAAQDAY XUKUNKA SOO SOCDA OO KU SAABSAN DACWADDII KU TAAGNAYD EEDEYSANAYAASHA KALA AH:

1. Inj. MAXAMED BAARUUD CALI L/31 Ina Cudbi Cali, ka shaqeeya Wershadda PEPSIGA Hargeysa-Qareenkiisa Ismaaciil Jumcaale.
2. AXMED MAXAMED YUUSUF"Jabane"L/33, ina Cawo Cilmi, Ex.Bare Jaamici ah Qareenkiisu ahaa Faysal X.Jaamac.
3. Dr.MAXAMED X.MAXAMUUD CUMAR L/33, ina Basra Ismaaciil, Ganacsade ah, Qareenkiisu ahaa Ismaaciil J.-
4. Dr.AADAN YUUSUF ABCKAR L/34, ina Xaali Yuusuf, ahna Maamulaha Isbitaalka Guud ee Hargeysa, Qareenkiisu ahaa Faysal Xaaji.
5. CABDIRAXMAAN CABDULAAHI X. AADAN, L/26, Ina Dahabo Maxamuud, ka shaqeeya Xafiiska Iskaada G/W/G, Qareenkiisu ahaa Faysal Xaaji.-
6. AXMED XUSEEN CAABI L/33, ina Faadumo Meecaad, ka shaqeeya Bankiga Ganacsiga & Keydka-Laanta Hargeysa.
7. XUSEEN MAXAMED DUCAALE"Berberaawi"L/32, ina Mako Ibraahim, ahna Bare Jaamici ah-Qareen.ahaa I.Jumc.-
8. Dr.MAXAMUUD SHEEKH XASAN TAANI,L/28, ina Maryan Beegsi, ka shaqeeya Isb.Hargeysa-Qareen.Ism.Jum.-
9. Dr.CABDULLAAHI CALI YUUSUF "Colaad",L/34, ina Caasha Cabdillaahi, ka shaqeeya Wak.Daaqa Qaranka ee Xamar, Qareenkiisu ahaa Xasan Sh.Ibraahim.
10. MAXAMED DAGAAL XIRSI, L/32, ina Muumina Maxamed, Ex.Bare Jaamici ah, Shaqo Laawe Qar.Xasan Sh.-
11. CALI CIGE FAARAX"Cali Biid" L/29, ina Ardo Kabar, ahna Maam.Wak. Dhismaha Hargeysa, Qareen.Xasan Sheekh.-

./...

........./2.

12. YUUSUF CABDULLAAHI KAAHIN L/29, ina Cibaado Warsame, Beeraale ah, Qareenkiisu ahaa Bashiir Cartan.

13. Dr.CISMAAN CABDI MEYGAAG, L/38, ina Kaaha Faarax, ahna Takhtar Shaqo Laawe, Qareen. Cusmaan Cabdi.

14. MAXAMED CABDI DUCAALE"Ayuub"L/35, ina Khadiija Xaaji, ka shaqeysta Sacuudiga, Qareen.Xuseen Bile.

15. AADEN WARSAME SACIID L/33, ina Cawa Ismaaciil, ahna Ganacsade, Qareenkiisu ahaa Ismaaciil J.

16. MAXAMED CALI IBRAAHIM L/35, ina Faaduma Ducaale, ka shaqeeya Xafiiska Iskaada G.W.G.,Qar.X.Bile.

17. AXMED MAXAMED MADAR L/28, ina Caasha Cali, ahna Bare Jaamici ah, Qareenkiisu ahaa X.Bile.-

18. CUMAR CIISE CAWAALE L/33, ina Aamina Nuur, ahna Xisaabiyaha Wak.Bad.Shaqaalaha ee Hargeysa, Qareenkiisu ahaa Cusmaan Cabdi.

19. Dr.MAXAMUUD CALI SULUB, L/30, ina Faaduma Muxumed, ka shaqeeya Isb.Hargeysa, Qareen.Bashiir Car.

20. BAASHE CABDI YUUSUF L/29, ina Aamina Ibraahim, ahna Ganacsade, Qareenkiisu ahaa Faysal Xaaji.-

21. ISMAACIIL CABDI HURRE, L/26, ina Xabiiba Mooge, u shaqeeya ganacsade X.Cali, Qareen.Bashiir.

22. XASAN CABDISALAAN SH.CALI, L/23, ina Cibaado Xaaji, ka shaqeeya Wershadda Pepsiga Har.Qareen.Bashiir.

23. AXMED XASAN MADAR, L/29, ina Faaduma Caabi, Shaqo Laawe, Qareenkiisu ahaa Ismaaciil Jumcaale.-

24. MAXAMUUD CABDI JICIIR, L/34, ina Khadiija Daarood, ahna Bare Jaamici ah, Qareenkiisu Xuseen Bile.

25. MAXAMED MACALLIN CISMAAN AXMED, L/32, ina Shukri Jaamac, ahna Bare Jaamici ah Qareen.Xuseen Bile.

26. SACIID MAXAMED IBRAAHIM, L/33, ina Mako Kaariye, ahna Bare Jaamici, Qareenkiisu Xuseen Bile.

27. G/Dhexe ISMAACIIL XAASHI MADAR, L/..., Madaxa Waaxda Sancada Qaybta 26aad XDS, Qareen.X.Bile.

28. XASAN CABDULLAAHI CALI "Ceelgeeye" L/36, ina Faaduma Muxumed, ahna Arile, Qareenkiisu ahaa Ismaaciil J.

L A X I R A Y:

Eed.1aad 4.11.81, Eed.2aad 2.11.81, Eed.10aad & 19aad 11.11.81, Eed. 3aad, 4aad, 5aad, 7aad, 8aad & 9aad 19.11.81, Eed.11aad, 12aad, 13aad, 14aad, 15aad, 16aad & 18aad 4.12.81, Eed.28aad 4.12.81, Eed.6aad

../..

......../3.-

5.12.81, Eed.17aad 14.12.81, Eed.20aad 29.12.81, Eed.24aad & 25aad 30.12.81, Eed.21aad & 22aad 9.1.82, Eed.23aad 10.1.82, Eed.26aad 6.2.82, Eed.27aad Dibed joog.-

K U E E D E Y S A N

B. Eedeysanaha 1aad (Inj.Maxamuud Baaruud Cali).
" 2aad (Axmed Maxamed Yuusuf "Jabane").&
" 3aad (Maxamed Xaaji Maxamuud Cumar), waxaa wadajir la idiinku eedeynayaa Dembiga ah "ABAABULID URUR XAARAAN AH", kana soo horjeeda Midnimada Ummadda Soomaaliyeed ee ku xusan qod.3aad qaybtiisa 1aad, X.L.Y.54 ee 10.9.1970kii oo xiriir la leh Qod.71aad X.C.S., sababtoo ah in aad Magaalada Hargeysa ka abaabusheen"URUR" ka soo horjeeda Midnimada Ummadda Soomaaliyeed oo aad ku magacowdeen R.U.D.M., kasoo micnihiisu yahay "Ragga U Dhashay Magaalada".

T. Eed.1aad & kan 2aad, waxaa gaar ahaan la idiinku eedeynayaa Dembiga ah QORID DACAAYADO KU LID AH QARANNIMADA ee ku xusan Qod.18aad (qaybtiisa 1aad) ee isla XLY.54 ee 10.9.1970kii, xiriirna la leh Qodobka 71aad X.C.S., sababtoo ah in idinkoo Madax u ah "Ururka RUDM" aad misna abaabusheen, daabacdeen, soo saarteen kaddibna qaybiseen Jornaal aad ku qorteen dacaayado ka dhan ah Midnimada oo aad kaga been sheegeysaan ujeedooyinka & Siyaasadda Kacaanka, Jornaalkaasoo aad u bixiseen "UFFO" oo aad micnaheeda ulajeeddeen Dabeysha ka soo horreysa roobka, idinkoo ulajeeda in "URURKA R.U.D.M." iyo Jornaal-kuba ay hordhac u yihiin Siyaasado Kacaanka lagu majo-xaabinayo, oo ay ka dambeeyaan Dad ku nool Dibedda kana soo horjeeda Qarannimada Soomaaliyeed.

J. Eed.3aad, waxaa gaar ahaan laguugu eedeynayaa dembiga ah "HAYSASHO QORAAL LID KU AH SIYAASADDA QARANKA" ee ku xusan Qod.19aad isla XLY.54 ee 10.9.1970kii, sababtoo ah in gurigaaga laga helay "Hal Koobi oo ah Jornaalka UFFO, oo ay soo saareen Eed.1aad & kan 2aad, kuwaas oo aad Madax ka wada tihiin Ururka Xaaraanta ah ee R.U.D.M.-

X. Eed.4aad Dr.AADEN YUUSUF ABOKOR, 5aad CAB/MAAN CAB/HI X.AADEN,
" 6aad AXMED XUSEEN CAABI , 7aad XUSEEN MAX'ED (BERBERAAWI),
" 8aad MAXAMUUD SH.X.TAANI , 9aad Dr.CABDILLAAHI CALI COLAAD,
" 10aad MAXAMED DAGAAL XIRSI , 11aad CALI CIGE FAARAX(C.Biid),
" 12aad YUUSUF CAB/HI "GEYDH" , 13aad Dr.CISMAAN CABDI MEYGAAG,
" 14aad MAX'ED CABDI "AYUUB" , 15aad AADEN WARSAME SACIID,
" 16aad MAXAMED CALI IBRAAHIM , 17aad AXMED MAXAMED MADAR,
" 18aad CUMAR CIISE CAWAALE , 19aad Dr.MAXAMUUD CALI SULUB,
" 20aad BAASHE CABDI YUUSUF , 21aad ISMAACIIL CABDI HURRE,
" 22aad XASAN CAB.SHEEKH CALI , 23aad AXMED XASAN MADAR,

../..

......../4.

Waxaa wadajir la idiinku eedeynayaa Dembiga ah ka "QAYB GELID URUR XAARAAN AH", kana soo horjeeda Midnimada Ummadda Soomaaliyeed, ee ku xusan Qod.3aad (Qaybtiisa 2aad) X.L.Y.54 ee 10.9.70kii, xiriirna la leh Qod.71 X.C.S., sababtoo ah in aad Xubno Fir-Fircoon ka ahaydeen "URURKA R.U.D.M.", ee Eedeysanayaasha 1aad, 2aad & 3aad ay ka abaabuleen Magaalada Hargeysa, ujeeddadiisuna ahayd in la wiiqo Siyaasadda Kacaanka, idiinkoo ka qayb galay Kulanno iyo Shirar kala duwan ee Ururkaasi yeeshay, go'aannadiisana si buuxda uga qayb gasheen, Fikradana uga dhiibteen.-

KH. Eedeysanaha 5aad (Cabdiraxmaan Cabdillaahi), waxaa gaar ahaan laguugu eedeynayaa Dembiga ah, "HAYSASHO QORAAL LID KU AH SIYAASADDA QARANKA ee ku xusan Qod.19aad X.L.Y. 54 ee 10.9.1970kii, sababtoo ah in Gurigaaga laga helay Gabay aad gacantaada ku qortay oo lagu canbaareynayo Siyaasadda iyo Mabda' Kacaanka.-

D. Eedeysanaha 16aad Maxamed Cali Ibraahim, waxaa gaar ahaan laguugu eedeynayaa Dembiga ah "HAYSASHO HUB SHARCI DARRO AH", oo ku xusan Qod.1aad X.L.Y.65 ee 3dii Nofembar 1977dii, sababtoo ah in Gurigaaga laga soo helay Bastooladda Maakaaroofka ah tirsigeedu yahay AY3138, iyo 6 (lix) xabbadood oo lagala soo galay Xad-ku sheegga.-

R. Eedeysanaha 17aad Axmed Maxamed Madar & Eedeysanaha 20aad Baashe Cabdi Yuusuf, waxaa si gaar ah la idiinku eedeynayaa Dembiyada kala ah 1)-ABAABULID URUR DEMBI FALE AH, ee ku xusan Qod.322 (1aad) ee X.C.S., 2)-KU CABSI GELIN QARXIN BOMBO GACMEED ee ku xusan Qod.325 ee X.C.S. iyo 3)- HALIS GELIN NABADGELYADA GUUD ee ku xusan Qod.332 ee X.C.S. oo xiriir la leh Qod.71aad X.C.S., sababtoo ah in aad abaabusheen Urur ujeeddadiisu tahay in lagu tallaabsado dembiyo kala duwan, isla markaana aad labadiina iyo eedeysanayaasha 24aad, 25aad, 26aad iyo 27aad, aad ku qarxiseen Guryo ay leeyihiin Dad isugu jira Madax iyo Shacab "BOMBOOYINKA" gacanta, isla mar ahaantaana aad halis geliseen Nabadgelyada Dadweynaha, idinkoo BOMBOOYINKA aad qarxiseen ku tuurey meelo aadnaan hubsan in dad joogo iyo in kale.-

S.- Eed.24aad (Maxamuud Cabdi Jiciir), Eed.25aad (Maxamed Macallin Cismaan), Eed.26aad (Saciid Maxamed Ibraahim) & Eed.27aad (G/Dhexe Ismaaciil Xaashi Madar), afartiina waxaa eedeysanayaasha 17aad iyo 20aad, la idiin kula eedeynayaa Dembiyada kala ah 1)- KA QAYB QAADASHO URUR DEMBI FALE AH ee ku xusan Qod.322 (Qy.2aad) X.C.S., 2)-KU CABSI GELIN QARXIN BOMBOOYIN GACMEED oo ku xusan Qod.325 X.C.S. iyo 3)- HALIS GELIN NABADGELYADA GUUD ee ku xusan Qod.332 X.C.S. oo xiriir la leh Qod.71 X.C.S., sababtoo ah in aad ka mid ahaydeen Urur Dembi

../..

......../5.

fale ah, kana qayb qaadateen, gacanna ka geysateen BOMBOOYIN GACMEED lagu qarxiyey Guryo ay kala deggen yihiin Dad Madax iyo Shacabba leh, isla markaana Bombooyinkaa aad halis ku geliseen Nabadgelyada Guud ee Dadweynaha.-

SH.-Eed.28aad Xasan Cabdullaahi Cali "Ceelgeeye", waxaa laguugu eedeynayaa Dembiga ah "AFMINSHAARNIMO", ee ku xusan Qod.21aad XLY. 54 ee 10.9.1970kii, sababtoo ah in markii dembiyada ay galeen dartood loo xiray eedeysanayaasha kor ku qoran qaarkood, aad ku dhaqaaqday, fidisayna dacaayado Lid ku ah Hawlaha Madaxda G.W.G. iyo Hay'adaha baarista, adigoo sheegay in eedeysanayaasha la xiray aysan wax dembi ah gelin, hase yeeshee la shirqoolayo iyo in qoraalka Jornaalka Uffo ay ka dambeeyaan isla Madaxda Dowladda ee G.W.G.-

Dembiyadaasu waxay ka dhaceen Magaalada Hargeysa 6dii (lixdii) bilood ee ugu dambeeyey Sannadkii 1981kii.-

F A L IYO X E E R

Garsooraha Maxkamadda markii la horkeenay Eedeysanayaasha kor ku xusan, una akhriyey warqadda EEDDA isagoo isla markaasna u sheegaya jawaabihii uu Sharcigu u banneeyey sida ay qorayaan Qodobada 103 & 104 XHCS, waxay Eedeysanayaashu ku kala jawaabeen dhammaantood DAFIRAAD, hase yeeshee Eedeysanaha 16aad Maxamed Cali Ibraahim oo ku wada eedeysnaa Dembiyada kala ah "KA QAYB QAADASHO URUR XAARAAN ah iyo HAYSASHO HUB SHARCI DARRO AH, wuxuu QIRTAY Dembiga ah Haysasho Hub Sharci darro ah.-

Kaddib waxay Maxkamaddu amartay Dadweyne U Doodaha inuu soo caddeeyo in DEMBI DHACAY, hadduu dhacayna ay galeen Eedeysanayaashani, sida waafaqsan Qodobada 110 & 163 XHCS.-

H O R D H A C

Dadweyne U Dooduhu wuxuu Maxkamadda u soo jeediyey Hordhac sida uu qoraayo Qod.114 XHCS, yirina sannadkii 1981kii ayey Debadda ka yimaadeen Dad Soomaaliyeed oo Qaranka ka soo horjeeda, lana kulmeen Eedeysanayaasha oo isugu jira Jaamiciyiin iyo Indheer garato ah, oo abaabulay Ururkan, qoreenna Jariidada Kacaanka liddiga ku ah, qabashadoodiinna waxaa dhacay dembiyada kale, waxaanan keenayaa maragta dacwaddan:

MARKHAATIGA 1AAD : DHAMME DAAHIR CIID CILMI: asagoo dhaarsan wuxuu yiri: Waxaan ahay Madaxa Xafiiska Nabadgelyada C.Q.S. ee Qaybta 26aad X.D.S., waxaa jirtay in bishii Oktoobar 1981kii, dhammadkeedii

.../...

......../6.-

warar lanagu soo gaarsiiyey in Hargeysa uu ka soo baxo Joornaal Dad Soomaaliyeed ay soo saaraan. Dad xog-ogaal noqon kara ayaan u dirnay. Nin la yiraahdo Cabdi Laangare wuxuu ii keenay Joornaal la yiraahdo "UFFO", Ururka soo saarana la yiraahdo R.U.D.M., waana akhriyey Jornaalkaas, kaddib waxaan u geeyey Jeneral GAANNI, Taliyaha Qaybta 26aad XDS. Markaan aragnay Joornaalka iyo Ururka soo saara magaciisa, waxay noogu muuqatay in aan u gudbino Taliyaha NSSka Gobolka W.Galbeed si ay u baaraan.-

IM/ DADWEYNE U DOODE & M/1AAD:

J. 5 (shan) warqadood oo la teebgareeyey oo isku xiran ayey ahayd, mana xusuusan karo sidii ay u qornayd, haddii aan arkose waan garan lahaa.

J. TUSID - Joornaalku waa asagii.

J. Waxaa ii keenay Joornaalkan nin la yiraahdo Aadan (oo Boliiska ka tirsanaan jiray) oo Cabdi Laangare la socday.

J. Aadan-kaas maalin ayuu Xafiiskayga iigu yimid wuxuuna ii sheegay inuu Xamar ka yimid oo uu la soo kulmay G/Dhexe Maxamuud Samatar oo Xafiiskayaga Xamar Madax ka ah, wuxuuna ii sheegay inuu jecelyahay inuu i arko ilana sheekaysto, wuxuuna la socday Cabdi Laangare.

J. Cabdi Laangare aniga ayaa u diray Joornaalka, wuxuuna igu yiri Aadan ayaa ii keenay iina soo helay.

J. Ma aanan weydiinin Aadan inuu asagu u dhiibay Cabdi Laangare Joornaalka.

J. Taliyaha Qaybta 26aad aniga ayaa Joornaalka u geeyey, asaga, Aadan iyo Cabdi Laangare si gaar ayey isku arkeen.-

IM/QAREEN ISMAACIIL JUMCAALE & M/1AAD:

J. Joornaal waxaa la yiraahda "Hadal daabacan oo ujeeddo la leeyahay,

J. Magaca UFFO ayaa ka dhigay Joornaal iyo Ururka soo saaray.

J. Maan arag cid daabacday iyo meesha lagu daabacay.

IM/QAREEN FAYSAL & M/1AAD:

S. Ma wax been ah ayaa ku qoran Joornaalka? MAXKAMADDU WEY KA JOOJISEY SU'AASHAAS QAREENKA.

S. Ma jiraan magacyo caddeynayaa dadkii qoray Joornaalka?

J. Ma jiraan wax magacyo ah oo ku qoran Joornaalka oo ah ciddii qortay.

J. Erayga UFFO IYO RUDM ayaa ku tusaaya inuu Joornaalka ka soo horjeedo Dowladda, waayoo waa Urur aan Dowladdu ogayn.-

../..

......./7.

J. Markii Joornaalka ay ii keeneen ayaan lacag siiyey Cabdi Laangare & Aadan.

IM/QAREEN XASAN SHEEKH & M/1AAD:

J. Waxaan ka marag furayaa Joornaalka, xogtayduna waa tan aan sheegay.

IM/QAREEN CUSMAAN & M/1AAD:

J. Wuxuu marag furkaygu ku egyahay Joornaalka.-

QAREEN BASHIIR: Ma su'aalayo.

IM/QAREEN BILE & M/1AAD:

J. Markii lacagta aan siiyey waxay ahayd markii ay Joornaalka ii keeneen ee way ahayn markaan u diray.

J. Waan fahmay UFFO siday u qoran tahayba.

J. Ciidanka Booliiska ayuu ka tegey Aadan, shaqose ma hayo.

IM/2AAD DADWEYNE U DOODAHA & M/1AAD:

J. Uffo waxaan u aqaanna "DABAYL KULUL"

S. Macno kale ma laguugu sheegay? J. Macnaheedu waa sidaas.

IM/MAXKAMADDA & M/1AAD:

J. Wax baaris ah kumaan samaynin Joornaalka cidda soo saartay.

J. Cabdi Laangare wuxuu yiri Aadan ayaa ii keenay. Aadanna wuxuu ii sheegay in niman dhallinyaro ah oo guux-guuxaaya ay jiraan Taliyaha Qaybta 26aad ayaan u sheegayaa ayuu i yiri.

J. Joornaalka Jeneral Gaanni ayaan u gudbiyey, asaga ayaa NSSka u gudbiyey.

J. Waxaan weydiiyey Cabdi Laangare wuxuuna ii sheegay in Joornaalka ay qoreen Maxamed Baaruud (Eed.1aad), Jabane (Eed.2aad) iyo Dr. Taanni (Ed.8aad), waxaana lagu daabacay Wershadda Pepsi Cola.

SOO JEEDIN DOOD QAREEN ISMAACIIL:

Haddii ay Maxkamaddu su'aal cusub keento, Eedeysanayaasha aan difaacayana wax ka sheegayso, Habka (Procedura) oo dhan ayaa isbedelaaya, marag kale hala weydiiyo su'aalahaas.-

JAAWAABTA MAXKAMADDA:

Maxkamaddu waxay raacdinaysaa garsoor daddaalad ku dhisan, wixii cusub ee ka soo baxa su'aasha, Maxkamadda u soo jeedi.

M/1AAD - CELIS JAWAAB:

Cabdi Laangare wuxuu ii sheegay in Dr.Taanni (Eed.8aad), Baaruud (Eed.1aad) iyo Jabane (Eed.2aad) ay Qoreen Joornaalka UFFO, kuna daabaceen Wershadda Pepsi Cola.-

..../...

........../8.

QAREEN ISMAACIIL & MAXKAMADDA:

Qareen Xasan Sheekh wuxuu maraggu ugu jawaabay waxaan ka marag ahay in warqaddu (Joornaalka) la ii keenay aanan raad-raacin, ma ogi eedeysanayaasha in ay xiriir la leeyihiin. Maxkamaddan wuxuu u sheegay in eedeysanayaasha 1aad, 2aad & 8aad ay qoreen Jornaalka UFFO iyamaa Run ah?

M/1aad: J. Labada su'aaloodba waan ka jawaabay.-

SOO JEEDIN QAREEN ISSMAACIIL:

Ha lagu dacweeyo maraggan Qod.291 XCS, waa markhaati Beenaale, isku arrin ayuu laba siyood uga kala jawaabay.

JAWAAB CELIN K/XEER ILAALIYAHA:

Been ma sheegin maraggu, su'aasha dambe hore looma weydiinin.

ADKEYN QAREEN ISMAACIIL:

Ha lagu qaado Qodobkan, ma aha Xeer Ilaaliyuhu inuu Difaaco maragga uu keensaday, Kitaabna waa lagu dhaariyey, Eeddu waa DIL ciyaar ma ah waa KIIS addunka oo dhan indhaha ay ku hayaan Verbaalahana 3 Kaaliye ayaa qoraaya.-

JAWAAB MAXKAMADDA:

3 (siddex) Kaaliye wey qorayaan, dhegeystayaasha Hoolka fadhiyaanna labada su'aalood & Jawaabahoodaba wey maqlaayeen. Maxkamaddu markay dhegaysatay codsiga Qareen Ismaaciil iyo Jawaabta K/X.I., way diidey soo jeedintii Qareenka kuna saabsan in Maraggu lagu dacweeyo Markhaati Beenaale.

MARAGGA 2AAD: G/SARE XASAN MAXAMED NUUR TALIYAHA NSSka G/W/G.:

Dhaar dabadeed wuxuu yiri:

Bishii Oktoobar dhammaadkeedii 1981 ayaa war nalagu soo gaarsiiyey in Joornaal magaalada Hargeysa gudaheeda laga soo saaro, isla markaana lagu akhristo Magaalada Joornaalka la yiraahdo S.N.M. oo ka soo baxa LONDON laguna daadiyey suuqa Hargeysa warqado dacaayad ah oo SNM leedahay. Markaas anagu Xafiis ahaan maannu helin, hase yeeshee Taliyaha Qaybta 26aad ayaa noo soo gudbiyey Joornaal la yiraahdo UFFO iyo cadad ka mid Joornaalka SNM.- Jaalle Cumar Jees oo ka tirsan G.S.K. ayaa lala socodsiiyey anaguna Xafiiskayaga Xamar ayaan gaarsiinnay. Kaddib Xamar ayaa laga soo amray in la baaro. Ninkii warka soo sheegay wuxuu sheegay in eedeysanaha 2aad (A.M.Y.) gurigiisa hal koobi Joornaalka UFFO laga soo qaaday, waxaanan soo xirnnay Eedeysanaha 2aad oo sheegay in asaga iyo eedeysanaha 1aad ay qoreen oo keliya Joornaalkaas. Maallintii markaan ku laabtay gelin-

../..

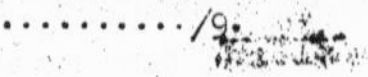

kii dambe Xafiiskayga, waxa la ii keenay qoraal uu eedeysanaha 2aad ii soo qoray oo uu iigu dhiibay Sarkaal Xafiiska joogay, wuxuuna ku qoray warkii hore la iga qoray waa been ee waxaan arrintan isku ognahay 20 (labaaton) Qof oo uu magacyadooda qaar sheegay, qaarna uu yiri wajiyadooda ayaan garanayaa, kadibna waxaan soo xirnay eedeysanaha 1aad, waxaana Xamar looga soo diray Guddi Baariseed, Eedeysanayaasha 1aad & 2aad iyo Dokumentiyadii ilaa markaas aan ka hayey, ayaga ayaan ku wareejiyey.-

IM/ DADWEYNE U DOODAHA & M/2AAD:

Wuxuu akhriyey maraggu Joornaalka wixii dusha kaga qornaa.

J. Ma xusuusan karo taariikhda la xiray Eedeysanaha 2aad.

J. Laba cisho ayaa u dhexeysay eedeysanaha 1aad & 2aad xarigooda.

J. Labaaton qof ayuu qoraal ku bixiyey eedeysanaha 2aad.

J. Eed.1aad sheegista eed.2aad ayaan ku soo xirnay.

J. Eed.2aad warqad magacayga ku qoran yahay ayuu ii soo diray oo uu gacantiisa ku qoray.

J. TUSID. Warqaddani waa tii uu ii soo qoray Eed.2aad.

J. Waxaa ku qoran: Ku: Col.Xasan Maxamed, waxaan xusuustay (anigoo aan mar wada xusuusan karin magacyada ku qornaa) ay kala yihiin Aadan Cali Faarax, Aadan Aw Saciid Warsame, Maxamed Baaruud Cali, Baashe Cabdi Yuusuf, Dr.Sulub, Dr.Bashiir, Dr.Xaddi, Daahir Faarax Jire iyo eedeysanaha 2aad laftiisa iyo qaar kale oo badan. Akhristayaasha Uffo way badan yihiin, inkastoo aysan koobiyadu badneyn, waxaana loo akhristaa si wareeg ah, Eedeysanaha ayaa qoray oo saxeexey warqaddan.

J. Su'aal keliya ayaan markaasi weydiiyey eedeysanaha, waxaannu iigu jawaabay inuu hubo in raggaani yihiin raggii ka mid ahaa raggii la ogaa.

J. Eed.1aad waxba anigu kama ogi.

J. Waxaan ku wareejiyey Guddi oo uu Madax ka yahay G/Sare Cali Xuseen, caddeyntii eed.2aad iyo labada eedeysane 1aad & 2aad.

IM/QAREEN FAYSAL & M/2AAD:

S. Qoraalka SNM iyo UFFO ayaa kuu soo gudbiyey?

J. Waxaa ii soo gudbiyey S/Guuto Gaanni.

S. Ma ogtahay cidda keentay labadaas Joornaal?

J. Ma ogaanin cidda u keentay General Gaanni.

S. Cabdi Laangare ma kuu sheegay in Aadan Joornalka keenay?

J. Maya, wuxuu Cabdi Laangare ii sheegay inuu ka soo qaaday asagu guriga eed.2aad.-

.../..

............/10.

S. Mala handaday mase la dilay Eed.2aad?

J. Inta aan ogahay lama dilin.

S. (TUSID) warqadda magaca ah SULUB ma qoraal ka geddisanaa farta kale?

J. Jawaab waa maya ee biirsha (Qalinka) ayaa lagu celceliyey.

S. Liiskan Eed.2aad qoray Cabdi Langare ma ku jiray? J. Haa.

S. Joornalka SNM ma ogtahay cidda laga soo qaaday?

J. Ma ogaanin.

S. Ragga liiska ku qoran ma wada xirteen?

J. Rag xiran iyo rag kaleba waa ku qoran yihiin.

IM/QAREEN ISMAACIIL & M/2AAD:

S. Warqaddan (Joornaalka) ma hab Xafiiseed ayaa laguugu soo gudbiyey mise waa laguu dhiibay?

J. Gacanta ayaa la iiga dhiibay.

S. Markii hore warbixin ayaa laga qoray eed.2aad markii dambena warbixin 2aad ayaa laga qoray, midkoodeedbuu xor ahaa?

J. Tan hore si xornimo ah ayaa looga qoray, tan labaadna la mid.

S. Ma waafaqsan yihiin labada caddeymood qod.201 XHCS?

J. Labada caddeymoodba Xeer Ilaaliyaha ayaa haya.

S. Eed.1aad goormaa ayaa la soo xiray?

J. Dhammaadkii Oktaobar ayaa la soo xiray, markuu sheegay Eed.2aad.

S. Eed.1aad wax maka qortay? J. Maya.-

IM/QAREEN XASAN SHEEKH & M/2AAD:

S. Qoraalka farta ah ee eed.2aad ma hortaada ayuu ku saxeexay, mise ayada oo saxeexan ayaa laguu keenay?

J. Ayada oo saxeexan ayaa la ii keenay.

S. Qallinka saxeexa iyo Qallinka qoraalka kale ma is leeyihiin?

J. Ma kala garan karo in ay kala duwan yihiin iyo in kale.

S. Baaristaadii ma ogaatay in ay laba qallin ahaayeen mise mid?

J. Ma baarin.

S. Sow waajib kuguma ay ahayn in aad baarto oo aad ogaato?

J. Sababta aan u baari waayey waxay ahayd waxaan ku wareejiyey Guddiga.-

IM/QAREEN CUSMAAN & M/2AAD:

S. Warbixinta Joornaalka makuu soo gudbisay ciddii keentay? Mise ma la socotay ciddii keentay?

J. Maya ee hore ayaan u ogaa dadka keenay.-

../..

......,,,./11.

S. Ma adiga ayaa u yeertay Dadkii keenay Joornaalka?

J. Cabdi Laangare ayaa igu yiri aniga ayaa keenay.

S. Ururku ma jiraa, mase ogaatay?

J. Urur waxba kama sheegin ee waxaan ka hadlay Joornaalka iyo xarigga Eed.1aad iyo 2aad.-

IM/QAREEN BASHIIR & M/2AAD:

S. Cabdi Laangare wax ma qortay?

J. Haa, wuxuu ii sheegay inuu guriga Eed.2aad ka soo qaaday Joornaalka UFFO sariirtiisa hoosteeda.

S. Cabdi Laangare meesha uu jiro ma ogaatay? J. Maya.

S. Taariikhdiisa ma taqaanaa? J. Waxba kama sheegi karo taariikhda Cabdi Laangare.

S. Imisa Eedeysane ayaa xirnaa markaad Guddiga dacwadda ku wareejisey? J. Waxaa xirnaa Eed.1aad & 2aad.-

IM/QAREEN XUSEEN BILE & M/2AAD:

S. Wax kale ma ka aragtay Joornaalkan?-

J. Koobigan hore iyo koobi Guddigu i tustay.

S. Idiinku ma baarteen oo ma hesheen meesha Joornaalka uu ka yimid?

J. War ahaan annaga oo u haynnaa ayaa la ii soo gudbiyey Joornaalka SNM iyo UFFO min hal koobi.

S. Ma baarteen halka dhabta ah ee ay ka soo baxdo UFFO?

J. Maya ee ninkii la iigu sheegay ayaan soo qabtay.

S. Eed.2aad markaad wax ka qoreyseen wax ma la gaarsiyey?

J. Markaan wax ka qoraayey Sarkaal ayaa ila joogay, wax la gaarsiyey ma-jiraan, isna waxba iima sheegin , midda kale wuxuu ku xirnaa bannaanka Xafiiska NSSka hortiisa, laba cishona wuu xirnaa.

S. Joornaalka ayaa keenay ayaa lagugu yiri?

J. Rag badan ayaa lagu tilmaamay, laakin Cabdi Laangare ayaan la kulmey.

S. Maka warhaysaa meel uu jiro Cabdi Laangare?

J. Meel uu jiro kama war hayo Cabdi Laangare.-

IM/MAXKAMADDA & M/2AAD:

S. Ma weydiisay eedeysanaha inuu saga qoray caddeynta labaad?

J. Haa, wuxuuna ii sheegay inuu asagu qoray.-

QAREEN CUSMAAN: Maxkamaddu waxaan ka codsanayaa in ay maraggu ii sulaasho.

S. Xageebuu ka ka keenay Cabdi Laangare Joornaalka UFFO?

.../..

........./12.

J. Cabdi Laangare wuxuu yiri Joornaalka anagoo wada qayilaynnaa Eed.2aad ayaan barkimo meesha taallay ka hoos helay.

QAREEN BILE : Maxkamaddu waxaan ka codsanayaa in ay maraggu ii su'aasho:

S. Caddeymo hore maka qorteen eed.2aad?

J. Ma jiraan 2dan caddaymood kuwa ka horreeyey.-

MARAGGA 3AAD L/X. QAASIM YUUSUF CALI: Dhaar kadib wuxuu yiri: Waxaan ka tirsanahay Qaybta Baarista NSSka ee Xamar. 8.11.81 ayaa Guddi aan ka tirsanahay oo ka kooban NSSka iyo Boliiska lanoo soo diray Hargeysa si aannu u baarno arrin ka dhacay. Waxaa madax noo ahaa G/Sare Cali Xuseen Diinle. 11.11.81, waxaa lanagu soo wareejiyey Dokumenti sheegaayo inuu jiro Hargeysa Urur qarsoodi ah oo ujeedadiisu tahay Midnimada Ummadda Soomaaliyeed in la qaybiyo, Hab Qabiil iyo Hab Gobol. Dokumentigu wuxuu sheegayaa in ay ka dambeeyaan Urur deggen Yurubta Galbeed, khaliijka iyo Xabashida. Joornaal ay ku qoran tahay UFFO waxaana ku qoran dushiisa: UFFO WAA JOORNAAL KA SOO BAXA GURIGA QABYADA AH EE XISBIGA, laba nin oo xiran ayaa lanagu soo wareejiyey, Eed.2aad (Jabane) oo macallin ahaan jiray iyo Eed.1aad (Inj.Maxamed Baaruud) oo ka shaqeeya Wershadda Pepsi Cola, ragga ka dambeeya waxaa laga hayaa ayaa la yiri labadaas nin. Wareysi ayaan la yeelannay Eed.2aad oo Bannaanka Xafiiska NSSka ku xirnaa, waxaa lanagu soo wareejiyey caddeyn uu gacantiisa ku qoray, wuxuu noo sheegay eedeysanaha in asaga iyo eedeysanaha 1aad ay Joornaalka UFFO ay gacantooda ku qoreen. Liis magacyo ah ayuu noo qoray. Waxaannu weydiinnay labada caddaymood (tan hore iyo tan labaad), wuxuu noo sheegay markaas eedeysanaha 2aad sidan: Niman Ciido gale ah ayaan hawshan la galay, markii la igu qabtayna wey igaga baxeen, markaan ogaaday in 2 (laba) nin oo Ciida Gale ahi lacag nagu qaateen kelidayna aan shabag ku dhacay, anna sirta kale waan sheegayaa: Wuxuu yiri dhaqdhaqaaqa Indheer garadku wuxuu bilawday 1977kii, markii Ruushka la eryay oo Adduunkii hore nooga reebay, haddii mabaadi'iisii la tuuri waayey niyaddiina wey naga xumaatay, waxaan marnay Heerar, waxaana la keenay Barasaab la yiraahdo AFAR JEEBLE oo dhaqaalihii Gobolka qaatay oo Xamar Wershado kaga dhistay, waxaa la keenay haddana G/Sare Cabdiraxmaan (M.Cab.) oo lacagtii geliyey Buur halkan ah oo magaaladu u taqaanno QOOR JAR ama JEEGA XIIR, lacagtaas Magaaladu u baahnayd, Maamulkii waan sii nacnnay.

..../...

........../13.

Wuxuu yiri Eed.2aad muddadii dambe waxaan ogaannay in S.N.M. laga furay Debadda Madaxna uu ka yahay DUQSI, Demuqraadiyadiina soo celinaya waxaanan doonnay inaan taageero siinno. Arooskii Eed.1aad oo lagu qabtay Eed.28aad walaalkii guri uu leeyahay, waxaan guddoonsannay in aan wax qabsano oo aan Dowladda wax ka sugin. Maallintii labaad waxaan guddoonsannay in Urur SAMAFAL ah samaysano dadweynahana ugu muujinno in aan danahooda u wadno, si inoo raacaan. Guryaha aan ku shiray oo ay wada degenaayeen Eedeysanayaasha 5aad, 6aad iyo 4aad oo saldhig noo ahaa. Guriga Eed.4aad (Dr.Aadan) anagoo fadhina ayuu Eed.1aad igala hadlay in aan arrimahayaga aan qoraal u bedelno, waxaanan ku niri cadadka hore soo diyaari. Eed.1aad ayaa ii keenay cadadkii 1aad oo laba koobi i siiyey, cadadkii 2aad waxbaan ka qoray ayuu yiri, cadadka hore makiinadda Wershadda Pepsi Cola ayaa lagu qoray 5 koobi ayey ahayd, cadadka 2aad waxaan ku qornay makiinad uu leeyahay Maxamuud Qaallib nin la yiraahdo, lagana soo qaaday gurigiisa, cadadka 3aad waxaa qoray Eed.1aad, wuxuuna ku qoray Wershadda Pepsi Cola, waxaanan siiyey ayuu yiri koobi Eed.3aad, koobi kalena waxaan siiyey nin la yiraahdo Aadan Waalli, koobiyadii kale waan qaybiyey dhammaantood, Eed.2aad wuxuu sheegay inuu la kulmay nin la yiraahdo Maxamed Nuur Xandulle (CARAB) uu la shiray Eedeysanayaasha 5aad, 11aad, 10aad & 7aad, wuxuuna na soo gaarsiiyey farriinno uu DUQSI iyo INA-WADAAD-DIID oo la shiray Isaaqa Sucuudiga degennaa. Dadkii aqoonta lahaa wey raaceen ayuu yiri, hase yeeshee kuwii diiday ee yiri Dalkayaga ka hor iman meyno wuxuu ku magacaabay REER SABLAALE, markaas wuxuu yiri buu yiri Maxamed Nuur Xandulle markuu eedeysanayaashaasi la shiraayey, idinkuna ha noqonina Reer Sablaale, Aadan Waalli si toos ah ayuu ugu xirnaa DUQSI, wuxuu yiri Reer kasta Jabhad ayuu sameystay Jabhadda ISAAQA adkeeya oo Ciida Gale soo raaciya Isaqa kale oo daba dhilif u ah Mareexaanka, ha iskana daayaan waxa uu Madaxa ugu yahay Cabdi Waraabe, farrintii taasi ayey ahayd. Waxaan goosannay ayuu yiri Eed.2aad inaan WAXDADDA isku xirno si xagga Diinta dadka uga soo galno, fadhi gogol dhig ah ayaan yeellannay, waxaana maallintaasi la is weydiiyey oo Waxdada ay ka waraysteen: Maxay saacadda midigta ugu xirtaan, Hilibka inay cunin iyo arrimo kale oo caadooyin ah. Waxdaddu 3 nin ayey ahaayoen, waxaana Madax u ahaa Eed.22aad iyo 23aad iyo nin Macallin (P.P.) ah oo Burco ka shaqayn jiray oo baxsaday. Maallintii dambe waxaa canuumad sameeyey WAXDADDA, wuxuu

......

........./14.

yiri Eed.2aad anaga ayaa waraysannay, waxayna yiraahdeen Urur Dowladdu diidan ayaannu nahay, waxay na weydiiyeen maxaad tihiin? Waxaanan ugu jawaabnay ayuu yiri: Dad saaxiib ah ayaan nahay oo Iskuulada mar kawada baxay, waxayna na weydiiyeen ujeedayada kadibna waan ka warwareegnay, adigu markii dambe waxaan ku heshiinnay ayuu yiri: ISKAASHI, kulana tallinnay Waxdada in ay ISTAKOORKA Bulshada iska bi'iyaan.-

IM/KXIG IYO M/3AAD:

J. Carab ninka la yiraahdo wuu la qayilay, waxaanan ahayn ayuu yiri Eed.2aad asaga ah, Eed.5, 7, 9, 10 & 11.

J. Waxdada waxaa la shiray Eed.1, 2, 3, 5, 6, 7, 8, 9, 11, 12, 14, 15, 22, 17 & 20 ayaan ka xusuusta oo Shirka ka qayb galay.

J. Su'aal khaas ah ma xusuusto cid weydiisay.-

J. Guriga Eed.22aad gurigiisa ayaa lagu shiray wuxuuna ka mid ahaa raggii wax u yeeray Eed.21aad oo Waxdada ah ayaa Madax u ahaa iyo 2 kale ayaa guriga Eed.1aad shirka uga qayb galay.

J. Eed.21 & 23 aad ayaa WAXDADA uga qayb galay.

J. Eed.22aad wuxuu sheegay in niman Waxdada ah isla shireen, markaan waxaan goostay ayuu yiri markayga inaan ka qayb qaato.

J. Eed.23aad ayaa Waxdada weydiiyey Dowladda ay rabaan habkeed, waxayna ugu jawaabeen "DOWLO ISLAAM AH", eedeysanaha 3aad wuxuu weydiiyey ma ta KHUMAYNI oo kale, waxayna yiraahdeen MAYA, middii KHLAFADA oo kale. Eed.3aad ayuu ku celiyey: ma ugu dhaqmi kartaan CASRIGAN, islaamku sidii uu u dhaqmi jiray? Waxay ugu jawaabeen in buugag Islaamka deggen Pakistaan iyo Masar oo culimo ahi ay qoreen lagu dhaqmi karo dhaqan dhaqaale ahaan.

J. Wuxdadu waxay weydiiyeen maxaad aragtay markaad Waddanka ku soo noqotay (waxaa la weydiiyey Eed.3aad), wuxuuna ku jawaabay: waxaan arkay: INANTII oo Qarsato ah, INANKII oo Kabagle ah, ISLAANTII oo Qaadley ah, ODAYGII oo Qurbaawi ah.-

Eed.1aad wuxuu noo sheegay in uu asagu abaabulay Wargeyska UFFO kii ugu horreeyey cadad ahaan aniga ayaa daabacay ayuu yiri, Makiinada Pepsi Cola ayaanan ku qoray, 3 Koobi Jabane ayaan u dhiibay. Cadadkii 2aad aniga iyo Eed.2aad (Jabane) ayaa gurigeyga ku qornnay, cadadka 2aad qaybintiisa waxaan ku beegnnay 21.10.1981,

.../..

........../13.

cadadkii 3aadna aniga ayaa ku qoray Makiinadda Pepsi Cola.-
Eed.1aad wuxuu sheegay in eed.4aad gurigiisa geyn jiray Joornaalka Eed.2aad gurigiisa dhigi jiray, eed.7aad uu koobi siiyey. Shirarkii Waxdada aniga ayaa qaban qaabiyey ayuu yiri eed.1aad, waxaanan la xiriiray ayuu yiri Eed.21 iyo 22 oo isku shaqo ahaayeen. Eed.1aad wuxuu sheegay in asaga iyo eed.4aad ay soo jeediyeen in ay u diraan Dacaayado Dowladda qaban karta, si toos ahna Dadku u qaadan karo, wuxuu yiri eed.1aad ninka Jariidada SNM qoraa muxuu Af Soomaali ugu qori waayey.-
TUSID: Joornaalka waa SNM, waana kii Mafrishyada lagu akhrisan jiray Eed.4aad ayaa yiri deed: Af Soomaali halagu soo qoro Dadku ma wada yaqaanno Afka Ingiriiska ah. Eed.1aad wuxuu yiri: Dacaayad Cusub oo Dowladda qaban karta ha loo diro.-
AKHRID: Joornaalka UFFO Qod.1aad Berbera waa la qabsaday.....Col. Cabdicasiis Bilad geesi ayuu mutaystay markii uu adhigii Mareexaanka raray.......Qod.2 Qaramaynta Gobolka, Mareexaan oo Madax ka wada ah Xafiisyada (tirin Xafiisyadaas) NNS iyo Guulwadayaasha ...LA SOCOTO....
S/J. Eed.1aad wuxuu sheegay inuu asagu fikiray kiligiina qoray UFFO Xafiiska Pepsi Cola waxaan ka helnnay BLOCK NOTE uu lahaa eed.1aad waxaanan ka helnay warar ku qoran oo uu ku soo saaray cadadka 2aad IYO 3aad ee UFFO ku soo baxay, waxaanan ka xusuusanahay: Gaanni oo Caasha Juusto ninkeedu beddelaayo, waxaannu yiri Eed.1aad SAADAALO ayey ahaayeen. Makiinaddii waannu helnay Guriga Maxamuud Qaalib nin la yiraahdo ayaanan ka soo qaadnay, Eed.1 & 2aad wey noo xaqiijiyeen. Xaaska Maxamuud Qaalib way sheegtay in Makiinadda uu qaaday Eed.2aad oo Macallin u ahaan jiray. Cadadadii kale maannu helin ee UFFO.-
EEDEYSANAHA SEDDEXAAD:
Eed.2aad siduu sheegay wuxuu ahaa nin qayb weyn ka qaatay Shirkii Guriga Eed.1aad, kadib markii Eed.2aad qiraal ku caddeeyey. Guriga Eed.3aad waxaan ka helnnay Hal koobi oo ah Joornaalka UFFO, wuxuuna noo sheegay inuu ka qaaday Eed.2aad ay akhristeenna Eed.8, 15, 6aad asaga oo geeyey guriga Eed.6aad. Muddo dheer ayuu ENGLAND wax ku baranaayey, markii dambena Bangiga Islaamka oo Sucuudiga ku yaalla ayuu ka shaqayn jiray, waxaan u malaynayaa inuu bartay "KOBCINTA DHAQAALAHA" Waddamada 3aad, kadibna Waddanka ayuu ku soo laabtay.-

.../..

........./16.

Wuxuu Shirkii ka sheegay in Bangiga Islaamku markuu uu ka shaqeyn jiray Soomaaliya u ogolaaday NALAYNTA 6 Magaalo, kadib markii Dowladda Soomaalidu soo weydiisatay. Haddana magaaladan wax nal ah lama gelinin, dadkana waa u dullinimo, Dowladdana waa u karti xumo. Socdaallo uu ku tegay Mareykanka, Ingiriiska iyo Sucuudiga cid maan arag ayuu yiri cid aan la kulmayna ma jirto.-

EEDEYSANA 4AAD:

Ilaa 18 qof oo eedeysanayaasha ka mid ahi waxay qiraal ku bixiyeen in ay guriga Eed.4aad lagu shiri jiray. Waa shaqaale eed.4aad, gurigana Dowladda ayaa leh. Ta labaad shirarka lagu qabanaayey waxay ahaayeen Hab Urur iyo waxyaabihii looga hadli jiray. Eed.4aad wuxuu sheegay in gurigiisa lagu shiri jiray. Danahoodana lagaga hadli jiray . Joornaalka UFFO gurigeyga waan ku maqlay ayuu yiri ciddii haysana ma xusuusto ayuu yiri. Joornaalka SNM waan akhristay ayuu yiri, waxaa kale oo akhristay ayuu yiri Eedeysanayaasha kala ah: 1, 2, 5, 6, 7, 8, 9, 10, 11. 13, 15 iyo 17aad.-

EEDEYSANAHA 5AAD:

Ugu horreyntii waxaa sababay qabashadiisii markuu Eed.2aad ku caddeeyey qiraalkiisa inuu ka mid yahay Ururka R.U.D.M., waxayna ku jireen asaga iyo Eed.2aad laba guri oo iska soo horjeeda (Indian Line) ku yaalla, guriga Eed.4aad wuu tegi jiray, shirkii Waxdada wuu ka qayb galay, wax dood ahna kama jeedin. Gurigiisa waxaan ka helnnay warqad oo ku qoran yahay GABAY oo gacantiisa uu ku qoray, Dacaayad ah kana dhan ah Madaxweynaha JDS. Eed.5aad wuxuu gurigiisa kula kulmay Maxamed Nuur Xandulle (CARAB) iyo Aadan Cali Faarax (Aadan Waalli) oo DUQSI farriin ka siday, wuxuu sheegay in rag u riyaaqay ay jireen farriintii, rag aan wax ku darsanna ay jireen. Wuxuu sheegay in uu laba cadad oo UFFO ah uu Eed.2aad koenay gurigiisa oo lagu akhristay. Joornaalka SNM oo barnaamij ah lagu akhristay, Qiraalna uu ku bixiyey arrintaas.-

WUXUU MARAGGU YAR AKHRIYEY GABAYGII LAGA HELAY GURIGA EEDEYSANAHA...
.......Eedeysanuhu wuxuu yiri nin Macallin ahaan jiray ayaa tiriyey oo hore Gabaygan awgii Maxkamadda Badbaadada Hargeysa ugu xukuntay 10 sano oo xarig. Wuxuu yiri eedeysanuhu ma garanaayo cidda ii akhriday iina yeerisay ee aan Gabayga ka qortay.-

DADWEYNE U DOODE:& M/3AAD:

S. Gabayga maxaad u fasirateen?

J. Gabaygu wuxuu ka mid ahaa gabayo isdaba joog ahaa oo la oran jiray

....../..

........../17.

"DEELAY" kana soo horjeeday Dowladda. Eed.5aad wuxuu yiri Urur aan ka mid ahaa ma jiro, hase yeeshee Shirarka waan iska fadhiyi jiray.

EEDEYSANAHA 6AAD:

Gurigiisa si joogta ah waxaa / tegi jiray Xubno Ururka ka tirsan, maalin ayaa eed.6, 8 & 15aad oo wada fadhiya ayaa eed.3aad ula yimid Joornaalka UFFO, kuna akhriyey, Eed.8aad, 15aad & 3aad wey wada akhristeen. Markii la xiray Eed.4aad wuxuu yri "WAR INALADA WAX AAN U QABANNO".

EEDEYSANAHA 7AAD:

S. Maxaad ku soo qabateen, maxaana idin gaarsiiyey qabashadiisa?

J. Eed.2aad wuxuu noo sheegay in cadad UFFO ka mid ah uu siiyey eed.1aad & 7aad. Eed.1aad wuxuu yiri ma xusuusto taasi. Eedeysanahani shirar badan ayuu ka qayb galay, gaar ahaan shirkii aroos ka Maxamed Baaruud, shirkii Waxdada. Wuxuuna ka mid ahaa raggii la kulmay Maxamed Nuur Xandulle (CARAB) sida ay sheegeen Eed.5° iyo 9aad. Eedeysanahani waxba kama jiraan ayuu yiri, hase yeeshee wuxuu sheegay inuu kula qayilay guriga Eed.4 iyo 5aad. Eed.2aad wax gaar ah noogama sheegin eedeysanaha, ka qayb gal shir mooyene.-

EEDEYSANAHA 8AAD:

Wuxuu ka mid ahaa Ururka, sida uu eed.2aad qiraal ku bixiyey. Waxaan ka warsannay oo dhan siday ahayd ayuu noogu sheegay. Guriga eed.2aad 4, 5 iyo 6aad, waan ka qayb galay ayuu yiri shirarkoodii. Shirkii Waxdada wuu ka qayb galay. CARAB (Maxamed Nuur Xandulle) oo ah ninkii Debadda ka yimid si gaar ah ayuu ula kulmay, marna kuwa kale ayuu kala mid ahaa. Xagga Caafimaadka ayuu ka hadlay shirkii Eed. 1aad gurigiisa lagu qabtay. Warqad niman kale ujeedo ka lahaayeen ayaa loo yeeriyey oo uu gacantiisa ku qoray, warqadda waxaa loo diraayey Dowladda Dhexe, waxaana soo diyaariyey Eedeysanayaasha: 10, 7, 15, 17aad oo lahaa ra'yigeeda, waxaana loo qoraayey oo dan ka lahaa Eed.28aad oo yiri saaxibaday ayaan rabey si kastaba ha u dhacee inaan siidaayo, wuxuuna sheegay in eed.28aad ugu yimid BAAR HARGEYSA kuna yiri, Masiir Xigeenka Gaadiidka Badda Jaalle Jaamac Gaas Mucaawiye wuxuu yiri soo diyaariya qoraal aad ku matalaysaan Dadweynaha. Eed.28aad ayuu weydiistay in ay soo qoraan warqaddaasi kadibna ay tegeen guriga eed.4aad oo markaas xirnaa, halkaasina ku

.../...

..........18.

qoreen warqaddaasi, kadibna warqaddii eed.28aad gurigiisa ku teeb-gareeyey, Jaamac Gaasna uu u dhiibay. Danta eedeysanaha 28aad waxay ahayd ayuu yiri Taani (Eed.8aad) waxay Ina-adeer ahaayeen eed.£aad, kadibna uu u qoray ra'yiga dhallinyaradu u yeerisay. Eed.28aad, in-kasta oo aysan ii sugnayn waxaan filayaa inuu ka shaqayn jiray Rug-ta Ganacsiga. Taani wuxuu noo sheegay inuu Aabihiis ka shaan jiray Gobolkan Qaadi, inuu Iskuullo badan ka galay Gobolkaan meelo ka tirsan, saxiibbo badan leeyahay, wax Qabiil ahina xiriirin, wuxuuna sheegay in Dhallinyarada ka xiriiran xagga Famliga Hoyadii ka dha-latay. Eed.8aad wuxuu sidaas ku bixiyey Qiraal, Qiraalkaasna way is waafaqeen ka eed.2aad.-

EEDEYSANAHA 9AAD:

Eed.2aad Qiraalka uu bixiyey ayaan raacnay. Waxaa jirtay intii an-nu Guddigayagani imaanin ayey NSSka yimaadeen asaga iyo eedeysana-yaasha 7, 8, 9aad, waxayna la kulmeen Eed.2aad oo halkaasi ku xir-naa. Eed.9aad wuxuu weydiiyey kan labaad "Arrintii lagugu xiray ka warran", waxaannu eed.2aad sheegay inuu ku yiri: markii hore idinka ayaa i geliyey, markii la i qabtayna waa la igaga dhuuntay, waxna la iima qabanin, aniguna waxaan ogaa oo dhan waan sheegay. Kadib maalmo dabadeed ayaa la ii yimid ayuu yiri eed.2aad, waxayna igu yiraahdeen ayuu yiri eed.7, 9aad oo ii yimid, dhallinyaradii waxay yiraahdeen, noona kaa soo fareen: waxaad u baahato waa laguu dham-maynayaa, waxaad badisaa liiska dadka aad magacyadooda sheegtay, si baadigoobka iyo baarista loogu jahwareero, arrintuna qoys kasta u taabato, arrintaasi Qiraal ayuu ku bixiyey Eed.9aad. Wuxuu kaloo eed.9aad sheegay in asaga iyo eed.18aad, Cabdi Laangare iyo Aadan Cali Guhaad ay ka wada hadleen arrimo, sida Ciida-galaha Mareexaanka looga reebi lahaa ee ISAAQA loo soo raacin lahaa. Wuxuuna ka mid ahaa raggii CARAB kula shiray guriga eed.5aad. Eedeysanahaan markii intooda badan la xiray uu ka mid ahaa Guddi loo magacaabay inay odeyaasha la shirsan, intii aanu wax qabanna la xiray.-

EEDEYSANAHA 10AAD:

Eed/sha intooda badan Qiraal ayey ku bixiyeen inu eed.10aad ka mid ahaa Ururka. Eedeysanuhu waan la qayili jiray ayuu ku daayey warkii-sa, hase yeeshee wuxuu ka mid ahaa raggii wax ka qoray warqadda Eed.28aad. Eedeysanuhu wuxuu ka qayb galay shirarkii lagu guddoomiyey in haddii Jabane (Eed.2), raggii sheegay inuu badiyo magacyada dadka iyo shirkii lagu guddoomiyey in odeysasha lala shiro.-

.....

......../19.

EEDEYSANAHA 11AAD:

Shirarkii wuu ka qayb galay siduu Jabane (eed.2) sheegay. Eed.11aad inuu Ururka ka tirsanaa la nooma sheegin, wuxuuna qoraal ku bixiyey inuu shirar ka qayb galay iyo inuu akhriyey Joornaalka UFFO & SNM.-

EEDEYSANAHA 12AAD:

Ugu horreyntii Jabane (eed.2) ayaa sheegay, wuxuu ka qayb galay shirarkii, wuxuuna akhriyey Joornaalka UFFO, wuxuu sheegay inuu shirar ka qayb geli jiray, hase yeeshee la sooonin ujeedooyin ka hooseeyey. Ragga kale waxba noogama sheegin. Wuxuu ahaa ninkani Beeraley, wuxuu yiri waqti ma haysaninba, wixii lagu sheekaysanaayey wax dareen ah ima gelinin,. Raggan markii la xiray wuxuu ka mid ahaa raggii loo diray in ay Madaxda Gobolka ka arkaan arrinta inamada.-

EEDEYSANAHA:13AAD.

Debadda ayuu wax ku soo bartay, Jabane (eed.2) ayaa Qiraalkiisa ku daray. Qiraalada eedeysanayaashu bixiyeenna wey ku sheegeen, wuxuu ka qayb galay shirarkii guriga eed.4aad oo uu la deggenaa. Wuxuu caddeeyey inuu akhristey UFFO & SNM, wuxuu shirkooda ka weydiiyey Odeyaashu maxay yiraahdeen: waxaa loogu jawaabay INAMO AFKOODA HAYSAN WAAYEY MA GALNO ARRIMAHOODA AYEY ODEYAASHU YIRAAHDEEN, wuxuuna yiri WAA CRIMINALS odeyaasha ee aan laynno Madaxda Gobolka, arrintaasi waxaa noo sheegay eed.20aad Baashe Cabdi Yuusuf. Eedeysanuhu wuxuu sheegay inuusan ra'yi ku darsan jirin lugna ku lahayn, hase yeeshee uu akhristay Joornaaladii gurigiisa la keenay.-

EEDEYSANAHA 14AAD:

Jabane (eed.2) wuxuu ku daray Qiraalkiisa, eedeysanayaal dhawr ahina caddeeyeen inuu eed/hani ka mid ahaa Ururka RUDM. Eedeysanuhu wuxuu sheegay inuu tegi jiray Eed.13aad oo Takhtar u ahaa, asaga oo wadnaha xanuun ka hayey awgeed, Eed.14aad ma tegin shirka Waxdada.-

EEDEYSANAHA 15AAD:

Wuxuu qoraal ku caddeeyey eed.2aad inuu ka qayb galay shirkii Waxdada iyo fadhigii Guryasamo, gurigа eed.6aad & 8aad ku akhriyey Joornaal UFFO, asna waa qiraal.-

EEDEYSANAHA 16AAD:

Waxaa qiraal ku caddeeyey eed.2AAD guriga eed.5aad uu ka qayb geli jiray shirarka, midna waxba kama sheegin. Gurigiisa waxaa laga soo helay mar la fatishay bistoolad Makarof ah. Ma jirto cid wax ka sheegayaa inuu eray ka yiri ama ra'yi ka geystay shirarkaas.-

../..

......../20.

EEDEYSANAHA 17AAD:
Jabane (eed.2) wuu caddeeyey inuu shirarkii oo dhan ka qayb galay, eedeysanahani kaallin muuqata markaan ka weynnay inuu ka jiro ayaan qabashadiisa dib u dhigannay . Wax ra'yi kama geysan fadhiyada. Waxay wada shireen Eed.20aad. Rag ilaa 13 gaarayaa waxay qiraal ku bixiyeen inuu Ururka ka mid ahaa, kana qayb galay shirarka, anaga oo qabashada la sugaynaa ayaa waxa la qarxiyey guriga Kaaliyaha 1aad ee X.H.K.S. G/W/G oo lagu tuurey BOMBO. Mar labaad waxa guri uu degen yahay nin ganacsade ah oo la yiraahdo TINDHEER lagu tuurey BOMBO, isla maalmahaas lagu tuuray 2 Bombo guriga Taliyaha Qaybta 26aad XDS, hase yeeshee aan qarxin. Warqado ayaa lagu daadiyey Xafiiska Socdaalka, Guulwadayaasha iyo meelo kale, waxaana warqadahaas ku qornaa "GUUSHA SNM AYAA LEH, GEERIDANA AFWEYNE" Xuuraanku wuxuu noo sheegay in raggaasi Ururka ah qaybta aan la xirin ay ka danbeeyaan qaraxyadaas. Eedeysanuhu 9.12.81 ilaa 14.12.81 baxsad ayuu ahaa, wuxuuna socod uga jiray Hargeysa/ Berbera/Hargeysa, kadibna waan qabannay. Markaan qabannay ayaan toos wax uga weydiinay Bombooyinka wuxuuna qirtay inuu qaybintooda iyo abaabulkooda uu ka danbeeyo, go'aanna ay sidaas ku gaareen asaga iyo eedeysanayaasha 20, 24 & 25 oo ay wadajir uga shireen. Shirkaasi oo ay ku qaateen Baar Hargeysa, guriga Eed.4aad iyo H.Q. agtiisa, ujeedadoodna ay ahayd in aanay wax dilin, hase yeeshee ay argagax geliyaan ciddii ka danbaysay xarigga saaxibadood, kadib markii waan-waantii soconweysay.-----------
Eed.17aad wuxuu sheegay inuu la kulmay Eed.27aad oo ay ILMA-ADEER yihiin ahna Madaxda Waaxda Sancada ee Qaybta 26aad XDS, waxaan ka codsadey ayuu yiri inuu ii keeno ilaa 10 (toban) xabbo oo waxyaabaha qarxa, si beer uu saaxiibkii oo xidhani leeyahay (eed.12) oo ay bahalo cunaan si uu ugu DIDIYO. Wuxuu eed.27aad ii sheegay ayuu yiri in ay tahay waxaan suurtoobi karin nin asaga oo kale ahna wax la weydiisto aysan ahayn. Mar labaad ayaan weydiiyey ayuu yiri, waanu iigu xanaaqay. Mar seddaxaadkii ayaan ku calaacalay ayuu yiri, wuxuuna iigu keenay markaas dambe gurigeyga, wuxuuna igu yiri eed.27aad, HA KORDHISANIN DHIBAATOOYINKA haddaadan beer ku isticmaalayn. Waxaan dhigay ayuu yiri guriga eed.24aad lana kulmay isla eed/ha gurigiisa uu dhigay kan 25aad, 20aad & 26aad. Waxaan qarxiyey ayuu yiri 9kii Diisambar 1981 guriga Kaaliyaha 1aad ee X.H.K.S. Gobolka W.G., eed. 20aad waxaan u xilsaarey ayuu yiri guriga Taliyaha Qaybta 26aad XDS,

.../..

........./21.-

Eed.24aad inuu qarxiyo sidoo kale guriga ninka TINDHEER la yiraahdo, ciddii raacday nooma sheegin, haso yeeshee asaga ayaa isa sheegay. Waanay wada fuleen ayuu yiri qorshihii oo dhan.-

EEDEYSANAHA 18AAD:

Jabane (eed.2) ayaa markii hore sheegay. Marna eed.20aad ayaa Qiraal ku bixiyey. Guriga eed.18aad waxaa lagu guddoonsaday in HAB GOBOL la isku habeeyo oo looga hortago Dowladda. Shirkii arooska wuu ka qayb galay. Jariidada SNM nin Jidda ka yimid koobi uu sitay ayaan mar akhristay ayuu yiri. Shirka gurigiisa lagu qabtay wuu dafiray iyo ka guriga Tr.Aadan (eed.4).-

EEDEYSANAHA 19AAD:

Marka hore Jabane ayaa Qiraalkiisii ku daray, wuxuuna guriga kula jiray eed.4aad, kana qayb galay shirkii Guryasamo ee arooskii eed. 1aad. Wuxuu guri kula jiray Eed.4aad laba bilood oo dambe mooyane. Kama uu qayb gelin shirka Waxdada Ururkii Samafalka wuu ka qayb galay Qiraalna wuu ku bixiyey.-

EEDEYSANAHA 20AAD:

Anaga oo raacayna qiraalka eed.2aad bixiyey, markii hore waan weyn-nay, waxanaan ka dirnnay BAADI GOOB. Markaan soo qabannay, caddeyn iyo qiraal ayuu ku bixiyey inuu ka mid ahaa Ururka, kana qayb galay dooddii, isla markaasna akhristey Joornaalada oo dhan.------------- Wuxuu sheegay in muddadii la xiray eedeysanayaasha kale ay wada shi reen eed/sha 24 iyo 25aad ay xoogna ula wada xiriireen eed.17aad oo ay saaxiibo ahaayeen, guriga eed.4aad ay ku kulmi jireen.-------- Wuxuu noo sheegay inuu maallin raacay baabuur uu watay eed.17aad oo uu la socdey eed.24aad asaga oo gaarsiinaayey meel uu guri ka dhi-sanaayey. Wuxu yiri in eed.17 ku yiri, war inamadii xirnaa wax ma u qabannaa, annagaa debadda joognaa, anna waxaan ku iri anigu idin kulama jiro, arrinta uu leeyahay kulama jiro waxay ahayd ayuu yiri go'aankii ugu danbeeyey ee uu soo jeediyey eed.13aad ee ahaa in Ma-daxda Gobolka la laayo, waxaa arrintaasi ku raacay ayuu yiri eed.24°.-

EEDEYSANAYAASHA 21, 22 & 23AAD:

Waxay ahaayeen Waxdada. Eed.21aad wuxuu ka qayb galay fadhigii RUDM iyo Waxdaddu yeelatay. Eed.1aad ayaa shirkaasi soo qaban qaabiyey, waxaana shirka hore ka soo qayb galay eed.21 & 23aad, waxayna markii dambe la xiriireen eed.22aad oo fadhiga dambe qaban qaabiyey. Sed-

.../...

............/22.-

dexduba caddeymo iyo qiraallo ayoy ku bixiyeen, waxaana fadhiyadaa la yeeshay ku saabsanaayeen: ISBARASHO, WADA SHAQAYN & AFKAAR IS-DHAAFASHO.-

EEDEYSANAHA 24AAD:

Jabane (eed.2) ayaa ugu horreyntii sheegay oo caddeeyey inuu ka mid ahaa Ururka. Wax hadal ah ama ficil ah lama yeelan. Asaga iyo eed.25aad kadib markuu caddeeyey eed.17aad inuu u xilsaaray qarxinta guriga TINDHEER, waxaan weydiinnay eed/sha 17, 20 & 25aad, wuxuu na yiri kuwan midna ma aqaanno. Kadibna waan u keenay oo soo horjoojinnay, wuxuuna yiri kuwan waxaan u kala aqaannaa JOHNY, BAASHE-YARE IYO MACALLIN CUSMAAN, siday u kala horreeyaan, wuxuu yiri kadib, Xarunta Gobolka agtiisa ayaan iska raacnay aniga & eed.20 iyo kan 17°, waxaan la soconnay baabuurka eed.17aad, wuxuuna na weydiiyey oo uu yiri INAMADII XIRNAA WAX MA U QABANNA, BAMBOOYIN MA ISTICMAALNAA, Baashe Cabdi Eed.20aad ayaa yiri annaga shuqul kuma lihi. Maalmo dabadeed, anigoo maallintii hore diiday, ayaan ogolaaday. Eed.17aad wuxuu noo qaybiyey Bombooyin, waxaa la ii xilsaaray inaan qarxiyo guriga Guryasamo ku yaal ee uu leeyahy TINDHEER, waxaana aniga gurigaasi ila fuliyey qarxintiisa eed.25aad oo Bombada gacantiisa ku tuuray. Isla hawshaas waxaa qarxiyey guriga Kaaliyaha Koowaad eed.17 & 26aad oo la socday. Guriga Taliyaha Qaybta 26aad XDS, waxaa loo xilsaaray eed.20aad, hase yeeshee habeenimadii ballanku ahaa inuu qarxiyo waa laga maqli waayey magaalada wax qarax ah. Subaxnimadii waxaannu ogaannay in guriga Taliyaha Qaybta 26aad laga helay bombo dheeraad ah, marka loo eego bombooyinkii aan haysannay. Kafib waxaan qabsannay eed.20aad Baashe oo xilkaas lahaa, waxaanan weydiinnay maxay bombooyinku u qarxi-waayeen iyo bombada dheeraad ah, wuxuu nagu yiri bombada dheeraad ah waxaa ii dhiibay eed.17aad, mar haddii aan tuurayna anigu waajibkayga waan gutay. Guriga Tindheer darbigiisu wuxuu ahaa 1,80 metir, waxaana ku tuuray bombada Maxamed Macallin Cusmaan ah, kadibna Maxamed gurigiisii ayuu u lugeeyey, aniguna waxaan soo raacay Baska.-

EEDEYSANAHA 25aad:

Wuxuu sheegay in ay aqoon ka shexeysay raggan kale, isla markaasna ay kulmi jireen, hase yeeshee waa uu dafirey inuu asagu bombadaasi wax ka ogaa, shaqona ku lahayn arrintaasi, hase yeeshee wuxuu noo sheegay in asaga iyo eed.24aad ay israaceen oo ay u soo qaadeen eed.17

../..

........../23.-

mushaharkiisii oo ay u geeyeen xaaskiisa oo ka shaqeysa Xafiiska Xanshuuraha Berriga ee Hargeysa, wuxuuna noo sheegay in xaaska eed. 17aad ay u sheegaty in ninkeedu u xiran yahay Bombooyinka. Eed.17aad markaan raadinaynnay waxaan ku doonaynnay magaciisa ah Axmed Maxamed Madar, hase yeeshee magac kale ayaan helnnay oo aanan hadda xusuus-nayn oo uu Dowladda ugu shaqeeyo kuna mushahar qaato.-

EEDEYSANAHA 26AAD:

Eed.24aad wuxuu qiraalkiisa ku sheegay in eed.17aad yiri waxaa i raacaya eed.26aad. Eed.17aad cid la socotay ma sheegin. Sidoo kale Eedeysanahani wuu dafiray in ay arrintaasi wax ka jiraan.-

EEDEYSANAHA 27AAD:

Eed.24aad ayaa noo sheegay in eed.17aad ku yiri bombooyinka waxaan ka soo qaadi doonaa INA XAASHI MADAR, wuxuuna yiri eed.24aad waxaan ogaaday in ninkaasi yahay G/Dhexe Ismaaciil oo Ilma adeerna ay yihiin eed.17. Eedaysanuhu wuu dafiray waxna kama sheegin bombooyinkaasi, isla markaasna wuxuu caddeeyey in aysan bombada weerarku asaga haw-shiisa hoos iman, wuxuuna sheegay inuu maallin keliya rawixiyey eed. 17aad xaaskiisa.-

EEDEYSANAHA 28AAD:

Urur kuma jiro. Waxaa xirhaa eed.1aad oo INA-ADEERKIIS AH, waxaannu eedeysanahani la xiriiray Jaalle Jaamac Gaas, warqadda saaxiibadii ayaa qoray, asaguna wuu TEEB GAREEYEY, waxaannu u dhiibay Jaamac Gaas oo Xamar tegaaya. Warqadda waxaa ku qornaa arrimo looga been sheegaa-yo dacwadda la baarayey, taasi oo ay ku qoreen in Madaxda Gobolku ka dambeyso arrinta Joornaalka UFFO oo ay soo direen Qurmis.-

IM/QAREEN ISMAACIIL & M/3AAD:

S. Maxaad ku xaqiijisay jiritaanka Ururka lagu eedeynaayo eed.1aad?

J. Baaristayda bilawgeedi eed.2aad waraysiga aan la yeellannay wuxuu noo sheegay inuu jiro Ururka RUDM iyo in eed.1aad uu ku jiro.

S. Ma hesheen qalabkii iyo Xafiisyada Ururka aad sheegtay ?

J. Maannu helin qalab iyo Xafiisyo Ururku uu ku shaqeeyo.

S. Ma jiraan wax aad ku caddeyn karto Ururka oo aan ahayn warka Eed.2?

J. Waxaan saldhig ugu dhignay laba arrimood: (1) Warbixinta Eed.2aad, iyo (2) Joornaalka UFFO.

S. Sida qod.199 XHCS sheegaayo warbixin eedeysane kan kale ee la eeday san wax kaga sheegaayo ay marag noqoneyso marka la helo marag kale oo lagu kaabo arrintaasi, ma hesheen cid kale oo caddeynaysa?

J. Ma haynno cid kale oo caddeynaysa.

.. ..

............/24.

S. Makiinadda maxaa soo geliyey?

J. Waxaa soo geliyey eed.1aad ayaa noo sheegay in makiinad Xafiis-kiisa taala uu ku qoray Joornaalka, asaga ayaana geeyey Xafiiska oo noo sheegay inay tan tahay makiinadii uu ku qoray, kadib mar-kaan xarfaha makiinadda iyo farta ku qoran jariidada isku eeg-nay waxba uma dhexeeyaan.

S. Sida uu qoraayo qod.161 XHCS, ma istiomaasheen KHABIIR garaacis-ta makiinadda aqoon u leh?

J. Maya.

S. Warqaddan (TUSID) qoraalka ku qoran ma makiinadda Pepsi Cola mise ku kale?

J. Haddaan makiinadda kale u eego ma sheegi karo.

S. Cabdi Laangare hadda ka hor Maxkamadda ma la keenay?

J. Waan maqlay in ayada oo dagaal cadow lagula jiro inuu gacan sii-yey kadibna Maxkamad la saaray.

S. Cabdi Laangare meel uu jiro ma ka warhaysaa?

J. Maya horeba aqoon ugume lahayn.

S. Ma martay Cabdi Laangare in marag looga baahan yahay awgeed aan-nu ka bixin Waddanka?

J. Maya maan amrin.

S. Maxkamad ma weydiisatay joogista Cabdi Laangare oo marag noqon doona?

J. Maya maan weydiisan.

S. Aadan Cali Guhaad ma la kullantay, mana ogtahay inuu wax ka keenay Joornaalka.

J. Aadan lamaan kulmin, hase yeeshee Cabdi Laangare wuxuu ii shee-gay inuu la fariistay nin la yiraahdo BARE GEEYE, eed.2aad iyo rag kale iyo inuu isla gurigé eed.2aad ka helay Joornaalka UFFO.

S. Ma weydiisay Cabdi Laangare in loo diray Joornaalka?

J. Maya ma hubo in loo diray iyo in kale, hase yeeshee wuxuu ii sheegay in nin la yiraahdo Faysal Cali Waraabe uu kula dardaar-may inuu la shaqeeyo Dowladda.

S. Haddii qalabkii dembi muujinta la waayo ma jiraa dembi mise ma jiro?

J. Ma aanan helin qalabka dembi muujinta ah.

S. Ma jiraa dembi dhacay?

J. Waa jirtaa.

.../..

......../25.

S. Haddaba ma hesheen dembigaas loo haysto wax marag ah oo ka baxsan iyaga?

J. Qiraalkooda maahee wax kale uma hayno.

S. Qirsalka eedeysanayaasha inaanu ku fileyn caddeynta dembiga ma
la socotaa?

J. Haa waan la socodaa sharciyan.

S. Eedeysanaha 3aad muxuu kaga duwan yahay kan 1aad & 2aad?

J. Waxba kagama duwana.

S. Qoraalka gurigiisa laga soo qaaday maxaad ka leedahay, mase
amar Maxkamadeed ma u hayseen baarista guriga?

J. Maya amar Maxkamadeed ma arkin, ciidanka baarayna kama mid ahayn
anigu mana sheegi karo inuu raalli ka ahaa iyo in kale.

S. Eed.23aad wuxuu ka duwan yahay kuwii hore ee ka qayb galka ahaa?

J. Waxba kagama duwan, 8aadna isna waxba kagama duwana, sidoo kale
Aadan Warsame Nuur.

S. Eed.28aad ma kuu yiri waxaan doonayaa inaan la hadlo Wasiir Ku-
xigeen?

J. Ma xusuusto..

S. Ma weydiisay inuu Wasiir Ku-xigeenku yiri qoraal ka soo dhig?

J. Sida uu ii sheegay eed.28aad.

S. Ma hubiseen in Wasiir Ku-xigeenku sidaas yiri?

J. Ma hubin sidaasi inay jirto.

S. Ma kuula muuqatay inay tahay cabasho loo qortay Madax, maxayse
kuula muuqatay?

J. Maya cabasho uma qaadan ee waxy iila muuqatay cambaareyn Madax
iyo been ka sheegid.

S. Maxaad ku diiday inaad rumeysato in qoraalka UFFO Kulmis soo
saartay maadaama uu Cabdi Laangaro oo cadow kalkaal ahi ka soo
fushay arrintu?

J. Waa mid meesha ku jirta.

S. Baaris ma ku haboonayd iyo hubsiimo?

J. Haa laakin kuma arag wax cilad ah oo uu dadweynaha kaga duwan
yahay.

S. Ma ku yiri eed.28aad rag baa warqadda qoray?

J. Haa waa ii sheegay.

S. Maxaa loogu eedeyay Afmiinshaarnimo?

J. Sababtu waxay ahayd isaga ayaa dan gaar ah ka lahaa.-

.../..

........../26.

S. Inuu wax qoro iyo in kale ma ka warqabtaa?

J. Maya.

S. Warqaddii ma la hayaa?

J. Ilaa iyo inta aan la socodo maya.

S. Warqadda iyo isagu ma is-arkeen?

J. Maya, waxaanu ku ogaanay raggii qoray iyo isaga oo keliya wax kalese looma hayo.-

IM/QAREEN XASAN SHEEKH & M/3AAD:

S. Maxkamadda u sheeg eed.9aad waxa uu ka shaqeeye maadama aad muddo dheer baareysay?

J. Xanaanada Xoolaha ayuu ka shaqeeyay, fasax ayuu ku yimid Hargeysa si uu u guursado, waana guursaday.

S. Wax ma ka weydiiseen qoraaladda UFFO & SNM?

J. Akhriska labada Joornaal wuu ka qayb qaatay.

S. Caddeynta eed.2aad oo keliya miyay ku saleysan tahay eeddu?

J. Haa waa sidaas.

S. Ma sababta Guddigii la yiri Dowladda hala hadasho baa lagu xiray ?

J. Guddiga ku jirideedu dembi ma aha, lama wada xirina Guddiga intii ahayd.

S. Dhibaato ma u geysateen inuu xirnaa, mase la socotaa inuu Dastuurku mam-nuucaayo ciqaabta jirka.

J. Haa waa mam-nuuc dilistu, dhibaatada la gaarsiiyeyna lama socdo.

S. Muxuu ku sugnaa markaad qabaneyseen & waxa uu ka shaqeynaayey?

J. Bare ayuu ahaa wuu ka ruqseystay, waxbana kama qabaneynin Har/ysa.

S. Wax argagaxisnimo ah ma ku kacay, nooma qiran ayaa tiri.

J. Eed.2aad ayaa saldhig u ah, waxna nooma qiran.

S. Wakhtiga aad qabateen xageebuu joogay?

J. Xerada Guulwadayaasha oo ay ku xiran yihiin eed.1aad ayey u dhaceen iyagoo kula jirana waa lagu qabtay.

S. Wax caddaan ma u hayseen?

J. Caddeyn iyo Qiraal buu bixiyey.

S. Waxaa ii qoran ma bixin qiraal ma jirtaa?

J. Waa dhici kartaa.

S. Ma jirtaa in eed.10aad nabaro kuu sheegtay?

J. Ma xusuusto laakin 20.11.81 aniga amray in katiinad lagu xiro.

../...

......../27.

QAREEN XASAN: Waxaan Maxkamadda ka codsanayaa iney aragto oogada eed.10aad, si caddaaladda loo daryeelo, waayo waxaanu haynaa "CAD HILIB AH" oo jirkiisa ka go'ay.-

DADWEYNE U DOODE: Ma ogolin arrintan haddii aannu caddeynin eedeysanuhu cid u geystay dhibaatada. Asaga ayaa xor u ah jirkiisa, arritan oo sideeba XASAASI AHAYD ama BEER LA-XAWSI AH, yaanan Maxkamadda ogolaanin.-

QAREEN XASAN: Sida qod.150 XHCS uu sheegaayo Qiraal lagu bixiyey TAHDIID iyo wax la mid ah, ballan qaad iyo Lacag waa waxba kama jiraan. Jaalle Guddoomiye, caddeynta ka weyn inaan keenno JIRKIISA CADIHII KA GO'AY IYO NABARADII WAA MAXAY? Maxkamaddu ha noo ogolaato. Eedeysanaha Difaaciisa Dowladda ayaa ii magacawday.

MAXKAMADDU: Iyadoo dhegeysatay dooddii dhinacyada, waxay garatay in aan Maxkamadda gudaheeda lagu qaabinin eedeysanaha, lagana ogolanin codsiga Qareenka, balse ay Maxkamaddu meel u gooni ah ay ku eegto haddii ay u aragto in ay lagama maarmaan tahay caddaaladda darteed.

QAREEN XASAN & M/3AAD:

S. Ma la kulanteen qoraal lagu magacaabay Xubno, Madax iyo Jagooyin uu kala leeyahay Ururka, ha ahaado qarsoosi mise caadi?

J. Maya maan helin qoraalkaasi.-

IM/ QAREEN CUSMAAN & M/3AAD:

S. Maxaad ku ogaatay shirkaasi caynka ay ahaayeen? Wax lagu tilmaamo Urur maxaad ku ogaatay?

MAXKAMADDU: SU'AASHAAS HORE AYAA LOO WEYDIIYEY, Su'aal kale weydiy.

S. Waxaad warqaddan iga tustaa meesha uu ku qoran yahay magaca eed.13?

J. Warqaddan waxba kamaan sheegin ee Qiraalka eed.2aad ayuu ahaakii wax ka sheegay eed.13aad.

S. Maxaad uga jeedday dhawaan ayuu Waddanka soo galay eed.13?

J. Inuu Debadda ka yimid oo waqti aan fogayn uu yimid, mase xusuusto waqtigii uu yimid.

S. Maxaa caddeyn ah ee aad ku haysaa?

J. Caddeyn iyo Qiraal Garsoore hortiisa uu ka bixiyey, wuxuuna akhriyey Joornaalada UFFO & SNM.

S. Ma sheegi kartaa meen aan gurigiisa ahayn ee uu fariistay?

J. Wuxuu fariistay Guriga eed.4aad ee uu la degnaa.-

../..

......../23.

S. Shirku ma shir caadi ah ayuu ahaa miso qayilaad la wada fadhi-
yo?

J. Shir caadi ah ma sheegin, hase yeeshee qayilaad Joornaal lagu akhrisanaayo, xanta lagu kala qaadanayo war la isugu sheegaayo ayey ahayd.

S. Waqtigeebuu ahaa shirka uu ka yiri eed.13 wax hala laayo?

J. Intii u dhexaysay 4tii ilaa 19.12.81 ayey ahayd.

S. Goormaa la xiray eed.13aad?

J. Waxaa la soo xiray 4.12.1981.

S. Ma intuu xirnaabuu hadalkaasi yiri?

J. Maya taariikhda kale ayaan ku khaldamay, ninka shirka wax nooga sheegay ayaa taariikhdaas baafis ku jiray.

S. Ma jirtaa wax dhibaato ah oo loo geystay eed.13aad?

J. Ma jirto in wax loo geystay ogaalkayga.

S. Eed.18aad sideebaad ku ogaatay, ma jirtaase inuu Ururka ka mid ahaa, cid idiin sheegtay oo marag ah?

J. Eed.2aad oo keliya ayaa noo sheegay, wax marag ah umanaan cuska-
nin.

S. Maxaad ku caddeyneysa in eed.18aad markaad lahayd nin Debadda ka yimid ayaa Huteel ku tusay Jariidadda SNM oo uu akhristay?

J. Xataa in ay jirto ma ogin ee asaga ayuunbaa noo sheegay.

S. Maxaad ku sugi weyday ama aad u xaqiiqsan weyday inuu noqon karo marag lagama maarmaan ah Cabdi Laangare?

J. <u>XEER ILAALIYE "DOOD AYAAN KA QABAA</u>. Su'aashaas hore ayaa looga jawaabay.

S. Ma jiraan wax aad ku hayso eed.13 & 18aad oo ka duwan qiraalka eed.2aad?

J. Ma hayo.

<u>IM/ QAREEN BASHIIR CARTA & M/3AAD:</u>

S. Mar haddii la waayey habkii Urur, Qalab I.W.M., maxay ku eedey-
san yihiin eedeysanayaasha aan Qareenka u ahay (12, 19, 21 iyo 22aad)?

J. Qalab ayaanan helin.

S. Wax caddeyn ah ma u haydaa eed/shan aan difaacayo oo <u>PROVA AH</u> oo aan ahayn Qiraalka Eed.2aad?

J. Maya uma hayo.

S. Waxdada oo aan dhowr jeer maqlaayey hadda, maxaad uga deeddaa, inkastoo aysan ku jirin eedda?

../..

............/29.

J. Haddii aysan eedda ku jirin, maxaad iga weydiin.

IN/QAREEN FAYSAL XAAJI & M/3AAD:

S. Imisa warbixinood ayaad ka qorteen eed.2aad?

J. Ilaa 5 caddeymood ayaan ka qornay.

S. Teebaad saldhig uga dhigateen baaristiina 5taas warbixinood?

J. Tii ugu horreysay ee aan annaku ka qornay ayaan saldhig uga dhigannay.

S. Ragga ku qoran warbixintaas aad saldhigga ka dhigteen ma wada xirteen?

J. Maya, maannu xirin.

S. Ma sheegtay wax ka geddisan warbixinta eed.2aad oo aad ku soo xirteen ma jiraan?

J. Warbixinta eed.2aad ayaan u cuskannay.

S. Maxaad u soo xiri weyday kuwan kale ee liiska ku jira?

XEER ILAALIYE: DOOD AYAAN KA QABAA SU'AASHAN:

Qab-qabashada eedeysanayaasha, saldhig ayey u ahayd ayuu yiri. Maraggu wuxuu sheegay in ay soo qabteen inta goobood ee qof waliba ka qaatay meesha ay ku soo qabteen. In badan ayuu maraggu taagnaa, Jaalle Guddoomiye waan iska hortaagayaa su'aashan oo waa ka jawaabay maraggu.

QAREEN FAYSAL: Jawaab celin:

Maxkamadda sharafta leh, in badan ayuu maraggu ku celceliyey Maxkamadda horteeda in saldhigga dacwad-du uu ahaa Qiraalka Eed.2aad, gaar ahaan su'aalaha uu weydiiyey Qareen Ismaaciil. Maraggu ayuu ka war-wareegin jawaabta ee Maxkamadda ha ka sheego.

M A X K A M A D D U:

Markay dhegeysatay su'aasha la weydiyey Maraggu, doodii uu soo jeediyey Xeer Ilaaliyaha iyo jawaab celintii Qareen Faysal, waxay amreysaa markhaatiga inuu ka jawaabo su'aasha Qareenka ee ah: HADDII AAD RAACDEEN QIRAALKA EED.2AAD MAXAA DADKA UU SHEEGAY LOO KALA REEBAY?

MARAGGA:

J. Qabashadu anigu igama soo fusho, warka Jabane (eed.2aad) mooyee ninkii war kale loo haynin maannu qabanin.-

.../..

......../30.

S. Urur in la abaabulay, lagana abaabulay Arooskii Eed.1aad, haddaan ku iraahdo ma hagaagsana? Maxaad ka qabtaa?

J. Maan odhanin halkaas ayaa Urur laga abaabulay, waxaan markii hore idhi "HALKAA WAXA LAGA ABAABULAY ARRIMO LA XIRIIRA URURKA.

S. Goormaa ayaa la abaabulay Ururkaan aad sheegayso?

J. Ururka sida Jabane sheegay (eed.2) waxaa la abaabulay 1977kii.

S. Ma kuu sheegay cidda abaabushay?

J. Eed.2aad iima uusan sheegin cidda abaabushay. Rag aannu sheegin ayaa abaabulay.

S. Eed.1, 2 & 3aad, waxaad ku soo eedeyseen in ay Urur abaabuleen? Maxaad ugu eedeyseen haddii aannu cidna sheegin?

J. Sannadkii 1977kii ayaa la abaabulay, cidda abaabusha iima sheegin.

S. Eedda waxaa ku qoran in dembigu dhacay 6dii Bilod ee ugu danbeeyey sannadka 1981kii, ma sheegi kartaa inta shir ee ay isugu yimaadeen?

J. Cidina nooma sheegin tirada shirarka.

S. Guriga eed.5aad imisa shirbaa lagu yeeshay?

J. 3 jeer ayaa lagu shiray.

S. Guriga eed.2aad imisa jeer ayaa lagu shiray?

J. Ma xusuusto.

S. Guriga eed.4aad imisa shirbaa lagu yeeshay?

J. Ma xusuusto.

S. Eed.2aad ma ku ogaatay baaristaadii inuu ka tirsanaa Guddiga Samafalka?

J. Kumaan ogaanin inuu ka tirsanaa.

S. Kulamada aad sheegtay in ay yeesheen Eed/shan Maxkamadda ma u sheegi kartaa, waxa Midnimada Ummadda wax u dhimaaya oo loo yeelay?

J. Haa. Kulan lagu yeeshay guriga eed.18aad, waxaa la isla soo qaaday sida ay ugu habaynayaan Ururka: "MA HAB QABIIL, HAB GOBOL MISE HAB QARAMEED.

S. Ma sheegi kartaa wax lagu wiiqay awoodda Dowladda oo ay ku kaceen eed/shu?

J. Guri Guryasamo ah shir ay ku yeesheen, waxaa go'aan ku gaareen in ay Guddi Samafal ah sameystaan, hase yeeshee Dowladdu aanay ogayn la yeeshaan dadweynaha

../..

........./31.

S. Yaa kuu caddeeyey inay sidaas yeeleen?

J. Caddeynta Jabane (eed.2aad).

S. Wax tillaabo ah oo awoodda Dowladda ku wiiqayaan ma qaadeen?

J. In ay sameeyeen Guddi Samafal ah, uruuriyeen daawooyin, lacago, qalab, xeaqeen, nidaamiyeen Isbitaalka Hargeysa, gaadhna ka qabteen. Maamulka Gobolkuna ma ogayn Samafalkaas.

S. Ma hubtaa in Maamulka Gobolku oggolaanin Ururka Samafalka?

J. Mar dambe ayaa loo oggolaaday.

S. Inuu eed.2aad muddo 5 cisho ah qatanaa isla markaana aad bistoolad ku hadadeen?

J. Ma ogi taas, meel aanan joogin waxba isaga lagama qorin.

S. Xiriirka dadweynaha iyo iyaga ma wiiqayaa awoodda Dowladda?

J. Taasi waxay ku tuseysaa Madax banaanidooda iyadoo Gobolka ogeyn.

S. Cadadka SNM ayaad ku soo qabateen?

J. Cidna kuma aanan soo qabanin, edd/shan ayaanu tuseynay in ay la mid tahay tii akhristeen iyo in kale.

S. Sida aad sheegteen Eed.4aad fadhiyada kama qayb geli jirin, si kale marna ma loo sheegay wuxuu ka qayb galay?

J. Mar buu sheegay asagu inuu ka qayb galay shirarkaas lagu qaban jiray gurigiisa. Maxamed Sh.Xasan Taani wuxuu noo sheegay inuu mar ra'yi dhiibtay.

S. Ma jiraan cid kale oon ahayn kuwan la xiran oo wax ka sheegaysa?

J. Maya.

S. Ma la scootay markii guriga eed.5aad la baarayey?

J. Maya ee Cabdirashiid nin la yiyaahdo ayaa arrintaas baarista nooga qayb galay.

S. Eed.20aad inuu Ururka ka mid yahay ma caddeynta eed.2aad baa tixgeliseen?

J. Haa, inkastoo isna noo qirtay.

S. Ururka Waxdada & Samafalku wey ka jawaabi kari waayeen ujeedooyinkooda ayaa mar hore tiri. Iminkana waxaad leedahay waa Urur dhisan ma iskhilaafsan yihiin?

J. Haa wey is khilaafsan yihiin.

S. [illegible] ka baxsan [illegible] dambiyada oo dhan ma u haysaan?

J. Maya wax ka baxsan uma hayno.-

.../...

........../32.

<u>CODSI QAREEN XUSEEN BILE:</u>

Eedeysanayaasha 26, 27 & 28aad waxay EG-MADEEN INAAN KA DIFAACO dembiyada loo kala haysto ee Maxkamaddu ha iga aqbasho.

<u>MAXKAMADDU:</u>

Way aqbashay codsiga Qareenka.-

<u>IM/QAREEN XUSEEN BILE & M/3AAD:</u>

S. Ma kuu sheegay eed.2aad wakhtiga ay Shirarka qaban jireen?

J. Ma garan karo wakhtiyada, hase yeeshee wuxuu xusay eed.[illegible] qadad dabadeed.

S. Ma sheegi kartaa Xubnaha Ururka sida ay Hawlaha u kala qaabil-san yihiin cida Madaxda u ah, kharajkooda iyo tirada guud ahaan?

J. Maya midna ma garanaayo isna iima uusan sheegin.

S. Ma ka qayb galeen shirarka Cabdi Laangare iyo Aadan Waalli?

J. Cabdi Laangare ayaa maallin fadhiistay shir lagu qabtay guriga eed.2aad.

S. Aadan Cali Guhaad ma la fadhiistay marna?

J. Maalin ayuu la fariistay eed.9aad.

S. Aadan inuu baxsaday ma la socotaa xaalkiisu se waa sidee?

J. Waanu ka maqnayn Hargeysa markuu baxsaday, waan qaban lahayn waa eedeysane maqan hadda.

S. Cabdi Laangare ma qaban lahaydeen?

J. Maya wax xadgudub ah oo uu sameeyay ayaan jirin.

S. Shirarka uu ka qayb galay maxaa lagu qaban waayey?

J. Sababto waxay tahay isagoo hawl loo diray ka soo qabanaayey mar-kasta.

S. Cabdi Laangare ma ku yiri aniga ayaa soo qaaday Joornaalka UFFO?

J. Haa aniga ayaa soo saaray ayuu i yiri.

S. Hadduu yiri anigu ma soo qaadin maxaad ka qabtaa?

J. Anigu qoraal aan ka qoray ayaan hayaa.

S. Wax dibada ka ah eed/sha oo caddeynaya jiriteanka dembiga ma jira?

J. Maya.

S. Baaristiinii maxaad ugu ogaan weydeen?

J. In Jornaalka ay qoraan ayaga ayaa soo sheegay (eed.1/2aad).

S. Eed.6aad inta goor ee gurigiisa la fadhiistay ma garaneysa?

J. Maya ma garanaayo.

S. Labada shir ee Waxdada kee buu ka qayb galay?

.../...

........./33.

J. Kii dambe ayuu ka qayb galay.

S. Eed.14aad sida uu sheegay wadno xanuun ma leeyahay?

J. Haa intii xabsiga ku jiray dhowr jeer ayaanu kula kulanay.

S. Wax hadal ama ra'yi ah ma dhiiban jiray?

J. Maya.

S. Ma idin sheegay eed.16aad inuu bistooladda sabab gaar ah u iibsaday?

J. Wax caddeynaya in xadku sheega laga keenay ma jiro, noomana sheegin.

S. Ururka dembi Falada ah ayaa caddeynayaa?

J. Qiraalkooda ma ahaa wax kale uma hayno.

S. Ma ka warhaysaa in la ciqaabay eed.17aad?

J. Maya inta aan ogahay.

S. Guddigii madaxda la hadleysay soo ka mid muu ahayn?

J. Ma ogi inuu ka mid ahaa iyo in kale.

S. Ma dhutinaayey eed.17aad markii la soo xiray?

J. Ma dhutineynin.

S. Hadda ma dhutinayaa?

J. Ma ogi.

S. Wax kale oo lagu caddeynaayo bomboojinka ma jirean?

J. Hadalkooda ma-hee, wax kale ma jiraan.

S. Eed.24aad caddeyntiisa mooyee wax kale ma loo hayaa?

J. Maya.

S. Ma ciqaabteen isagana?

J. Ma ogi.

S. Eed.25aad caddeyntiisa ka baxsan isna ma u haysaan?

J. Maya qiraalkiisa mooyee wax kale looma hayo.

S. Eed.27aad ayaa isaga wax ka sheegaya?

J. Cidna wax kama sheegeyso isna waxba nooma qiran shegidii eed.17aad mooyee.

S. Labo magac miyuu leeyahay eed.17aad?

J. Waxaannu ku baafinay magaca Axmed Maxamuud Madar.

S. Goorma ayaad hesheen eed.17aad?

J. Berbera oo walaalkii uga dhoofinaayey markuu ka soo noqday.

<u>CODSI QAREEN FAYS XAAJI:</u>

Waxaan codsanayaa in eed.20aad in la eego jirkiisa Maxk.horteeda.

<u>DADWEYNE UU DOODE:</u> Haddii cidda dhibaatada sheegeysaa aysan caddeynin dhibaatada qofkii u geystay, iyaga ayaa

../..

........./34.

mas'uul ka ahaa. Haddii aysan dhibtaas la sheegaayo aysan caddeynin eed/sha & Qareenadu oo markaas loo ciqaabi doono cidda dhibka geystay. Hore waxaani wey u jireen oo Dad aan xilka ahayn ba suuqa la wareegaayey oo doonayaa inay Dowladda iyo Dadweynaha kala dilaan. Rabashadii Magaalada Hargeysa ka dhacdayna ka mid ayey ahayd arrinta. Sidaas darteed ha la diido sababahaas darteed in eed/sha jirkooda Maxkamadda horteeda laga eego, dacwaddanina halkeeda ha ka socoto.-

<u>IM/MAXKAMADDA & M/3AAD</u>:

S. Ed.26aad waxba kamaadan sheegin Xeer Ilaaliyahana waxba kaagama su'aalin, bal noo caddey sababta lagu xiray?

J. Eed.24aad ayaa sheegay inuu la socday eed/hani kan 17aad habeenkii la qaybinaayey bombooyinka.

S. Asaga maxaad ka qorteen?

J. Waxaa uu noo sheegay inuusan waxba ka ogeyn arrintaas. Eed.17 aad isna waxba kama sheegin.

S. Joornaalka SNM ma yahay kaad sheegtay in lagu akhristay guryaha eed/sha: 4, 5, 6 & 7aad?

J. Joornaalka SNM ee aanu hayno cidna laguma soo qaban ee waanu tuseynay keliya.

S. Magaca RUDM & UFFO ma hesheen [illegible]?

J. Eed/sha 1aad & 2aad.

S. Ma ogaateen in Xubnaha kale ee Ururku ogaayeen soo saarka UFFO iyo in kale?

J. Ma ogeyn soo saarkiisa, hase yeeshee in ay arkeen ayey noo sheegeen.

S. Joornaalka SNM halkee baad ka hesheen?

J. Ma ogi ee waxaa keenay G/Sare Cali Xuseen oo laga xiriiri kara.

<u>MARAGGA 4AAD MAXAMUUD AXMED WILI[illegible]</u>: Dhaar dabadee wuxuu yiri:

Waan aqaana eed.1aad (Maxamed Baaruud) wuxuuna ka shaqeyn jiray Wershadda Pepsi Cola. Makiinad ay Wershaddu lahayd ayaa maalin Ciidamada Nabadsugidduu iga qaadeen baaris dartee oo ay yiraahdeen waxay baaristaasi la xiriirtaa eed.1aad, kadibna makiinadii ayaan siiyey, Xafiiska ayaa lahaa.-

<u>IM/QAREEN ISMAACIIL & M/4AAD</u>:

S. Ayaa makiinadan ku sheqeyn jiray Xafiiskiina?

J. Wiil iyo gabar ayaa shaqadaas u-qornaa, Madaxdana u garaaci jiray.

../..

......../35.

S. Ma aragtay Baaruud oo galab ama habeen ku soo noqonaya Xafiiska?

J. Ma arag weli.

MARAGGA 5AAD CABDIRASHIID YAASIIN MAXAMED: Dhaar dabadeed wuxuu yiri: Qoraalkan ah GABAYGA DEYLEEDA AH, wuxuu ka mid ahaa waraaqooyin annu ka soo qaadnay guriga Eed.5aad baaris mar aanu ku sameynay. Gabeygaas aniga ayaa helay una gartay inuu yahay GABAY ka soo horjeeda danaha Qaranka, ku qoranna farta eed.5aad. Markii aan akhristay una gartay inuu dembi ahaa ayaan garaacay oo tan makiinada ku qoran aniga ayaa qoray. Markii arrintaas aanu wax ka weydiinay eed.5aad wuxuu noo sheegay inuu isagu qoray Gabeyga fartiisiina ay tahay, hase yeeshee uu nin kale ii yeerinaayey oo ka qortay, waxaana tiriyey buu yiri nin macallin ah oo Maxkamaddaani horey u xukuntay. Anagoo wadana baarista eed/sha, waxaanu ka soo helnay bistoolad MAKAAROOF ah oo nooca Ruushka guriga eed.16aad. Sida aanu u helnay bistooladu waxay ahayd in aanu weydiinay HUB ma haystaa, wuxuuna noogu jawaabay Bistooladdan aniga ayaa waa hore iibsaday, hase yeeshee wax sharci ah ilaa hadda uma haysto, sidaas ayaanu bistooladda kaga soo qaadnay.-

IM/QAREEN FAYSAL & M/5AAD:

S. Amarka baarista gurigiisa ayaa idin siiyay, mase haysateen awood baaris oo idiin oggolaatay Maxkamadda?

J. Madaxda oo keliya ayaa amar nagu siisay soo qabashadiisa iyo baarista gurigiisaba.

S. Ma idinla socoday eed.5aad marka aad gurigiisa baareyseen?

J. Haa waa nala socoday.

S. Gabeygan maxaad ku garatay inuu Qaranka ka soo horjeedo?

J. Magaca AF-WEYNE oo uu Madaxweynaha loo jeedo iyo noociyadiisa oo DEYLE ah.

IM/QAREEN XUSEEN BILE & M/5AAD:

S. Ma kuu sheegay eed.16aad inuu lacago Dowladeed xuduud ku sheega agteeda iyo meelo kale oo badan uu geeyo, isuguna ilaaliyo?

J. Maya iima sheegin.

MARAGGA 6AAD DHAMME CALI GAANI AXMED: Dhaar dabadeed wuxuu yiri: Anigu waxaan ka mid ahaa Guddiggii loo soo magacaabay baarista eed/SHAN, waa jirtay in aanu labo nuqul oo Joornaalka UFFO ah oo aanu Xeer Ilaalinta u soo gudbinay, waxayna kala ahaayeen mid markii aanu Magaaladda nimid ayey NSSka Hargeysa noo soo gudbiyeen, kan

.../..

........./36'

kalena baaristeydii aanu ku holnay, waxaanan ka soo qaaday guriga eed.3aad habeenkii aanu qabaneyney isaga laftiisa.-

IM/QAREEN ISMAACIIL & M/6AAD:

S. Saacadda aad guriga tegteen waa goorma?

J. 13,30 ee habeenimo ayey ahayd.

S. Wax fasax baaris ah ma haysateen?

J. Inkastoo aanan waraaqo u haysanin haddana waxaa noo fasaxaya Qod.58 XHCS.

MARAGGA 7AAD KHADRA ISMAACIIL NUUR: dhaar dabadeed waxay tiri: Qaybta 26ka Juun ayaan deggenahay. Habeen saq-dhexe ay tahay ayaa waxaa gurigeygii iigu yimid eed.2aad iyo ciidan la socoda, waxaana layga qaaday teeb uu ninkeygu lahaa. Eed.2aad iyo ninkeygu wey wada sheqeyn jireen, markaa haddii uu joogo iyo haddii uu maqanya-hayba ninkeyga eedeysanaha wakhtiguu doono ayuu teebka qaadan jirey inkastoo aanan teebka waxba ka aqoonin haddana qubkii ama galkii uu ku jiray teebku waa kan Maxkamadda hor yaal.-

MARAGGA 8AAD MUXUMED SHEEKH CABDULLAAHI JIBRIIL: dhaar dabadeed wuxuu yiri: Anigu waxaan ahay waardiyaha guriga Kaaliyaha 1aad ee Gobolka W/G. Habeen anigoo barandada hoosteeda fadhiya ayaa goor fiid ah qarax ka dhacay kobta sibidhka ka soo horreysa hoosada baabuurka loo hooyo, cid kale guriga gudahiisa iyo dibadiisaba ma joogin waan sara kacay oon eegay dhankii aan islahaa waxa qarxay ayaa laga soo tuuray cid waan arki waayay, kadibna waan baqay in aan dibada u baxo soona eego cid meelahaas mareysay, kadibna dib ayaan gurigii ugu noqoday waxaanan baqtiyey nalalkii gudaha iyo di-badaba ku yaallay, waxaanan u soo sheegay gabadh Saciido la yiraah-do oo uu Kaaliyuhu abti u yahay oo nagu dhoweyd markaas iyana tele-foon ayey u dirtay Ciidamada Nabadgelyada, waana la yimid lana baa-ray lana masawiray, wax dhibaato ah oo weyn ma ahayn FALIIDH sibir-kii gaaray oo keliya ayaa khasaarey u ahaa qaraxaas.-

MARAGGA 9AAD FAADUMO MAXAMED XIRSI: Dhaar dabadeed waxay tiri: Anigu waxaan degganahay guri ku yaal Waaxda Guryasamo, goor aan anigu jiifsaday ayey ahayd oo habeenimo, waxaan maqlay QARAX dha-cay waan soo kacay waxaanan la kulmay siigo iyo BOOR kacay baranda-dii gurigii aan degganaa, iridka dibada ayaan furay cid ma arag waxna ma maqal wax dhibaato ah haba yaraatee nama gaarsiinin qara-xaasi, dadka joogay gurigana waa ay hurdeen oo qololkooda ayey ku jireen.

.../...

........../37.

MARAGGA 10AAD L/X.MAXAMED AXMED DHOCRE: Dhaar dabadeed wuxuu yiri: Ururka 18aad ee Sancada ayaan Taliye ka ahay, waxayna hoos timaa- da Waaxda Sancada ee Qaybta 26aad XDS oo uu Madax ka yahay Eed.27 aad, anigoo jooga Xafiiskeyga ayaa ii yimid L/X.Cabdillaahi Shaa- rub iyo M/le la socoday, waxayna ii sheegeen in BOMBO ay sideen oo ay yiraahdeen waxaanu ka soo qaadnay guriga S/Guuto Gaani, bom badaas ammankeedu badankeeda waa ka baxsanaa. Bombadu waa tan wee rarka ee C.Q.Sida. Labo ammaan ayey leedahay weyna kala sareeyaan, midka biinka ah ee kala jeeda waa toosiyey. Bombadii waxaanu tus- nay Ciidanka Laanta Baarista Dembiyada, weyna masawirteen, kadibna daryeel darteed ayaan meel banaan ah ku qarxiyey, kadibna waxaan u imid S/Guuto Gaani iyo G/Dh.Ismaaciil Xaashi Madar oo ah eed.27 aad, anagoo la fadhina Taliyaha Qaybta 26aad ayaa mar labaad lana horkeenay bombo labaad oo laga soo helay isla guriga S/Guuto Gaani dibadiisa oo aan isna qarxin. Labada bombo waa isku nooc ah RBG oo ah Sancada Ruushka, sidii tii hore ayey ahayd, haddii meel kakan lagu tuuri lahaa wey qarxin lahayd, meesha ay ku dhacday waa meel jilicsan dhul bilow ma laha, rako ahaa ayey ahayd oo diisan, meel bombada banaanku ah ayaa la dhigay, sidii tii hore oo kale ayaa Ciidan L.B.D. loo diray hawlahoodiina ay ka qabsadeen, kadibna ani ga iyo eed.27aad waan soo qaadnay waanan qarxinay.-

MARAGGA 11AAD AXMED CALI JAAMAC: Dhaar dabadeed wuxuu yiri: Waxaan ahay Xisaabiyaha Wasaaradda Waxbarashada & Barbaarinta ee G/W/G, waan aqaanna eed.17aad waa nin macallin ah magaca aanu mu- shaharka ku siinno waxaa la yiraahda Cabdiraxmaan Cabdillaahi Ma- dar. Dugsiga Faarax Oomaar ayuu bare ka yahay intii uu xirnaa mar Bil mushaharkeed ayaan ugu dhiibay eed/sha 24 & 25aad oo isla soco da waanu isticmaalnaa inuu macalimiinta iskugu dhiibno mushaharka.

IM/QAREEN XUSEEN BILE & M/11AAD:

S. Goormaad musharka iskugu dhiibtaan, magaca kale inuu leeyahay ma ogaatay?

J. Magaca Dowladda uu u shaqeeyo ayaa sidaas ah, Foolyo baagada ayey ugu qoran tahay magacaasi, markii isgaarsiin la'aani dhac- do ayaa loyskugu dhiiba.

DADWEYNE U DOODE:

Xeer ilaalinta marageedii intaas ayey kaga egtahay, waxaanan Max- kamadda u soo jeedinayaa sida uu qabo Qod.155 XHCS in aan soo gud-

.../...

............/38.

biyo caddeyntii laga qoray marag Cabdi Muxumed (Laangare) oo hadda maqane ah, sababtoo ah in aan maragaas haba yaraatee la helin karin, samankana lala heli waayey in loo geeyo isaga.-

DOOD: QAREEN ISMAACIIL:

Qod.155 XHCS, habkiisa lama raacin, waxaanan Maxkamadda ka codsanayaa in laga diido codsiga Dadweyne u Doodaha si loo dhowro caddaalada.

DOOD: QAREEN XASAN SHEEKH:

BI-MASLAX CADDAALA, ayaan isu hor taagayaa codsiga Dadweyne U Doodaha, waxayna dhaawaceysaa Qod'obada 184 & 188 XHCS, Hab ka marag furka. Qod.155 XHCS wuxuu sheegayaa xiriir caddeyn ah(sida qofka dhintay & qof la waayey marka habkeeda loo maro waana mid MAJHUUL AH.

DOOD: QAREEN CISMAAN:

Qoraalka uu qoray Cabdi Laangare, sida uu qoraayo qod.197 XHCS, shakh-siyadiisa oo xun awgeed, marag looma qaadan karo haddii qoraalkiisu waafaqsan yahay nin loo ballan-qaaday ama lacag la siiyey mana noqon karo marag ha la diido codsiga Dadweyne u Doodaha.

DOOD: QAREEN XUSEEN BILE:

Sida uu qabo Qod.155 XHCS, mid dhintay (xubnaha A/B) ee isla qodobkaas ayaa diidaya, ma ka hadal adduunyo oo la diidaayo sidaas darteed ha la diido codsiga Dadweyne u Doodaha.-

JAWAAB: DADWEYNE U DOODE:

Sida uu sheegayo Qod.155 XHCS ee aan hore u cuskaday maraggaas waa la soo waayay. Arrinta ay ka doodayaan Qareenhaduna waa la sheegay inuu ITOOBIYA u baxsaday si aanu maragga u furin, baxsashadiisiina waxaa ka dambeeya dad magaalada Hargeysa deggan. Abaalgudka la siiyeyna waa uu ka horreeyey xarigga dadkan. Eedeysanayaasha xiranna waxba kama hadlayo. Sidaa darteed waxaan ku ADKEYSANAYAA in nalaga aqbalo qabashada caddeynta ee Maxkamadda, lagana diido Qareennada codsigooda ay ku diidan yihiin in Maxkamaddu aqoonsato caddeynta Cabdi Laangare.-

DOOD: QAREEN ISMAACIIL:

Iyadoo ay arrintani ku timid sahlasho ay sahladeen baarayaasha iyo X/Ilaalintu iima muuqato sabab hadda nalooga dhigo

../..

...../39.

muhiim caddeynta Cabdi Laangare, sidaa daraadeed waxaan Maxkamadda ka codsanayaa ineysan oggolaan u soo gudbinta caddeyntaas iyada ah.-

<u>MAXKAMADDU:</u>

Markay dhegeysatay codsiga Xeer Ilaalinta kuna saabsan soo gudbinta caddeynta Cabdi Laangare iyo doodii Qareennada, aragtayna Qodobada 155, 184, 186 iyo 197 ee XHC., waxay oggolaatay in caddeynta Cabdi Laangare loo soo gudbiyo Maxkamadda.-

<u>DADWEYNE U DOODE:</u>

Waxaan Maxkamadda u soo gudbinayaa Qalabka marag muujinta iyo Dokumentiga isugu jira oo kala ah: 2 (labo) Makiinadood oo kuwa qoraalka ah, Bistoolad Makaaroof iyo 6 (lix) xabbadood, warqaddii Warshadda Pepsi Cola ay ku caddeynayeen inay Makiinadda qoraalka leeyihiin, hal koobi oo ah Jariidada S.N.M. ay soo saarto, Blok Note "VICTOR" ah oo ay ku qoran yihiin daraafyo caddadyo UFFO ah ku soo baxay, warqadda Taliyaha Nabadsugidda oo ka hadleysa qa[illegible]rixii Magaalada ka dhacay, Manifeesto ay ku qoran tahay Guusha SNM baa leh GEERIDANA AFWEYNAA LEH, taar baafin ah iyo caddeynti Cabdi Laangare.- Waxaan kaloo soo gudbinayaa GAL u gaar ah Eed.1aad oo ay ku jiraan 5 (shan) caddeymo, 2 (labo) qiraal Maxkamadeed, Farihiisa iyo sawirkiisa.- GALKA Eed.2aad oo ay ku jiraan 5 (shan) caddeymo oo uu mid gacantiisa ku qoray iyo 2 (labo) qiraal Maxkamadeed.

GALKA EED.3AAD [illegible] iyo 2 caddeymood.

" " 4aad " " " qiraal iyo 2 caddeymood
" " 5 " " " qiraal & caddeyn iyo gabay fartiisa ah.
" " 6 " " " qiraal iyo caddeyn.
" " 7 " " " qiraal iyo caddeyn.
" " 8 " " " qiraal iyo caddeyn.
" " 9 " " " qiraal iyo caddeymo.
" " 10 " " " qiraal iyo caddeymo.
" " 11 " " " qiraal iyo caddeymo.
" " 12 " " " qiraal iyo caddeymo.
" " 13 " " " qiraal iyo caddeymo.
" " 14 " " " qiraal iyo caddeyn.
" " 15 " " " qiraal iyo caddeymo.
" " 16 " " " qiraal iyo caddeymo.
" " 17 " " " qiraal iyo caddeymo.

.../..

......../40.

GALKA	EED.	18AAD	uu	ku	jiro	qiraal iyo caddeymo.
"	"	19	"	"	"	qiraal iyo caddeymo.
"	"	20	"	"	"	qiraallo iyo caddeymo.
"	"	21	"	"	"	qiraallo iyo caddeymo.
"	"	22	"	"	"	qiraallo iyo caddeymo.
"	"	23	"	"	"	qiraallo iyo caddeymo.
"	"	24	"	"	"	qiraallo iyo caddeymo.
"	"	25	"	"	"	qiraallo iyo caddeymo

iyo 2 Koobi oo ah Joornaalka UFFO oo kala ah mid laga soo qaaday aqalka eed.3aad iyo tii baarayaashu X/Ilaalintan u soo gudbiyeen.-

CODSI: QAREEN ISMAACIIL:

Si aannu uga boganno qoraallada iyo Dokumentiga Maxkamadda loo soo gudbiyey, waxaan codsanayaa in dib naloogu dhigo ilaa 30 daqiiqadood oo aannu xaaladda ku derisno.-

MAXKAMADDU:

Markii ay dhogeysatay codsiga Qareen Ismaaciil, waxay oggolaatay in hal saac dib loogu dhigo Qareennada si ay xaaladda u dersan..

DOOD: QAREEN ISMAACIIL:

7da eedeysane aan daafacayo 6 ka mid ah waxaa Galalkooda loo soo gudbiyey Maxkamadda. Eed.1, 3, 7, 8, 15 & 23aad midkood na kama hadlin Joornaalka UFFO iyo RUDM isla mar ahaantaas eed.3aad oe lagu eedeeyay in laga helay Joornaalka UFFO ma racsani habka Sharciga ah helitaanku sida u dhacay, bacdamaa aan lagu gelin aqalka oggolaansho Maxkamadeed wax kale oo sababana ayan muuqan.

DOOD: QAREEN XASAN SHEEKH:

X/Ilaalintu waxay ku egtahay Qod.114 XHCS, Qareennaduna waxay ku eg yihiin Qod.116, waxaa noo dhaxeeya Qod.115 XHCS, Maxkamaddu ha nagu dhaqdo qodobka noo dhaxeeya. Waxaa kale oo jirta qiraallada 3da nin ee Maxkamaddu ii magacawday, Maxamed Dagaal (eed.10) qiraal kuma kuma jiro Galkiisa, mana jiraan wax uu isku caddeynayo, sidaa awgeed ma qabo in Maxkamadda loo gudbiyo Galkiisa. Eed.9aad & 11aad isma laha caddeymadooda iyo Eedeynta, midda kale Qiraal marka la leeyahay waa in lagu hor qoraa Garsoore, taas wax muujinaya ma hayno, xitaa haddii ay noqon lahayd Shaabad keliya amaba

../..

........./41.

Saxiix Garsoore caddeynaya inuu goob joog u ahaa. Xeer Ilaaliyuhu wuxuu kaloo soo gudbiyey warqad Taliyaha N.Sugidda G/W/G qoray, Manifesto, caddad ka mid ah Jariidada S.N.M. & warqado kale. Haddaba sida ku cad Qod.172 XHCS, wixii Maxkamadda loo soo gudbinayo waa inay ahaadaan kuwo qof khuseeya, HA LA II SHEEGO INAY KHUSEEYAAN 3DA NIN EE AAN DAAFACAYO IYO IN KALE, haddii ayan khuseyn gaar ahaan ama guud ahaan eedeysanayaasha oo dhan waxaan codsanayaa in dib loogu celiyo X/Ilaaliyaha.-

DOOD: QAREEN CUSMAAN:

Waxaa jira in galka lagu soo gudbiyey waxyaabo aan daowadda khuseyn, caddeynta Cabdi Laangare waa 12 Bog oo bogga 12aad oo keli ahi saxiixan yahay oo aan xitaa lahayn shaabad muujineysa ciddii qortay. Taas waxay na tusaysaa in caddeynta Cabdi Laangare loo aqoonsan yahay bogga 12aad oo keliya, isla caddeyntaas boggeeda 5aad wuxuu Laangare leeyahay markii la i yiri soo raadi waxaan sheegay inaan hayo 2 Nuqul oo UFFO ah oo aan Aaden ku ogahay, dabadeed uu keenay, taas waxaan u qaadan karnaa inuu isagu mas'uul ka ahaa gebi ahaanba xaaladda UFFO loona baahnaa in isaga lagu eedeeyo abaabulka Jariidada UFFO.-

DOOD: QAREEN XUSEEN BILE:

Sida la ogyahay Qod.149 ee XHCS oo qeexaya Qiraalka waxa loola jeedo. Waxaa muuqata in eed/sha aan daafacayo 6 ka mid ah Maxkamadda looga soo gudbiyey 3 qiraal, seddexda kale 3 caddeymood. Haddaba waxaa muuqata inaanu jirin wax qiraal ah ee ay seddaxda hore yihiin caddeymo iska caadi ah kuwa kalena ay caddeymaba ahaayeen, midkoodna aan waafaqsanayn Qod.172 ee XHCS, hase yeeshee ay yihiin hadal ay bixiyeen oo keliya. Sidaas daraadeed, waxaa Maxkamadda ka codsanayaa inay dhammaanba Xeer Ilaalinta dib ugu celiso, iyadoo aan qabo kuna kalsoonahay in lagu dirqiyey.-

JAWAAB: DADWEYNE U DOODE:

Jaalle Guddoomiye, sida ku cad Qod.10aad ee XLY 8 soona baxay. 26.1.70, haddii dhegeysiga dacwaddu tahay awoodda MBD uma baahna in Qiraalka uu Garsoore goob joog u ahaado. Waxaan aad ula yaabanahay sababta Qareen Xuseen Bile uu u rumaysan la'yahay Saxiixa Qoraalka ama caddeymaha ee uu sheegayo in lagu

../..

........./42.

dirqiyey. Haddii aan u soo noqdo Qod.172 XHCS, Maxkamadda waa loo soo gudbin karaa wax allaale wixii khuseeya dacwadda, taas waxaan ulajeedaa si buuxdana aan rabaa inaan Maxkamadda iyo dadweynahaba ka dhaadhiciyo bacdamaa ay jirto EEDEYN la leeyahay waxaa uu Ururku RUDM ka shidaal qaata ka kaleɟ ee xaaraanta ah ee la yiraahdo S.N.M., inaan Maxkamadda u muujiyo astaan dhab ah meenaheeduna yahay Jariidada S.N.M. iyo Manifestadaba. Sidaas awgeed waxaa Maxkamadda ka codsanayaa in ay ii oggolaato inaan u soo gudbiyo si aan Eedda u soo gabagabeeyo.-

MAXKAMADDU:

Markay dhegaysatay dooddii Qareennada iyo jawaab celintii K/Xeer Ilaaliyaha Guud MBD Gobolka W/G kuna saabsan gudbinta caddeymaha eedeysanayaasha, marka aragtay Qod. 10aad XLY 8 ee 26.1.70 oo lala akhriyo Qod.151 XHCS, waxay GO'AAMISAY in la qaado lana tixgeliyo caddeymaha eedeysanayaasha.

Midda ku saabsan Qiraalada Eedeysanayaasha ee Garsooraha hortiisa ay ka bixiyeen ee Qareen Xasan Sheekh ka hadlay. Maxkamaddu iyadoo tixgelisay Qod.68 XHCS, waxay u muuqatay in loo raacay habkii loo baahnaa waafaqsan yahayna Shirciga.

Midda seddaxaad ee ku saabsan Joornaalka S.N.M., waraaqihii Taliyaha NSSka G/W/G iyo tol Xafiiska Nabadgelyada C.B.S. ee K/Xeer Ilaaliyaha Guud MBD Hargeysa Maxkamadda u soo gudbiyey, Maxkamaddu markay aragtay Qod.172 XHCS, waxay go'aamisay in dib loogu celiyo Xeer Ilaalinta, maadama aysan xiriir la lahayn EEDDA loo haysto eedeysanayaasha.-

CODSI: DADWEYNE U DOODE:

Maxkamadda waxaan u soo jeedinayaa sida uu qabo Qod.112 XHC, in aan Eedeynta kala noqdo Eedeysanayaasha kala ah: Eed.26aad Saciid Max'd Nuur oo lagu caddeyn waayey ka tirsanaanta Ururka RUDM iyo Qaraxa, Eed.27aad G/Dh.Ismaaciil Xaashi Madar oo isagana lagu soo caddeyn waayey dembigii lagu soo oogay oo ah ka QAYB GELID URUR DEMBI FALE AH IYO KU CABSI GELIN WAXAX BOMBO GACMEED iyo eed.28aad Xasan Cali "Ceelgeeye" oo lagu soo

.../..

caddeyn waayey AFMINSHAARNIMO oo ah dembigii lagu soo eedeeyey.-

MAXKAMADDU:

Markay dhegeysatay codsigii Xeer Ilaaliyaha ee ku saabsan kala noqoshada Eedda ku taagan eed/sha kala ah 26,
27 & 28aad, aragtay Qod.112 (2) ee XHCS, way ka oggolaatay Xeer Ilaaliyaha inuu eedda eed:sha kor ku xusan kala noqdo.-

GABAGABADII DADWEYNE U DOODAHA

"""Jaalle Guddoomiye, Garsoorayaal iyo Maxkamadda Sharafka leh, ani
goo bilaabaya soo jeedinta eedeyntayda, Eed/sha 1aad, 2aad & 3aad,
waxaa si wadajir ah ugu eedeynayaa inay ABAABULEEN Urur ku sheegga
xaaraanta ah ee lagu magacaabay R.U.D.M., kuna tallaabsadeen qoraal
ka iyo Faafinta Joornaalka UFFO oo Ururkoodu soo saaro, muddadii
ay baaristu socoteyna waxaa la ogaadey iney xiriir sokeeye la lee-
yihiinUrur ku sheegga S.N.M. ee Londan ka fura. Cabdi Laangare
wuxuu ahaa nin hadda ka hor lagu soo eedeeyey BASAASNIMO oo ay MBD
W/G ku xukuntay DIL, hase yeeshee markii dambe isla MBD W/G ciqaab-
taas ka sii deysey, taasi waxaan filayaa inay inooga filan tahay
qiimeynta maragga MAQANAHA AH oo haddii DILKII lagu waayey ayan
suurtagal noqon inuu ciqaab kale kala kulmo Maxkamadda horteeda ha
ahaato Xabsi daa'im ama xabsi dheerba, waxaana habboon inay Qareen-
nadu sidaas u fahmaan qiimaynta uu leeyahay maragga MAQANAHA AH.
Sida caddeyntiisa ku qoran Cabdi Laangare wuxuu caddeeyey inuusan
RUDM magaalada ku xidhnayn Aadan Waallina uu la damacsanaa inuu
Dowladdu ku soo xidho sidii uu ula shaqeyn lahaa mar hadii uu SNM
aad ugu dhowaa xogogaalna u ahaa ujeedooyinka wecsan ee RUDM. Eed/
sha 1, 2 & 3aad waxay kaloo ahaayeen raggii la shiray Maxamed Nuur
Xandulle (Carab) oo isagu Jidda kula kulmay DUQSI iyo INA-WADAAD
DIID oo ah Madax ku sheegga SNM sheegayna in labadaas nin ay dha-
waan Dalka Sacuudiga kula kulmeen ISAAQA jooga Dalkaas, kuwaasoo
intooda badan ee waxgaradka ahi raaceen RERR SABLAALE MOOYE. Reer
Sablaale waxaa loola jeedaa Dadkii Soomaaliyeed ee ku tabaaloobay
abaartii daba dheer, kaddibna ku caato baxay gargaarkii Dowlad iyo
[illegible] ee ay ka heleen Ummadda Soomaaliyeed iyo xukumadooda
Kacaanka ah [illegible] Dibadaha u shaqa tegey si ay qiimaha noloshoo-

........../44.

da wax ugu taraan ee ku gacan seydhay DUQSI iyo INA-WADAAD D[illegible], iyagoo ku hal qabsanaya kuna qanacsan gacantii ay dadkooda iyo dal-koodaba ka heleen markii ay tabaaleysnaayeen una sheegay in ayan wax gacan ah ku siin doonin fikradooda iyo hadafkooda lidka ku ah Midnimada iyo Qarannimada Ummadda Soomaaliyeed, isagoo weliba intaas raaciyey in loo baahan yahay in CIIDAGALE lagu soo xiro ISAAqa intiisa kale lagana soo gooyo dabadhilifnimada MAREEXAANKA, taas oo aan wax sal ah lahayn siyaabaha ay isugu taxallujinayaan. Waxaa tusaale ugu filan waxyaabihii Maxkamadda horteeda laga akhrinaayey ee ku qornaa Joornaalka UFFO ee ay ka mid ahaayeen Qaraneynta Gobolka, Berbera waa la qabsaday iyo la SOCOTO. La socoto waxaa ceddan ah loola jeedo QOF ALLA QOFKII si xilkasnimo ah uga soo baxa waajibaadka ciidiisa iyo Calankiisa ka saaran inuu ku tilmaanaado LA SOCOTO oo micnaheedu yahay dabadhilifka MAREEXAAN, nuxurka ka dambeeyaana uu yahay Niyad Jab ceadooyin haraa ah oo kala goynaya Qarannimada Ummadda Soomaaliyeed loo abaabuli lahaa dhaawacna loogu geysan lahaa dadka diyaarka u ah waajib gudashada dadkooda iyo dalkoodaba. Si ay ujeedooyinka Urur ku sheeggaas u hirgeliyaanna waxay isla garteen iney dadka Soomaaliyeed aad ugu jajaban yihiin xagga Diinta loona baahan yahay in Diinta loogu soo dhuunto, si arrinta weji kale loogu yeelo, waxaana dhacday in eed.1aad Shir la yeeshay dhallinyarada Waxdada oo uu u arkaayey inay Dowladda ka soo horjeedaan, isla mar ahaantaasna uu eed.3aad oo ah Maxamed Xaaji Maxamuud shirkaas kaga hadlay erayo ay ka mid yihiin: "GABADHII WAXAY NOQOTAY QARSATO, [illegible]IILKIINA WUXUU NOQDAY XABAGLE, ODAYGIINA WUXUU NOQDAY QURBAAWI, HABARTIINA WAXAY NOQOTAY JAADLEY, una nisbeeyey in Dowladdu dhaqan xumadaas mas'uul ka tahay isagoo uga gol xaaraya sidii uu u abaabuli lahaa QAS la isaga hor geynayo Dadweynaha iyo Dowladda, kaasoo aan run ahaantii qabo in natiijadiisu aaney maanta shaki lahayn Qaskii iyo Weerarkii uu beryahan ay ka dhasheen Hargeysa, dhibaatooyiinkii dhawaan dhacay ee loogu soo gabbaday xadhigga eed/sha iyadoo la isla dhexmaray been aan sal lahayn oo la leeyahay eed/shii xidhnaa oo kuwan ah badh baa DIL lagu xukumay intii kale XABSI DAA'IM, wixii ka dhashayna aannu u wada joognay. Waxyaabahaas oo dhan iyo kuwo kaloo fara badaniba waxa ay na tusayaan jiritaanka Ururka, kasoo ay xarun u ahaayeen [illegible] Adan, Jabane, Cabduraxmaan iyo Caabi. Eed.4aad ilaa eed.20aad waxa-

..../...

......../45.

an iyagana si wadajir ah ugu eedeynayaa inay yihiin Xubnihii Ururka R.U.D.M.. Eed/sha 21, 22 iyo 23aad arrintoodu waa xadaysan tahay waxayna ahaayeen Xubnihii Wazdada oo iyagu RUDM la waafaqay inay iskaashi aan xalaal ahayn la sameystaan. Dunuubta gaarka ah Eed.16aad waa u qirtay Dembiga loo haysto ee ah Haysasho Hub Sharci Darro. Dhinaca Qaraxyada waxaannu abaabulkooda ku eedeynayaa Eed.17aad iyo 20aad, isla mar ahaanteasna sida ay iyagu sheegeen waxaa la fuliyey waajibaadkii Qaraxyadaas eed.24 iyo 25aad, waxaanan idiin xusuusinaysa in habka uu qaraxu u dhacay laga dareemi karo inuu daba joogo qoraalladii UFFO, maxaa yeelay 3dii nin ee Joornaalka ku qornaa ee loo malayn karay iney xarigga eed/sha ka dambeeyeen ayaa aqalladoodii la qarxiyey. Ragan xidhan markii aan qiimeeyo waa inta u dhaxeysa 28 jir ilaa 38 jir ugu yaraan uu ninka ugu aqoon gaabani haysato shahaadadda Dugsiga Sare, waa ay wanaagsanaan lahayd haddii ay ujeedadoodu tahay sidii ay SAMAFAL & wax qabasho daacad ah dadkooda ugu geysan lahaayeen, hase yeeshee taas ma hayno, waxaanuse haynaa inay ahaayeen rag doonaya inay dhistaan Dowlad toleed una guntaday sidii ay Dowladda iyo dadweynaha isaga horkeeni lahaayeen. Sidaas awgeed Eed/sha 1aad, 2aad iyo 3aad waxaan ku adkeysanayaa in eedda naloo raaco. Eed.4aad ilaa eed.20aad waxaan u weydiinayaa in MIN 30 SANADOOD OO XARIG AH LAGU XUKUMO. Eed/21, 22 iyo 23aad waxaan u deynayaa go'aankooda Maxkamadda, isla mar ahaantaas waxaan kaloo Qodobka eedda u deynayaa eed.24 iyo 25aad. Maxkamaddu waa mahadsantahay.-

DIFAACA QAREEN ISMAACIIL

Sida uu X/Ilaalintu sheegtay raggani waa rag dhallinyaro ah maantana qiimo gaar ah inoogu fadhiya marka loo eego xagga aqoonta iyo xagga hawlahaba taas oo aannu ka dhadhansan karno, inay yihiin Takhaatiir, Injineero iyo ganacsato aqoon leh oo hore hawlwadeeno Qaranka ugu ahaan jirey haddana wax ka kobcinaya dhaqaalaha Dalka. Waxaa kaloo la sheegay Urur, Qod.322 XCS iyo Qod.3 ee YLY 54 midkoodna Eeddu ma waafaqsana maxaa yeelay ilaa hadda ma hayno wax Urur ah oo dhisan. X/Ilaalintu waxay kaloo ka hadashay Ciraal haddaba [illegible] uu qorayo Qod.68 ee XHCS waxaan ayidsanahay in aanay wax qiimo ah lahayn caddeymaha galalka Maxkamadda loo gudbiyey ku jira oo ku saleysan tahdiid, cabsi gelin IM.., una weheliso baarista

../..

........./46.

naftirkeed oo ay dhaliilo fara badani ka muuqdaan. Dad fara badan baa ka Qayb-gal Urur lagu eedeynayaa, bal aan is weydiinee maxaa keenay Urur aan dhismihiisuba jirin in ka qaybgalkiisa dad lagu eedeeyo. Eed.23aad eedeyntiisa ma waafaqsani kan 3aadna waxaa muuqata in aqalkiisa si Sharci darro ah lagu baaray taasina waxay .. qiima dhac u keeneysaa eedeynta Joornaalka. Xaggeese laga keenay Joornaalka UFFO? Daahir Ciid, wuxuu sheegay in markii uu warka helay kaddib uu dad u dirsaday loona keenay UFFO oo uu si khalad ah ugu gudbiyey Taliyaha Qaybta 26aad, markii dambena ay khaladkii hore la mid ah ugu gudubtay NSSta. Madaxda Pepsi Cola waxay sheegeen in makiinadda tahay toodi, hase yeeshee sidii Sharcigu ahaa maxaa khabiir aqoon u leh hawsha looga baahnaa in lagu xaqiijiyo in qoraalku keeda yahay loogu gudbin sida ku cad Qod.161. Marka la leeyahay eed/shu waxay ka hadleen biyo la'aan, nal la'aan iyo dhaliilo kale oo jira oo xagga Dowladda ku lug leh, ma waxaa la oran kara waa Urur Qaranka lid ku ah, taasi ma bannaana waayo waa wax xaqiiq ah inay jiraan dhibaatooyinka ay ka hadleen.. Xaley miyaanay Maxkamaddu nagu madoobaan, miyaanay nasiib darro weyn ahayn in Tuulada Wanla-Weyn ay si joogto ah u hesho xoog koranto oo ku filan, Magaala-madaxdii 2aad ee Hargeysana ayan maalintii gelinkiisa dambe wax koronto ah lahayn, saacadaha uu doonana uu bakhtiyo sidii xaleyba Maxkamadda dhexdeeda nagu qabsatay iyadoo weliba xuduud ku sheegga aan waxba u jirin. Maragga 3aad wuxuu sheegay inay Ururka Samafalka dhallinyaradu abaabuleen markii dambena uu Maamulka Gobolku aqoonsaday wax qabadkiisa iyo jiritaankiisaba. Manifestada waxaa ciddii ka dambeysay ugu talagaleen QAS iyo xasilooni la'aan taasina waa dhacdayba. Maxkamadda waxaan ka codsanayaa in 6da nin ee aan daafacayo oo aan midna lagu hayn eedeynta RUDM laga sii daayo xabsiga si ay danahooda qabsadaan.-

DIFAACA QAREEN FAYSAL

Iyadoo aan Qareen u ahay Eed.2, 4, 5 iyo 20aad in aanay kaafi ahayn caddeyntii X/Ilaalinta looga baahnaa. Waxaa kaloo jirta in eed.2aad markhaatigiisu aanay saldhig u ahayn eedda. Eed-2aad waxaa lagu eedeeyey Qod.3 XLY 54 iyo Joornaalka Uffo, haddaba maxay X/Ilaalintu ku codsatay Dilka. Caddeymo, warbixintii Laangare iyo maraggii 3aad oo sheegay in eed.2aad uu Abaabuley Urur, hase ahaatee mar dambe waxaa la ogaaday in Ururku la abaabulay 1977kii cid abaabushayna

.../..

......../47.

lama sheegin, maragguna wuxuu sheegay inayan hayn wax kale oo raad ah oo ka duwan markhaatiga Laangare. Warbixinta Eed.2aad ee Saldhigga u noqotay abuurista dacwaddan waxaa jira rag ku qoran oo aan la soo xirin lamana caddeyn sababta, Maxkamadda waxaan ka codsanayaa inaanay tixgelin qoraallada Eed.2aad. Eedeysanaha 2aad wuxuu sgeegay in ay jiraan dhallinyaro Urur Samafal ah sameysay hase yeeshee Laangare oo dhibaatooyin dhaqaale wadeen iyo Aadan oo sheegay in nin Feysal la yiraahdo oo Xamar jooga uu kula soo taliyey inuu Dowladda la sheqeeyo ay dhibaatada abuureen. Laangare wuxuu caddeyn tiisa ku sheegay in isagoo la qayilaya Taliyaha Qaybta 26aad uu ka codsaday inuu u keeno Joornaalka UFFO, hase yeeshee uu u sheegay inuu laba midh hayo una keeni doono, wuxuu kaloo sheegay inuu Hargeysa ka jiro Urur Samafal ah oo marmar Dowladda la hadla marnabana ma aanu sheegin wax Urur ah iyo RUDM toona. Waxaan aaminsanahay in arrintan loola jeedo sidii Dowladda iyo dadweynaha la isaga hor keeni lahaa, maragga 3aad waxa uu ka been sheegay inuu RUDM qirtay eed.2aad, welina ma hayno Urur iyo wax loola jeedo, taas waxaan u arkaa in aanu jirin wax eed.2aad ku cad marka Uffo laga hadlayana kuma filna Qodobka ceddaasi. Eed.4aad, wax kale oo aan ahayn caddeynta eed.2aad looma hayo mana garan sababta ay X/Ilaalintu eedda ugala noqon weyday. Eed.5aad isagana looma hayo wax aan maragga 3aad ahayn, loomana hayo eed.5aad wax sheegay inuu akhristay, helay ama hayey UFFO sida ku qoran eedda. Eed.20aad waxaa lagu soo xiray qaraxa wax ku filanna looma hayo, maxaa yeelay sida ku cad qodobada 322, 325 332 cid aan ahayn eed.17aad looma hayo. Dhigitaanka bombada Guriga S/Guuto Gaani cid aan ahayn eed.17aad kuma caddeyn karto. Hub ma yaqaan sida uu sheegay maragga 3aad, waxyaabahaas oo dhami waxay u baahan yihiin in Maxkamaddu ay qiimeyso. Waxaa kale oo muuqata inaanay X/Ilaalintu si buuxda uga soo bixin kaalintii looga baahnaa waxaan codsanayaa in Maxkamadda ay xabsiga ka sii deyso eed/sha aan daafacayo ee kala ah eed.2, 4, 5 iyo 20aad.-

DIFAACA QAREEN XUSEEN BILE

Magaca R.U.D.M. uma qalmo dacwaddan, maxaa yeelay Dr.Taani wuxuu ku dhashay Awaare Jabanena wuxuu ku dhashay Oodweyne, maragga 3aad wuxuu sheegay in Laangare u keenay Jariidada, wuxuu kaloo sheegay inay hayaan eed/sha oo keliya ee ayan jirin markhaatiyo kale, taasina waxay muujineysaa in ayan X/Ilaalintu wax caddeyn ah hayn,

.../../

......../48.

sidaa daraadeed waxaan codsanayaa in ay dib u raacdo nuxurka doodan oo ah eed.6aad waxba laguma caddeyn, kan 14aadna la sheegay inuu bukaan u tegi jiray guriga Dr.Aadan lana sheegay inay intuu xidhnaa xitaa Takhtarradu xabsiga ku daweyn jireen, kan 16aadna uu la mid yahay kuwaas hore oo aan waxba ku caddeyn, bistooladda mooyee taasoo ku xiriirsan (Ordinamento Pubblico Sicurezza). Eed. 17aadna aan wax qawl ah oo uu yiri laga hayn xagga Ururka lana caddeyn waayey meesha uu Hubka (bombada) ka keenay iyo in aan waxba ku caddeyn, kan 24aad oo aad loo caddibey kan 25aad waxba lagu caddeyn waayay in la sii daayo dhammaanba eed/sha aan daafacayo waxaanan gaar ahaan ula yaabsanahay sababta X/Ilaalintu ay dhinac arrinta uga rumeysan tahay dhinacna uga beeneyneyso bacdamaa eed. 26aad iyo kii 27aad oo lagu kala eedeynaayay: kan 27aad inuu Hubka keenay, kan 26aadna wax ka fuliyey Qaraxa ay eedeyntii kala noqotay, kuwana ugu soo eedeysay Qaraxa.-

DIFAACA QAREEN XASAN SHEEKH

Habka caddaaladda waafaqsan in loo derso Qodobada soo socoda ee X.C.S. ay qorayaan: Qod.1aad, 16aad iyo 20aad, Maxkamadduna ku dhisto dacwadda qaadisteeda. Waxaa iga su'aal ah: Maxaa dembi lagu tilmaami karaa? Shuruucda Jinaa'iga ahi waxay khuseysaa qofka Sharaftiisa iyo Xoriyadiisa, waxaana lagu tilmaamay Dembi iyo Ciqaab. Qodobku ma hadli karo ee waxa hadla Qofka. Eeddu ma ku fadhidaa Qodobadan, Jawaabtu waa MAYA, wuxuuna buxsamaa marka la helo Shuruudiisa oo dhan. Marka ficilku waxyeelo keenaayo, Maxkamadda horteeda Qofka taagani ma yahay kii isku xiray Silsiladda ficilka iyo dembiga (rapporto di causalità). Xubno firfircoon in ay ka ahaayeen Ururka R.U.D.M. waa in la helaa Qalab iyo Xafiis, sida Qodobka eeddu sheegaayo ujeedada lagu dhaawacayo Qaranka, laguna wiiqayo awoodda Dowladda, laguna curyaaminaayo, laguna daciifinaayo, TURJUMAD KHALAD ah weeyaan Hargeysa ayaa dhaawacaysa Midnimada Ummadda Soomaaliyeed, waayo Magaalooyin kale ayaa la isku shirqooli karaa, Dowladdana uma fiicna. Rabshadii Cabdi Laangare abuuray, meel kastaba ha jiree, wuxuu kallifay in Ciidanka waqtiga laga lumiyo ilaalinta Magaalada, Indheer-garatadii Adduunkoo dhammi fiirsanaayo lagu eedeeyo WAX AAN JIRIN. Sida Qod.149XHC qabo, Qiraalka la sheegay may caddeynin ereyga lagu eedeynaayo,

.../...

......../49.

ma aha wax kasta oo lagu horsaxeexay Garsoore ee wuxuu yahay mida asaga wax ka sheegaaya (liddi ku ah). Maxamed Dagaal Xirsi (eed. 10) waxaa laga qoray lana horkeenay Garsoore, hase yeeshee 3da kale ee aan u ahay Qareen may qorin waxa eedda ku qoran. Qod.146 XHCS wuxuu sheegaaya ineysan wax Qiraal ah nala tusin ee wax ku furayaa eed/shan waafaqsanna Qod.199 XHCS. MAJHUULNA waannu ka nahay , xuquuqdii Difaacuna waa dhimantahay. Eed/shu wax ay qirteen ma jiraan, waxna laguma caddeynin, X/Ilaaliyaha naftiisa waxaa lagu casumay Arooskii mana aha dembi, hala sii daayo Eed/shan.-

DIFAACA QAREEN CUSMAAN CABDI:

Maxkamaddu waxay ku qanci kartaa doodda Qareennada kale ee aannu wada difaacayno Eed/shan. Fikradaha iyo Hanuuninta ay Xeer Ilaalintu soo jeedisay Hay'ado kale ayaa iska leh, waxaan meesha u fadhinaana waa caddaalad iyo Sharci. Cabdi Laangare wuxuu ka mid yahay Urur Xaaraan ah oo ka soo horjeeda Qarankeena, ilaa haddana wuxuu ka soo hadla IDAACADDA CADOWGA, lagana dhegeystaa. Waxaa la yaab leh in Qofka ay shakhsiyaddaas leh warbixintiisa la rumeysto. Sida Qod.197 XHCS uu qoraayo, haddii laba warbixinood iska horyimaadaan waxa la raacayaa tan Eed/ha. Caddeynta Dr.Cusmaan wuxuu sheegay inuu qayili jiray, maadaama uusan dembi ku caddeyn eedeysanayaasha aan difaacayo (eed.13 & 18aad) ha la siidaayo.-

DIFAACA QAREEN BASHIIR CARTAN

Afarta eedeysane ee aan Qareenka u ahay (eed.19, 12, 21 & 22aad) lama weydiinin Ururka jiritaankiisa iyo ka qaybgalkiisa, mana jirto wax ay qirteen oo Garsoore hortiisa lagaga qoray, waxay ahayd arrintu in lagala noqdo eedda loo haysto. Jiritaanka Ururka lama caddeynin xataa wax raad ah looma helin. Qod.110 iyo Qod.163 XHCS, waajibaadkeedii kama soo bixin Xeer Ilaalintu. Wax marag lama horkeenin Maxkamadda. Xeer Ilaalintu way ka cabsatay inay kala noqoto eedda ee Maxkamadda ayey u deysay, wax aan la dhegeysan karin marag ahaan caddeynina dembiga meesha ku jiray ay Maxkamadda la horkeenay, baaruhuna waa warbixin uu qoray oo keliya ayuu ka waramayaa maadaama aysan wax jirin wax dembi ee lagu caddeeyey eed/sha aan daafacayo ha la siidaayo shaqooyinkoodiina ha lagu celiyo.-

../..

......../50.

GUNDHIG & ASBAAB XUKUN

Maxkamaddu markay dhegeysatay markhaatiyadii uu Dadweynaha u Dooduhu horkeenay wixii ay fureen iyo dooddii dhinacyada, aragtayna qoraalladii iyo dembi muujintii loo soo gudbiyey, waxaa u soo ifbaxay arrimaha soo socda:

1). Waxaa jirtay in muddadii u dhexaysay sannadkii 1977 ilaa 1978kii ay ka bilaabeen Hargeysa kulammo ay yeelanayeen qaar ka mid ah Ee/sha kor ku xusan oo isku tirinaayey "Indheer-Garadka Magaalada", isuguna iman jireen mafrishyada qayilaadda, ayagoo ka faaloonaayey Fikradaha, isweydaarsanaayeenna aragtida ay kala qabaan Guud ahaan Maamulka Dowladda Kacaanka, gaar ahaanna Maamulka Gobolka W/Galbeed, iyagoo ka faa'iidaysanaya guuxa ka jiray in muddo ahba Gobolka Hargeysa...

Iyadoo ay si caadi ah u soconaayeen kulamadoodii iyo shirarkoodii qarsoodiga ahaa, ayey bilaabeen in ay Dadweynaha ka dhaadhiciyaan mashaakilaadka Gobolkan ka taagnaa, markastana ka tusi jireen dadweynaha dhanka xun·ee dhaliisha leh, ayaa ugu danbeystii Bishii Juun 1981dii ay xoojiyeen kulamadoodii, shirar isdabajoog ahna yeesheen, lana samaysteen Iskaashi Xubno ka tirsan Ururka Xaaraanta ah ee S.N.M., xaruntiisuna tahay LONDON, Madaxna uu ka yahay nin la yiraahdo DUQSI ee ka yimaadeen Dalka Sucuudiga, kuwaas oo si qarsoodi ah ku soo geliyeen Wargeyska SNM, warbixinna ka bixiyeen sida dadka u dhashay"EX-ISAAQ" kuna dhaqan Khaliijka ay ugu biireen Urukooda Xaaraanta ah ee SNM.-.......................................

Xubnaha ka socday Ururka SNM ee Dibedda ka soo galay oo kala ahaayeen Aadan Cali Faarax (Aadan Waalli) iyo Maxamed Nuur Xandulle (Carab), baxsadeenna markay Ciidamada Nabadgelyadu bilaabeen baarista la xiriirta Dacwaddan, iyadoo loo soo xilsaaray in ay Magaalada Hargeysa ka abaabulaan Urur xaaraan ah kana soo horjeeda Himilooyinka Kacaanka, abuuraanna arrimo liddi ku ah xasiloonida iyo Nabadgelyada Guud ee Gobolka, isla markaasna ka soo horjeeda jiritaanka Ummadda Soomaaliyeed.—————————————

Kaddib markii si isdaba joog ah Kulammo ay la yeesheen Eed/shan qaarkood, iyagoo ka dhaadhicinaayey in Dadka ISAAQA ahi ee Sucuudiga ku nooli ku biireen Ururka Xaaraanta ah ee S.N.M. intaan ka ahayn CIIDAGALE, waxay ku booriyeen in Soomaali kala tagtay qolo walbana ay Jabhad samaysatay iyagana looga baahan yahay in ay toode (S.N.M.)

../..

......../51

xoojiyaan, iskana dhaafaan dabadhilifnimada MAREEXAANKA sida EX CIIDAGALE. Labadaas eedaysane (Aadan iyo Xandulle) oo ka wakiil ahaa Ururka SNM ee DUQSI uu Madax ka yahay, markii ay u meel martay ujeedooyinkoodii foosha xumaa, waxay ABAABULEEN Ururka Xaaraanta ah oo ay u bixiyeen R.U.D.M., micnihiisuna yahay RAGGA U DHASHAY MAGAALADA, waxaana Ururkaasi ku soo biiray Eed/sha kala ah:---------

- Edd. 1aad Maxamed Baaruud Cali,
- " 2aad Axmed Maxamed Yuusuf,
- " 3aad Maxamed Xaaji Maxamuud,
- " 4aad Aadan Yuusf Abookar,
- " 5aad Cabdiraxmaan Cabdullaahi Aadan,
- " 6aad Axmed Xuseen Caabi,
- " 7aad Xuseen Maxamed Ducaale,
- " 8aad Maxamuud Sheekh Xasan Taani,
- " 9aad Cabdullaahi Cali Yuusuf "Colaad",
- " 12aad Yuusuf Cabdillaahi Kaahin,
- " 13aad Cismaan Cabdi Megaag,
- " 20aad Baashe Cabdi Yuusuf,
- " 16aad Maxamed Cali Ibraahim,
- " 15aad Aadan Warsame Saciid.

Kulamadii ugu horreeyey ee ay rasmi ahaan u yeesheen Eed/shu kor ku xusani iyo ABAABULAYAASHA Ururka RUDM (Aadan Waalli & Xandulle) waxaa laysku baraarujiyey wax qabad la'aanta iyo dacdarrada ay Dawladdu ku haysay G/W/Galbeed, isla markaana waxay go'aansadeen in dadweynaha ku nool Magaalada Hargeysa isku tashadaan oo aysan Dawladda waxba ka sugin, kana hoos baxaan Jamhuuriyadda inteeda kale, ayaa waxay abuureen magacaabeenna Guddi ay ku sheegeen "SAMAFAL" oo ka Madax banaan Maamulka Gobolka, isla markaasna ay ka aruuriyeen Dadweynaha Lacag, Qalab, Dayactir iyo daawooyin lagu taakulaynaayo Isbitaalka Hargeysa, iyagoo ujeedadoodu ahayd inay iska horkeenan dadweynaha iyo Dawladda si kalsooni iyo gacan buuxda uga helaan dadweynaha, kaddibna ku soo biiraan Ururkooda Xaaraanta ah.--------

Waxaa intaas dheer in mudadii ay u socdeen shirarkoodu ayna isweydaarsanayeen fikradahooda ka dhanka ah Dawladda, waxay fursad u heleen in ay la kulmaan dadweynaha qaarkiis munaasabaddii arooska Eed.1aad (Maxamed Baaruud Cali) laguna qabtay Guri ku yaalla Xaafadda Guryasamo ee Magaalada Hargeysa, uuna lahaa Eed.28aad Xasan Cab-

.../...

Appendix IV

Full names and short bio of the My Friends and Fellow Prisoners

Further details on the profiles can be found in "A note on my teachers' group: news report of an injustice", Jama Musse Jama.

1. Abdillahi Ali Yussuf (Olaad), 1947-2001, Hargeisa.
2. Abdirahman Abdillahi H. Aden, 1955, Hargeisa.
3. Adan Yusuf Abokor, 1944, Hargeisa.
4. Aden Warsame Saeed, 1947, Hargeisa.
5. Ahmed Hussein Abby, 1946, Berbera.
6. Ahmed Mohamed Yusuf (Jabane), 1949.
7. Ahmed Muhumed Madar, 1952, Hargeisa.
8. Ali Egeh Farah (Ali Biid), 1953, Hargeisa.
9. Bashe Abdi Yussuf , 1953, Hargeisa.
10. Hussein Mohamed Dualeh (Berberawi), 1950, Berbera.
11. Mohamed Ali Ibrahim, 1945, Hargeisa.
12. Mohamed Ali Sulub, 1950, Hargeisa.
13. Mohamed Barud Ali , 1950, Aware.
14. Mohamed Haji Mohamoud Omer-Hashi, 1948, Hargeisa.
15. Mohamed Ma'allin Osman, 1949, Hargeisa.
16. Mohamoud Abdi Ji'ir, 1947.
17. Mohamoud Sheikh Hassan Taani, 1953, Aware.
18. Osman Abdi Maigag, 1943, Hargeisa.
19. Omer Isse Awale, 1948, Sheikh.
20. Yusuf Abdillahi Kahin, 1952, Hargeisa.

Appendix V

The list of prisoners at Labaatan-Jirow at one time or other from 1981-1989.

1. 14 of us named above	
2. Ismail Ali Abokor	Ex-Vice-President.
3. Omer Arte Galib	Ex-Minister of Foreign Affairs.
4. Osman Mohamed Jelle	Ex-Minister of Livestock/Range.
5. Dr. Mohamed Adan Shiekh	Ex-Minister of Information.
6. Mohamed Yusuf Wayrah	Ex-Minister of Finance.
7. Abdillahi Mohamed Nour	Army Major.
8. Warsame Ali Farah	Ex-Mayor of Mogadishu, died in prison in 1983.
9. Ali Easa Islam	Army Inspector.
10. Mohamed Ali Jama	Army Captain released from prison in 1984.
11. Mohamoud Islam (uncle of no. 9)	Army Captain.
12. Ahmed Hashi	Army Captain.
13. Gaboobeh	Army Captain.
14. Ahmed Dhore Farah	Businessman still in prison when we left.
15. Mohamoud Malin	Civil Servant.
16. Sheikh Mukhtar	Ex-Lawyer
17. Yusuf Osman Samater	In prison since 1968.
18. Hussein Ahmed	Ethiopian Air-Force colonel still in prison when we left.
19. Jama Ali Jama	Imprisoned since 1978.

The following ten were among a group of 21 people known to human rights group as "Parliamentarians" because there were a number of government ministers and a vice-president among them. 12 of the 21 all Issaqs, were sentenced, 8 of them to death, all the rest released including two of Siyaad Barre's cousins.

20. Abdi Ismail Yonus	Ex-Dean of College of Education. Somali National University.
21. Suleiman Nuh Ali	Engineer.

22. Mohamed Abdi Adan	Army Colonel.
23. Abdillahi Jama Galal	Army Colonel.
24. Ahmed Omer Abdalla	Businessman.
25. Abdi Abdillahi Madar	Unemployed at the moment of arrest.
26. Abdillahi Jama Samatar	Air-Force Colonel.
27. Ahmed Mohamed Halla	Police Colonel.
28. Hussein Adan Samakab	Army Major.
29. Hussein Ismail Abdi (Crash)	Army Major.

Bibliography and further reading

1. Africa Watch, *Somalia: A Government at War with Its Own People: Testimonies about the Killings and the Conflict in the North*, London, Africa Watch, January 1990.
2. Amnesty International, *Somalia: A long-term human rights crisis. 9/ 1988*. London: Amnesty International Publications, 1988.
3. Carol Corillon, ed., *Scientists and Human Rights in Somalia: Report of a Delegation*, Washington, DC, National Academy Press, 1988.
4. Robert Gersony, *Why Somalis Flee: Synthesis of Accounts of Conflict Experience in Northern Somalia by Somali Refugees, Displaced Persons and Others*, United States Department of State, August 1989.
5. Jama Musse Jama, *A note on my teacher's group: news report of an injustice*, Ponte Invisibile Ed. REDSEA-ONLINE Publishing Group, Pisa, 2003
6. Mohamoud Sheikh Ahmed Musa (translated by), *General Morgan's Letter of Death*, Somaliland Times, Issue 318, Hargeysa, Somaliland, February 23, 2008 (http://www.somalilandtimes.net/sl/2008/318/71.shtml - accessed 7/2/2010)
7. Somali National Movement, *Human Rights Violation in Somalia*. Occasional publications between 1984-1988

Stampato dalla Tipografia
Bandecchi & Vivaldi

Febbraio 2010